New Casebooks

BLEAK HOUSE

New Casebooks

Further titles are in preparation

New Casebooks Series
Series Standing Order ISBN 0–333–69345–0
(outside North America only)

You can receive future titles in this series as they are published by placing a standing order. Please contact your bookseller or, in case of difficulty, write to us at the address below with your name and address, the title of the series and the ISBN quoted above.

Customer Services Department, Macmillan Distribution Ltd
Houndmills, Basingstoke, Hampshire RG21 6XS, England

New Casebooks

BLEAK HOUSE

CHARLES DICKENS

EDITED BY JEREMY TAMBLING

First published 1998 by
MACMILLAN PRESS LTD
Houndmills, Basingstoke, Hampshire RG21 6XS
and London
Companies and representatives
throughout the world

ISBN 0-333-65858-2 hardcover
ISBN 0-333-65859-0 paperback

A catalogue record for this book is available
from the British Library.

This book is printed on paper suitable for recycling and
made from fully managed and sustained forest sources.

10 9 8 7 6 5 4 3 2 1
07 06 05 04 03 02 01 00 99 98

Printed in Hong Kong

Published in the United States of America 1998 by
ST. MARTIN'S PRESS, INC.,
Scholarly and Reference Division
175 Fifth Avenue, New York, N.Y. 10010

ISBN 0-312-21120-1

To all the Hong Kong students past and present who have followed the 'Reading the Nineteenth Century' course.

Contents

Acknowledgements

Thanks to Martin Coyle and John Peck for helpful comments on the Introduction, to the contributors for agreeing to the re-issue of their work, Kwong Yiu Fai for help with the book's production. Work on this Casebook has followed on from my *Dickens, Violence and the Modern State* (1995) and the many friends and colleagues who appear in the Acknowledgements for that book, are also to be thanked here for their help.

The editor and publishers wish to thank the following for permission to use copyright material:

Virginia Blain, for 'Double Vision and the Double Standard', *Literature and History*, 2:1 (1985), 31–46, by permission of the University of Greenwich; Katherine Cummings, for material from *Telling Tales*: The Hysteric's Seduction in Fiction and Theory (1991), pp. 191–229. Copyright © 1991 by the Board of Trustees of the Leland Stanford Junior University, by permission of Stanford University Press; Audrey Jaffe, for material from *Vanishing Points: Dickens, Narrative, and the Subject of Omniscience* (1985), pp. 128–149. Copyright © 1991 The Regents of the University of California, by permission of the University of California Press; Dominick LaCapra, for 'Ideology and Critique in Dickens's Bleak House', *Representations*, 6 (1984), 116–23. Copyright © 1984 by The Regents of the University of California, by permission of the University of California Press; Kevin McLaughlin, 'Losing One's Place: Displacement and Domesticity in Dickens's Bleak House', *Modern Language Notes*, 108 (1993), 875–90. Copyright © 1993 The Johns Hopkins University Press, by permission of The Johns Hopkins University Press; D. A. Miller, for material from *The Novel and the Police* (1988), pp. 58–106. Copyright © 1988 The

Regents of the University of California, by permission of the University of California Press; J. Hillis Miller, for material from *Victorian Subjects* (1990), pp. 179–99, Harvester Wheatsheaf. Copyright © Duke University Press, by permission of Prentice-Hall Europe and Duke University Press; Timothy Peltason, for 'Esther's Will', *English Literary History*, 59 (1991), 671–91. Copyright © 1991 The Johns Hopkins University Press, by permission of The Johns Hopkins University Press; Bruce Robbins, for 'Telescopic Philanthropy: Professionalism and Responsibility in Bleak House' from *Nation and Narration*, ed. Homi Bhabha (1990), by permission of Routledge; Christine van Boheemen Saaf, for material from *Psychiatry and the Humanities*: Vol. 6 *Interpreting Lacan*, ed. Joseph H. Smith and William J. Kerrigan (1983), pp. 225–57, by permission of Yale University Press.

Every effort has been made to trace the copyright holders but if any have been inadvertently overlooked the publishers will be pleased to make the necessary arrangement at the first opportunity.

General Editors' Preface

The purpose of this series of New Casebooks is to reveal some of the ways in which contemporary criticism has changed our understanding of commonly studied texts and writers and, indeed, of the nature of criticism itself. Central to the series is a concern with modern critical theory and its effect on current approaches to the study of literature. Each New Casebook editor has been asked to select a sequence of essays which will introduce the reader to the new critical approaches to the text or texts being discussed in the volume and also illuminate the rich interchange between critical theory and critical practice that characterises so much current writing about literature.

In this focus on modern critical thinking and practice New Casebooks aim not only to inform but also to stimulate, with volumes seeking to reflect both the controversy and the excitement of current criticism. Because much of this criticism is difficult and often employs an unfamiliar critical language, editors have been asked to give the reader as much help as they feel is appropriate, but without simplifying the essays or the issues they raise. Again, editors have been asked to supply a list of further reading which will enable readers to follow up issues raised by the essays in the volume.

The project of New Casebooks, then, is to bring together in an illuminating way those critics who best illustrate the ways in which contemporary criticism has established new methods of analysing texts and who have reinvigorated the important debate about how we 'read' literature. The hope is, of course, that New Casebooks will not only open up this debate to a wider audience, but will also encourage students to extend their own ideas, and think afresh about their responses to the texts they are studying.

John Peck and Martin Coyle
University of Wales, Cardiff

Introduction

JEREMY TAMBLING

The essays in this book have an interesting and significant starting-point. They begin with J. Hillis Miller's essay on *Bleak House* which first appeared as an introduction to the Penguin edition of the text in 1971, a year after the 1970 centenary of Dickens's death, when there were numerous celebratory – and generally very conservative – readings of Dickens. (The previous Casebook on *Bleak House* appeared a year before that, in 1969.)

If Hillis Miller made a big difference, it's worth reviewing the history of Dickens criticism up to then. Its influence, after all, still survives and perhaps is still pre-eminent. Writing on Dickens in Britain in the 1960s may be grouped within two traditions: firstly, the historical and scholarly approach of Humphry House in *The Dickens World* (1941) and Philip Collins (*Dickens and Crime*, 1962; *Dickens and Education*, 1964). The same approach is seen in Kathleen Tillotson's *Novels of the Eighteen-Forties* (1956) and *Dickens at Work* (1957) which, written with John Butt, traced Dickens's writing methods, based on a study of the number-plans which he wrote for each number of the later novels. This scholarship, which has also engendered a currently ongoing collection of Dickens's letters in several volumes, and scholarly editions of the novels and of Dickens's speeches, makes up one side of British writing on Dickens.

The second tradition is closely associated with F. R. Leavis, the most influential British critic of English literature for the greater part of the twentieth century, who in 1948 in *The Great Tradition* had called Dickens an 'entertainer' rather than a 'great' and 'serious' novelist, and found only *Hard Times* a 'wholly successful work of art'. Leavis's views on Dickens changed in his writings on him in the 1950s and 1960s, and in 1970 he and his wife, Q. D. Leavis, produced *Dickens the Novelist*, which contains Q. D. Leavis's remarkable chapter on *Bleak House*, notable for its defence of Esther Summerson as an important creation for Dickens and certainly not an unsuccessful part of the novel (as she had earlier been considered to be). The line that F. R. and Q. D. Leavis take is to stress Dickens as a romantic, anti-Utilitarian and anti-mechanisation. The novelist is seen as triumphantly sane and in touch with his own feelings, and the author of a critique of Benthamism as the society's ruling ideology.

Criticism of Dickens along Leavis's lines, as the popular entertainer who was also a great novelist, has continued to appear, but I feel that *Dickens the Novelist* began to mark the limits of this line of criticism's usefulness. The Leavises made a case for a 'normal' intelligent Dickens, in whom questions of sexuality and women were not problematic, and whose texts simply endorsed energy, art, imagination, intelligence and professionalism. They had, however, to ignore virtually all the more original or disconcerting criticism of Dickens written beforehand, particularly the views of the American critic Edmund Wilson, whose essay 'Dickens: The Two Scrooges' in *The Wound and the Bow* (1941) had asserted the presence of a Dickens psychologically deeply split and divided (both bourgeois-respectable and criminal). The Leavises ended up with a Dickens that needed reacting from just as much as the previous House/Collins models of Dickens which had also made him more an 'entertainer' than a 'serious' novelist.

There is, however, one British critic who stands out from these two traditions: the Marxist critic Raymond Williams. His work was in debt to Leavis, while being distant from it because of its Marxism, and he read Dickens in terms of a new form of novel writing that was able to perceive the new structures and forms of urban life (see *The English Novel from Dickens to Lawrence* and Williams's Introduction to *Dombey and Son* for Penguin, both appearing in 1970).[1] His influence is felt in this volume in Bruce Robbins's essay (7), which also makes interesting comments on Q. D. Leavis. With the exception of Williams, however, none of the earlier criticism is represented in this New Casebook. Instead the volume concentrates on recent moves in critical thinking which have called the assumptions of both of the earlier traditions into question. It is not coincidental that this volume actually reprints nothing from Britain[2] and takes much of its material from America.

Perhaps the critique of Britain Dickens offers is best read from outside – where Dickens is not part of the national ideology, whereas he is virtually made to embody it in Britain. But the US critics represented here are in turn influenced by three different emphases, all French-derived, from Derrida, Foucault and Lacan. Jacques Derrida's deconstruction influences Hillis Miller's essay of 1971, which is the first one included here, and it is also important for Katherine Cummings (essay 8). Michel Foucault's work lies behind D. A. Miller's essay taken from his book *The Novel and the Police*. The second and third essays use Lacan, as does Katherine Cummings. To complete the list: Virginia Blain's essay (3) looks at Dickens in the light of feminism. Audrey Jaffe (essay 7) focuses on issues central for narrative theory about the question of who narrates. The essays by Timothy Peltason (9) and by Kevin McLoughlin (10) are sophisticated re-readings of the text which use many points derived from the above, while owing fewer obvious allegiances. The headnotes to each essay discuss the presuppositions underpinning it, and point up the debate which can be developed going from essay to essay, noting contradictions, common obsessions and points of contact, and agreement on the important elements in the text.

What is noticeable is how these critics keep returning to similar themes – to Esther, to the policing at work in the novel, to the function of the law, and to questions of interpretation and resistance to interpretation. The earlier criticism which I have discussed, in contrast, went in for questions of the text's social criticism, the importance and symbolism of Chancery (as opposed to abstract 'law') and the role of the 'omniscient' narrator, as opposed to Esther as narrator. Indeed, Esther was largely neglected by the House/Collins tradition which was much more concerned with questions of how much Dickens exaggerated, and how far he was a writer of realist fiction. The question of realism has recently been taken up again but with considerably more theoretical backing, as we shall see. In the rest of this Introduction, rather than discussing each individual essay reprinted in the volume, something in any case covered in the headnotes, I want to sketch out the new directions Dickens criticism has taken by looking first at some of the recurrent key concepts or methodologies that underpin the essays reprinted – realism, deconstruction, psychoanalysis, feminism. Secondly, I want to ask where this criticism gets us, because, as it circles round some questions which it returns to insistently, in picking on these areas, it leaves others out. Finally, I want to suggest, by referring to the law and deconstruction, and to Walter Benjamin and his writings about the metropolis, that there are still other new ways for thinking about Dickens's text.

WRITING AS A WOMAN – REALISM

As the importance of Esther Summerson's narrative became recognised in the 1970s and 1980s, so *Bleak House* became more and more compelling for contemporary critics. Earlier critics, however, thought differently. Philip Collins, though he notes that Dickens was entirely original in writing as a woman (as opposed to writing the letters of a woman, as in, say, Samuel Richardson's novel of 1747–8, *Clarissa*),[3] is unconvinced by the result. Collins's dislike of Esther echoes that of John Forster, Dickens's biographer, writing in 1872:

> To represent a storyteller as giving the most surprising vividness to manners, motives, and characters of which we are to believe her all the time, as artlessly unconscious, as she is also entirely ignorant of the good qualities in herself she is naïvely revealing in the story, was a difficult enterprise, full of hazard in any case, not worth success and certainly not successful.[4]

It also echoes Charlotte Brontë (the author of *Jane Eyre*), writing in a letter of 11 March 1852, just after the first number of *Bleak House* had appeared (28 February 1852):

> Is the first number of *Bleak House* generally admired? I like the Chancery part, but when it passes into the autobiography form, and the young woman who announces that she is not 'bright' begins her history, it seems to me too often weak and twaddling; an amiable nature is caricatured, not faithfully rendered, in Miss Esther Summerson.[5]

With these critiques, consider also John Stuart Mill's contemptuous reference to 'that creature Dickens' on account of his portrayal of Mrs Jellyby.[6] Dickens's construction of women in *Bleak House* attracted no praise (I will return to Mrs Jellyby), but the question of Dickens and feminism haunts the essays collected here. Even though *Jane Eyre's* heroine, autobiographical structure and Gothicism influenced the avowedly non-realist *Bleak House*, which dwells on 'the *romantic* side of familiar things' (Preface, my emphasis), there was a clear antipathy between the Brontës and Dickens, who in conversation said he had not read *Wuthering Heights*, and 'he had not read *Jane Eyre* and said he never would as he disapproved of the whole school'.[7] Perhaps by 'the school' Dickens meant women's literature, perhaps just the Brontës.

Dickens's and Charlotte Brontë's disavowals of interest in the other suggest how contestatory the relation between new and modern writing and the narrative of women could be. Esther's autobiography may be an attempt to resituate women's discourse after Charlotte Brontë had so appropriated it and the woman's voice. Charlotte Brontë by implication uses the then new, 1850s, discourse of 'realism' when she uses the word 'caricature' about Dickens's writing. It is a criticism best expressed by George Eliot:

> We have one great novelist who is gifted with the utmost power of rendering the external traits of our town population; and if he could give us their psychological character – their conceptions of life, and their emotions – with the same *truth* as their idiom, and manners, his books would be the greatest contribution Art has ever made to the awakening of social sympathies. But while he can copy Mrs Plornish's colloquial style [in *Little Dorrit*] with the delicate accuracy of a sun-picture, while there is the same startling inspiration in his description of the gestures and phrases of 'Boots' [in 'Holly-Tree'] as in the speeches of Shakespeare's mobs or numbskulls, he scarcely ever passes from the humorous and external to the emotional and tragic without becoming as transcendent in his *unreality* as he was a moment before in his artistic *truthfulness*. But for the precious salt of his humour, which compels him to reproduce external traits that serve, in some degree, as a corrective to his frequently *false* psychology, his preternaturally virtuous poor children and artisans, his melodramatic boatmen and courtesans, would be as noxious as Eugène Sue's idealised proletaires in encouraging the miserable fallacy that high morality and refined sentiment can grow out of harsh social relations, ignorance and want; or that the working-classes are in a condition to enter at once into a millennial state of *altruism*, wherein everyone is caring for everyone else, and no one for himself.[8]

Realism, a critical term of the 1850s, found especially in the rationalist pages of the literary magazine *Westminster Review*, was also the stick G. H. Lewes (George Eliot's friend) took to Dickens over the scientific impossibility of 'spontaneous combustion' in chapter 32 of *Bleak House*.

'Realism' has been much discussed in modern critical theory: by Pierre Macherey, and Roland Barthes, for instance, in France and by Colin MacCabe and Terry Eagleton following them in Britain. Earlier, the Marxist critic George Lukács, in perhaps the most influential treatment of the topic, had used 'realism' to discuss nineteenth-century novels, arguing that the works of Balzac or Tolstoy could be admired even though they were written by a reactionary bourgeois, because of their ability to show the 'totality' of a society, its interconnectedness. The novels' realism was not simple description, passivity before the facts: it implied a critique of society, and a narrative drive showing a possible way forward out of the current problems of bourgeois society.[9] Against the claim that the realist novel offers a 'totality' – a complete representation of reality in the realist text, linking the parts to the whole, showing how the tiny parts of society help to add up to a whole – it could be argued that Lukács evaded questions of the codifications of reality and of narrative that take place in the text, and paid no attention to the text's silences, evasions and displacements of critical material. In a word, 'realism' concedes too much to the conscious voice that directs the narrative towards one end.

Though *Bleak House* might be dubbed by Lewes as deficient in realism, from the twentieth-century perspective it seems to fit that term only too well. Such appears to be the view, for example, of Catherine Belsey in her important study *Critical Practice* (1980), which takes *Bleak House* as nineteenth-century classic realism, finding in it a convergence of discourses that arrive at a single truth which confirms the wisdom of author and reader alike. She looks at the double narrative, observing in the first the 'worldly, knowing narrator' and in the second, Esther's strength of feeling:

> The reader is constantly prompted to supply the deficiencies of each narrative. The third person narration ... is strongly enigmatic, but provides enough clues for the reader to make guesses at the 'truth' before the story reveals it; Esther's narrative frequently invites an ironic reading: we are encouraged to trust her account of the 'facts' but not necessarily her judgement. ... Thus a third and privileged but literally unwritten discourse begins to emerge, the discourse of the reader which grasps a history and judges soundly.

Belsey thinks Esther's dismissal of Skimpole (ch. 61) brisk enough to be worthy of the ironic narrator, and finds the ironic narrator softens when dealing with the innocence of Jo, the Bagnets and Mr George. 'The three discourses thus converge to confirm the reader's apparently extra-discursive interpretation and judgment.' So:

By this means *Bleak House* constructs a reality which appears to be many-sided, too complex to be contained within a single point of view, but which is in fact so contained within the single and non-contradictory invisible discourse of the reader, a discourse which is confirmed and ratified as Esther and the ironic narrator come to share with the reader a 'recognition' of the true complexity of things. By thus smoothing over the contradictions it has so powerfully dramatised in the interests of a single, unified, coherent 'truth', *Bleak House*, however critical of the world it describes, offers the reader a position, an attitude which is given as non-contradictory, fixed in 'knowing' subjectivity.[10]

This is part of the case against 'realism' put by modern theorists, a case which is based mainly around the novels of George Eliot, but which includes Dickens: whatever local differences there may be in his work from Eliot's, he appears to write the same kind of material that assumes a knowable truth, a knowledgeable author, and a centred reader who can take in the whole impetus of the text.

There are, however, difficulties with this attack on nineteenth-century novels, especially in the case of Dickens. My inclination, for example, would be to contest Belsey's conclusion that the two narratives in *Bleak House* converge as much as she says, and I will want to show what I take to be a lack of unification – closure – in the rest of this Introduction. Perhaps Belsey forces her case by making the two narrative voices she describes more single, more monological (to use Bakhtin's term, which I explain below) than they actually are. Belsey may, that is, make Esther more Esther-like (more self-effacing) than she really is, and the narrator over-ironical, the two too different. And to argue that the text resolves contradictions seems problematic. If by contradictions we mean that, at the level of plot, everything is discovered and made plain, that seems reasonable, but if we mean that the text becomes aware of competing, contradictory discourses that mould it differently from moment to moment, then I do not think it true that these are resolved at all in terms of the text and its closure, its resolution.[11]

Esther's narrative, though it seems straightforward, calm and unironical, is more ambiguous, even duplicitous, than Belsey allows. Her past-tense progress, opposed to the present tense of the rest of the book, invites probing: and who is the 'unknown friend' to whom she writes? (ch. 67, p. 932)? Why does she conceal throughout the narrative that she is a happily married woman with two children, letting the reader assume that she is isolated, an orphan first and last? (It is not her only concealment.) What about her ending, which is not an ending (there can be no conclusion), which stops with an incomplete sentence, an Emily Dickinson-like hyphenated phrase '– even supposing –' which leaves the question open of what she wanted to say, and how often she has stopped herself short in the earlier part. Like Mr Tulkinghorn, she may be a 'silent depository' of noble secrets (ch. 2, p. 58) – in this case, her own. Dickens opts to write in a mode that suspends his 'normal' ebullience and excess for another which advertises its repression, and the question remains whether Esther has the same knowledge that the other narrator possesses: for instance, does Esther find out who her father was? Or why her mother is discovered at the entrance to the graveyard where Nemo is found? If she knows, she keeps it to herself. 'I proceed to other parts of my narrative', she writes (ch. 60, p. 869), after the discovery of her dead mother, in a style almost akin to that of Jane Austen in the last chapter of *Mansfield Park* ('Let other pens dwell on guilt and misery. I quit such odious subjects as fast as I can'), as if to suggest that there is a coherence, an order to her life. The evidence, however, suggests how fractured her life is, so much so that the happy marriage disappears from the narrative in place of the memory of the former days, as though the trauma was what remained, unworked through, requiring her to tell her autobiography, though not acknowledging even to herself that she is the subject of it.

In Esther, I suggest, may be found many of the contradictions the text cannot resolve. It is she who writes about Mrs Jellyby, and her opposition to Mrs Jellyby's chaos at home obviously contrasts with her own dedication to cleanliness, which itself asks, however, to be 'read' psychoanalytically.[12] The question of whether a single view emerges in the text of Mrs Jellyby, or of Mr Skimpole, who obviously contrasts strongly with Esther's attention to 'duty', is not clear. A realist reading, such as Catherine Belsey's, would see a closure in the text which permits a single reading to emerge. That, however, assumes the possibility of reading the text as classic realism, something contested by the novel itself, and also by more recent criticism which has questioned much of the traditional understanding of realism by drawing attention to, for example, how reality is codified, how texts often have gaps, silences, erasures. Such questioning has above all been evident in deconstructionist criticism which has also re-examined the art of criticism, as the next section discusses.

DECONSTRUCTION AND THE TEXT

Issues of realism are taken up in different ways by Hillis Miller (essay 1) and by D. A. Miller (essay 4), whose reading of the text uses Foucault's ideas on power and repression. Hillis Miller's essay, the first major deconstructive reading of Dickens, influences nearly every other in this collection, being topical, since, by 1971, deconstruction had begun to emerge in America, following the publication of Derrida's founding texts of deconstruction, *Writing and Difference* and *Of Grammatology*, both of which appeared in 1967.

Hillis Miller begins his essay by quoting from Nietzsche's *Genealogy of Morals* (1887), on those things which Nietzsche takes to be the 'essence of interpreting' – 'forcing, adjusting, abbreviating, omitting, padding, inventing, falsifying'.[13] Interpretation is regarded by Nietzsche as a process of violence, whose motivation is the 'will to truth' – i.e. the impulse to dominate, to use knowledge for control, to create knowledge where this does not exist in order to have a hold over people. Nietzsche's hostility to interpretation as a violent strategy appears in both Foucault and Derrida. Derrida for a while was Foucault's pupil, but broke from him in a review-essay of Foucault's *Madness and Civilization* (1961). Whereas Nietzsche's insights in the work of Foucault stressed how power and domination change their ways of working and surface strongly in the nineteenth century – in such path-breaking books as Foucault's *The Birth of the Clinc* (1963), in the case-history compiled on the murderer Pierre Rivière (*I, Pierre Rivière, Having Slaughtered My Mother, My Sister and My Brother ... A Case of Patriarchy in the Nineteenth Century*, 1973), and above all in *Discipline and Punish* (1975) and *The History of Sexuality* (1976) – Derrida went a different way. He accused Foucault of writing history which began with a pure moment of non-oppression before oppression started; secondly, of reading without noticing the plural possibilities of the text that he was using, a plural reading being one that illustrated the impossibility of the text being made to yield an oppressive message; and thirdly, he said Foucault was trying to do the impossible, and what, assuming he could, would be itself oppressive, i.e. of trying to speak for the silenced other, in this case, the 'mad'. Whether this is fair or not has been the subject of much debate which has separated admirers of Foucault's work from admirers of Derrida's.[14]

Yet deconstruction is a practice enabled by Foucault. It works by showing up the hidden violence involved in textual forms of interpretation. Derrida's hostility to single 'meaning' – to the idea that texts can ever be reduced to a set of coherent, unified meanings – is often caricatured so that it seems as if Derrida is saying there is no meaning to a text. It would be better to say that he feels there is too much meaning around, but that any meaning we give a text is imposed by ignoring the 'return' of the text, its otherness, the notion that the text is haunted by other traces within it, all of which interpretation must leave out. The interpretation generated serves ideology and the dominant ways of understanding that circulate within society, or within Western metaphysics. This unveiling of the way criticism represses the text by the very act of interpretation and so hides the uncertainty that permeates it, received Foucault's contempt: he called deconstruction a pedagogy, something suitable for the classroom, but of no political value outside.

The debate between Derrida and Foucault about violence, politics and meaning appears in the essays in this volume. In his essay 'Discipline in Different Voices: Bureaucracy, Police, Family and *Bleak House*' reprinted below, D. A. Miller finds it 'seriously misleading' for Hillis Miller, in a characteristically Derridean way, to take the text as exemplifying 'an interminable proliferation of readings' (p. 93). He adds that if Hillis Miller shows that the impossibility of reaching a conclusion in the case of *Jarndyce* v. *Jarndyce* demonstrates the impossibility of interpretation, that in itself is no consolation, for 'the hermeneutic problematic itself is an instrument in the legal establishment's will to power' (p. 126). The impossibility of a final interpretation, in other words, is one way in which the law secures power. D. A. Miller's essay is the response of a politically inflected Foucault-inspired criticism to deconstruction, and the debate continues in Dominick LaCapra's intervention (when D. A. Miller's essay was originally published in *Representations*, the 'New Historicist' Foucauldian journal, it attracted much attention, including LaCapra's reply, reprinted here as essay no. 5. Miller went on to respond to LaCapra. Miller's essay itself, which became the basis of his book *The Novel and the Police*, is most in debt to Foucault's *Discipline and Punish* and *The History of Sexuality*, both of which focus on the disciplinary technologies that use as their nineteenth-century symbols the prison (especially in its ideal form, the Panopticon, as a device for constant monitoring of prisoners), and the police (the first London police came on the streets in 1829). Discipline is produced through, for example, the calibrating of different forms of sexuality, linking these to character-types, so that sexual behaviour became in the nineteenth century the marker of a personality, of a subject to be treated as such (i.e. to be subjected, but also to be individualised, singled out). Miller argues that Foucault's use of the word 'discipline' implies a number of meanings that bear upon Dickens's novel:

> (1) an ideal of unseen but all-seeing surveillance, which, though partly realised in several, often interconnected institutions, is identified with none; (2) a regime of the norm, in which normalising perceptions, prescriptions and sanctions are diffused in discourses and practices throughout the social fabric; and (3) various technologies of the self and its sexuality, which administer the subject's own contribution to the intensive and continuous 'pastoral' care that liberal society proposes to take of each and every one of its charges.[15]

The purchase that Foucault's work has upon *Bleak House* is clear. The aristocratic law (represented by Tulkinghorn) gives way to the middle-class power of the detective police, Inspector Bucket, whose deceptiveness in his way of discovering the truth is apparent from his first appearance in chapter 22, tricking both Mr Snagsby and Jo. Dickens shows a shift of power at work. Bucket is aided unconsciously by other middle-class figures – Guppy, Weevle/Jobling, the Smallweeds – in tracking down and trapping Lady Dedlock. *Bleak House* becomes a detective novel after Tulkinghorn is shot, virtually the first in English (though Edgar Allan Poe's detective stories 'The Murders in the Rue Morgue' [1841] and 'The Purloined Letter' [1845] had already appeared). Bucket's actions fit with the *exposé* of the criminal/homosexual/degenerate/eventual policeman Vautrin (based on the thief turned Head of the French police force, and supposed author of *Les Vrais Mémoires de Vidocq* [1828] in the series of novels which were written by Balzac in the 1830s and 1840s: *Old Goriot, Lost Illusions, Splendours and Miseries of Courtesans* and *Cousin Bette*). Bucket symbolises a new type of surveillance working in society, and the detective form links with the drive for a 'will to truth', for a single, monopolistic wish to find out people's secrets and expose them, drive them out, or normalise them.

The detective story paradigm, however, may also be regarded as realism's last word. This is D. A. Miller's point: though *Bleak House* seems confusing in its proliferation of characters and settings, it all works towards one end, and everyone turns out to be related, connected to everyone else, crossing class and gender lines. Details – e.g. the handwriting that Lady Dedlock sees in chapter 2 – are picked up and used by the agents of surveillance. The realist novelist is himself a policeman, not least because he knows the secrets of everyone, as it is also implied that everyone is aware of Lady Dedlock as repressing a secret.

> She supposes herself to be an inscrutable being, quite out of the reach and ken of ordinary mortals ... Yet, every dim little star revolving about her, from her maid to the manager of the Italian Opera, knows her weaknesses, prejudices, follies, haughtinesses and caprices; and lives upon as accurate a calculation and as nice a measure of her moral nature, as her dressmaker takes of her physical proportions.
>
> (ch. 2, p. 59)

Through Miller's reading of the novel through Foucault we return to the politics of realism and its problems as a genre. Does *Bleak House* offer a resistance to the power of the police, or is Dickens – fascinated by the police force, and even accompanying them on their sleuthing work – writing as a policeman, siding with the forces of bourgeois hegemony, that would replace an inchoate, fog-bound, filthy, wasteful society with one organised, inspected and known, down to everyone's initimate secrets? At this point, the significance of the double narrative should be posed again, and Esther's secrecy, her attitude to her mother, her share in tracking her down, and her (excessive) care for duty, for cleanliness and her repression should be read again. A Foucauldian analysis would see the doctor as an emergent figure of normalisation and discipline in the nineteenth century: how does the portrayal of the doctor in *Bleak House*, Woodcourt, fit here? It might be argued that, as with the comparable figure of Physician in *Little Dorrit*, who discovers Mr Merdle's 'secret' (his swindling), Dickens's analysis goes soft, avoids the implications of the argument. But it might also be suggested that the text is opposed to systematicity of interpretation in general, and this returns us to the question of deconstruction.

Miller's Foucauldian analysis offers a sense of how Dickens's text is caught up in history and social change. As a result, we become aware of a more complicated view of realism than that offered by Lukács. Instead of thinking of realism in terms of a totality, Miller, dealing with the politics of realism, enables us to see why there are two narrators – that they represent the text's own conflicted politics and its lack of a synthesis. This, which is emphatically not a short-coming in *Bleak House* but part of its refusal to be confined to one genre (the French word is the same as gender), brings us back to divisions in the text, which need thinking about psychoanalytically.

PSYCHOANALYSIS, THE LAW AND DECONSTRUCTION

'Is there such a thing as principle, Mr Harold Skimpole?'
(Mr Boythorn, *Bleak House*, ch. 18, p. 306)

Several of the essays reprinted here use psychoanalysis, particularly the works of Jacques Lacan (1900–81), to think with: all of the essays are aware of its power as an interpretive discourse, one that looks at the hidden history of repression that structures people's lives. The novel lends itself to psychoanalysis in that it records a history which has taken place before the reading of the novel starts: psychoanalysis, like the detective force, uncovers that past. A danger of psychoanalysis, however, is that it claims to know, to possess the truth. In this way it could be said to serve realism, and underwrite a sense of narrative as capable of telling the truth about the dead past. This criticism has been made, for instance by Derrida, in discussing Jacques Lacan. It is not clear, however, whether a psychoanalytic reading does indeed produce a realist text committed to the will to truth, or whether it resists the power structures that operate within the text, in this case the power structures in *Bleak House*.[16]

In order to explore psychoanalytic criticism, I would like to look on the role of law in the text, drawing on a number of Lacan's ideas. Lacan discusses the child's entry into the symbolic order – the order of language, of sociality – and he stresses that this takes place through the 'name of the father' (the *nom du père*) where the word 'nom' (name) is a homonym for '*non*' (no). Learning the father's role within culture, as the embodiment of that system which assigns to each a subject position, and yet inscribes that subject with lack, so that he or she is motivated by desire, also implies the barring of the mother. She becomes the fantasised but excluded figure of pleni-tude (an important point for Lady Dedlock). The child is confined to absence and to language as an image of loss, founded on separa-tion from the mother.[17] Access to the symbolic, to the public order of language, thus entails a recognition of patriarchy, its name, its laws, its repression. Entry into the symbolic entails seeing language as patriarchally bound; it imposes a gender-position on the subject (the individual) who is subordinated to the law of the father, and that position in relation to the father can only be one of lack, felt both by those gendered as male and by those gendered as female, but doubly existent as lack for the female, since she can never attain patriarchal status, the phallus being in Lacan the marker of what *both* sexes, but especially the female, must for ever lack.[18] Esther's subjectivity is thus especially one of deprivation, and her narrative may be seen as the sign of her need to conform to that law, which means repressing her difference from it, and trying to speak and to act consciously in reference to it – hence her will to cheerfulness and to duty. Her relationship with Ada (see the end of ch. 36), which is outside patriarchy, is virtually the most tender – because less repressed – emotion felt in the book.

But the name of the father – the social, symbolic order – must, says Lacan, be asserted. Accordingly, in *Bleak House*, the criminal law, represented by Mr Bucket, who in this continues and develops the work done earlier by Mr Tulkinghorn, serves patriarchy. It is a woman who is hunted down, and though a woman shoots Mr Tulkinghorn, she too is caught through the agency of the detective law, empowered, in this case, by Sir Leicester Dedlock. Patriarchy, the order of society and the order of the police all come together. Mr Bucket's fat forefinger points in token of the phallic power of this law. Detective fiction works to map the law of the father, that unconscious force by which the child is gendered, socialised and repressed, onto the law of the land, except that it is interesting that in *Bleak House*, as in so much subsequent detective fiction and television police series, we never see Hortense, the murderess, brought to court; her arrest by Bucket is quite enough, as though the policeman, not the courts of justice, was himself the embodiment of that which protects patriarchy – that which is patriarchy itself.

The law-courts are a different proposition. In *Bleak House* the court described is Chancery, and early on we are told that 'the world of fashion and the Court of Chancery are things of precedent and usage' (ch. 2, p. 55). Historically, the Court of Chancery came into existence by the end of the twelfth century. It was concerned with actions arising out of the ownership and conveyancing of property, and it began by making decisions on the basis of equity – i.e. of looking at the particular merits of a case. In this it was separate from the common law, which rested on (unwritten) laws and practices. But after the seventeenth century, Court of Chancery decisions were written down, and then legal decisions appealed to precedents, which means that decisions rested upon interpretation. But to make any case a precedent is dangerous in that it involves the ability to say that one case can stand as an example for another, or for a set of cases, as though a part could represent a whole, and to use a previous case as a precedent involves the assumption that you can compare two narratives. Literary theory adapted to legal theory would suggest the impossibility of 'getting a story straight', of fixing what 'exactly' happened in any one case, let alone the impossibility of comparing two narratives, since to decide what is the 'same' and what is 'different' is not simply empirically available but rests on a decision of from what perspective the two narratives are being compared, and what contextual frameworks are being considered relevant for the comparison, while the choice to see things as the same or different rests on interpretation, which is Nietzsche's topic. Interpretation of a precedent is the more dangerous in that, covertly, it is not historical, something to be arrived at simply cognitively, but begins with present-day application to the case in hand, which then involves finding – or constructing – something that can be called a precedent.

The attack on precedents (compare the idea of origins, one of the concepts deconstruction is most sceptical of) is one way in which deconstruction has affected legal theory, and it remains a question how this material might be applied to *Bleak House* where the law as father and the law the lawyers cannot establish are imbricated with each other.[19] Since 'the one great principle of the English law is, to make business for itself' (ch. 39, p. 603), neither lawyers nor the police have any interest in establishing the law irrefragably: both professions exist by creating, constructing, criminality. Since the law, what is written, is, after all, rhetoric, its value is performative, i.e. it tries to bring about a state of affairs, to which it tries to make people subject. This gives it an inherent weakness, and it is certainly an ideological position of most contemporary television police series that if the 'criminal' got to court, s/he would be let off because of the court's indeterminacy (or 'softness'); hence the importance of the policeman/detective as a culture-hero, whose work, often enough outside the law, also reinstates the law. The policeman / detective thus turns into a figure of violence, establishing the law by lawlessness and violence. So, for example, Bucket becomes a marginal, covert, secret figure during Tulkinghorn's funeral (ch. 53), and his character has its destructive side even while he serves the interest of property.

In the Court of Chancery, property disappears, as happens obviously with *Jarndyce* v. *Jarndyce*, which means that the Court cannot maintain the concept of the 'proper', the correct, the right. To think of the proper may suggest how many forms of the non-proper there are in *Bleak House*. Esther is illegitimate (which means she is 'improper'), and her name, which could be Barbary, or Dedlock, or Summerson, or Hawdon, or Woodcourt, or Nemo, suggests that Chancery cannot fix identity: there is no law of the father there. Jo and Nemo exemplify in their own ways this failure of the law to impose its authority. An equal weakness afflicts John Jarndyce, who is in part the subject of several essays here, such as Peltason's (9). He is not the patriarch, and his philanthropy,[20] his sense of inability to do anything, his weak rebelliousness, most demonstrated in the way he sides with Skimpole, and his concessiveness all mark him out as both the failure of patriarchy and a figure that patriarchy has failed to place firmly within the symbolic. (Jarndyce and Boythorn in a sense are boys together: a sexlessness marks each, including possibly, Skimpole; they do not belong in any other relationship.) According to Lacan, where the law of the father fails to 'take' in the consciousness of the subject, the foreclosure (*déchéance* – the term partially translates Freud's *Verwerfung* – i.e. 'repudiation') means that the subject becomes psychotic – i.e. ego boundaries dissolve; the subject is unaware of the presence of the symbolic order outside in which it exists.[21] The situation is productive of schizophrenia, which would correspond to a failure at the level of the signifier, that is, of the word. The name of the father is the 'paternal metaphor' and it anchors the subject within the metonymic sequence of signifiers, all of which signify, in metaphorical form, the name of the father. To be outside that metaphorical signified means that the subject can take no single position within the symbolic order, and Lacan accordingly speaks of a hole opened up in the signified[22] which is filled by delusions, hallucinations, voices. Accordingly, madness and despair and suicide and hauntings are dominant motifs in *Bleak House*, as they are in Dickens throughout. The keynote of ruined lives is sounded in chapter 1 (p. 53): 'How many people out of the suit, Jarndyce and Jarndyce has stretched forth its unwholesome hand to spoil and corrupt, would be a very wide question.' Miss Flite – a mad figure of prophecy like Joanna Southcott – Gridley, Richard Carstone, Nemo, Esther in her delirium, the various forms of bodily deprivation that go through the text and the madness of Mrs Jellyby's household and of the Snagsbys', all suggest prevalent forms of melancholy-madness that structure *Bleak House*. Esther is told it were better she had not been born; Caddy wishes she were dead. Even the doctor, Woodcourt, suggests a double inadequacy in his name: he is not quite adequate for love (he cannot 'court') and not quite sufficient for the law (the law 'court'). There is failure everywhere, even in what seems an established state.

Richard commits himself to a will to truth, so he beggars himself and dies in trying to get beyond interpretation to justice, and Boythorn believes that a society can only be founded on principle, to which Skimpole, the *flâneur*, as Baudelaire would call him,[23] replies that he doesn't know what Boythorn means by that name, or where it is, or who possesses it. Skimpole's anarchism suggests that he recognises the constructed nature of any form of justice: he sees that principle is indeed a matter of possession: it ties in with property (and property rights). Boythorn, who is conducting a dispute over property with Sir Leicester, takes a simpler view, believing in the name of the father (this accounts for the first syllable of his surname) and he rebels against patriarchy as it takes the form of Sir Leicester, like an Oedipal figure, a mere 'boy' with pretensions to phallic domination (note his temper), which appear in the second syllable of his name, 'thorn'. (The second syllable of Skimpole's name also works like 'thorn' but 'skim' implies a basic superficiality, that someone with this name slides out of responsibility to the patriarchy.) Christine van Boheemen-Saaf (essay 2), similarly brings out the phallicism in Tulkinghorn's name. While patriarchy is vindicated, at the end with Lady Dedlock dead and Sir Leicester paralysed, it is an empty victory for all but the police, agents of a new, and more devious form of control, and designed to become independent of the aristocracy who in the 1840s and 1850s were hiring them to solve their domestic mysteries. If the novel colludes with the police, it shows its awareness that to do so is to become caught up in a new, efficient (i.e. unlike Chancery) and ruthless machinery, whose basis for existence does not involve the rule of principle. Bucket may respect patriarchy, but he deals Sir Leicester and his dying order several *coups de grâce* on the way. The basis of modernity is a new authoritarianism (inseparable from populism) lacking in the old Chancery regime.

URBAN EXPERIENCE. POSTMODERNISM AND 'SCHIZANALYSIS'

Bleak House is unique amongst English novels in mapping its double narrative, its gender-shift and its detective form onto its reading of urban experience. Its first word is 'London', and though it implies a wider geography, of Lincolnshire, St Albans just outside London and the industrial north for the Ironmaster (ch. 63), and probably, in the starving poor in the brickfields, the presence of Irish refugees, its main geography remains a tight labyrinth of streets around the district of Holborn and Seven Dials. The present-tense narrator asks:

> What connexion can there be, between the place in Lincolnshire, the house in town, the Mercury in powder, and the whereabouts of Jo the outlaw with the broom … What connexion can there have been between many people in the innumerable histories of this world, who from opposite sides of great gulfs, have, nevertheless, been very curiously brought together?
>
> (ch. 16, p. 272)

The word 'connexion' recalls Lukács arguing that realism relates the parts to a whole in its analysis of society. Asking what connection exists in this chapter, which brings Lady Dedlock and the dead Nemo's burial-place together through the agency of Jo, affirms a possibility of seeing the city whole, of making links, but the second sentence quoted is more puzzling, for the question about these unspecified people at unspecified times could be answered 'no connection', so that the stress would fall on the method – 'very curiously' – with which they were linked. The text would thus seem to suggest the importance of coincidence and chance, that if causality exists in the city, to be picked up by the careful detective/realist writer, so also does pure chance.

This would be an aspect of the text's modernity. Comparatively few nineteenth-century novels in English write intensively about the city: Dickens's London fits well with the writings of Walter Benjamin, who called Paris the 'capital of the nineteenth century' and discusses the city as imposing a whole mental life onto the urban dweller, the partaker of modernity. In *The Mysteries of Paris and London*, the critic Richard Maxwell, writing on Dickens, Victor Hugo and the popular novelist G. W. M. Reynolds, author of *The Mysteries of London* (1846), invokes the philosopher and sociologist Georg Simmel (1858–1918). Simmel was a profound influence on theorists of modernity such as Siegfried Kraucauer and Benjamin, and Maxwell quotes from him that in the modern metropolis 'what is public becomes ever more public, and what is private becomes ever more private'.[24] We noted that George Eliot says that Dickens writes about 'our town population', but she misreads his modernity: wishing Dickens to deal with the psychology of his characters, she cannot see how the external is all that can be read in the city: the conditions of the metropolis withdraw lives into a state of secrecy and unreadability. A unifying narrative becomes impossible; just so, *Bleak House* gives a broadly public narrative alongside a private one and suggests they cannot meet.

Benjamin partially borrows from Simmel when he makes gambling an important image for the city, for in gambling 'no game is dependent on the preceding one. Gambling cares about no assured position ... [it] gives short shrift to the weighty past on which work bases itself.'[25] *Bleak House* is full of gamblers – those who trust in Chancery (like Richard – 'And if the suit *should* make us rich Esther – which it may, you know!' he says early on [ch. 14, p. 234]), ridden with people who do no more than wait for something to happen. Harold Skimpole, a continuation of Mr Micawber in *David Copperfield* who like a gambler waits for 'something to turn up', lives his life as though gambling on the goodness of his friends, and not surprisingly, with Benjamin's contrasting of work and gambling. Esther, who commits herself to work and duty, scorns him. Gambling evokes a perpetual present with no chance to create a pattern: it destroys ideas of cause and effect on which linear narrative depends. Not coincidentally, the *Jarndyce* v. *Jarndyce* narrative of *Bleak House* peters out in the loss of everything – a loss which ends all planning and sense of purpose. George Eliot's complaint that Dickens gives no more than the external life of its inhabitants implies her wish that realism might provide a convincing narrative to link together such disparate beings and to represent them recognisably. The failures of narrative, its supplement through such devices as spontaneous combustion, imply that the text remains concerned rather with the unrepresentable.

At the beginning of *Bleak House* there is smoke with 'flakes of soot ... as big as full-grown snowflakes – gone into mourning, one might imagine, for the death of the sun' (ch. 1, p. 49). The death of the sun suggests an important theme for 'modernity' – the absence of authority (like the absence of law), the absence of the law of the father. Lacan's insights into schizophrenia are more relevant in that Gilles Deleuze and Felix Guattari describe capitalism in terms of 'decoding' or 'deterritorialisation' – the loss of fixed subject-positions.[26] Sir Leicester Dedlock's ruminations on the floodgates of society being opened, and all landmarks gone (ch. 28 – 'The Ironmaster') express comically the argument from the standpoint of one faded patriarch (hardly a patriarch, being officially childless). Benjamin writes about the metropolis because here the decoded, unstable, *laisser-faire* nature of modern life appears fully, with its succession of stimuli that make shock definitional for the city and for the state of modernity.[27] The police represent forces for reterritorialising, for fixing things back. The text is ambivalent about such an attempt to recode, to restabilise energies that the nineteenth century had seen open up, politically, economically, socially and in sexual, gender and libidinal terms.

Bleak House may be a schizophrenic text itself – at all levels: in the double narrative, in Dickens writing 'his' 'autobiography' (as in some sense he may be doing) as a woman, in terms of tense and temporal awareness, in terms of double and contradictory authorial positions, in its pattern of concealments and revealments. Taking one example: the text 'knows' the answer to the question 'What's that? Who fired a gun or pistol? What was it?' (ch. 48, p. 719) when Tulkinghorn is killed; but it holds back that knowledge: to repeat Maxwell's point, as certain things in the text become more obvious and open, so the text withdraws itself into its own secrecy. If the text is schizoid, which implies there can be no single knowledge of a society because there is no single subject who knows or who can observe, an argument about realism – the attempt to repress a more primary schizoid doubleness – would need restaging. Instead of reading *Bleak House* as two narratives, it might be worth trying to read it as the record of what we might call, punning on the book's mode of production, *serial* identity, as the subject of and in the text changes from moment to moment, sometimes taking on an unstable identity as 'Esther' and sometimes not even to be labelled as anything so specific.

Who is the hero(ine) of *Bleak House*? Baudelaire gives an answer, locating a new heroism in the writer/artist who can describe and report the beauty of modern life – transitory, passing beauty, that of the city. In his essay 'The Painter of Modern Life' (1859), the artist is the *flâneur*, the idler, the dandy who is aloof from the crowd, but is fascinated by it, and colludes with it, taking up no 'morality' towards it (none is possible). Harold Skimpole, who makes a sketch of 'Coavinses's' head while being arrested for debt and getting off again when the others pay his debts, on this basis would come nearest to being the hero. Skimpole may be the Romantic poet and radical Leigh Hunt (or rather, Leigh Hunt was sometimes like Skimpole), or he may be William Makepeace Thackeray (rival author to Dickens), or a representation of Dickens's own father (via the portrayal of the father figure Micawber in *David Copperfield*, Dickens's previous novel) – but he is the dandy, *blasé* about the big world – 'an agglomeration of practical people of business habits' (ch. 6, p. 120) – who in being so is of the modern world. The text is schizoid about him, criticising him through Esther (as though Esther stands for Dickens and Skimpole is old John Dickens, the feckless father who spent time in prison), yet it has also created him, as a counter-cultural representation critiquing the Bleak House-world as little else in Britain could do. Q. D. Leavis suggested that Oscar Wilde plagiarised him,[28] meaning this to be rude (being more like Esther than Esther in her commitment to morality and duty), because she failed to recognise Wilde's contestatory power – his critique of imperialism and its ideological masculinity, and of bourgeois repression.[29] Dickens, as the hero of modern life, includes Skimpole within the text. Here is Skimpole at work, commenting on Mrs Jellyby's endeavours to have 'from a hundred and fifty to two hundred healthy families cultivating coffee and educating the natives of Borrioboola-Gha, on the left bank of the Niger' (ch. 4, p. 86):[30]

> We have been mentioning Mrs Jellyby. There is a bright-eyed woman, of a strong will and immense power of business-detail, who throws herself into objects with surprising ardour! I can admire her without envy. I can sympathise with the objects. I can dream of them. I can lie down on the grass – in fine weather – and float along an African river, embracing all the natives I meet, as sensible of the deep silence, and sketching the dense overhanging tropical growth as accurately as if I was there. I don't know if it's of any direct use my doing so ...
>
> (ch. 6, p. 120)

This is dialogism in Bakhtin's sense,[31] where all speech is the speech of the other, where the opinions of someone Esther does not agree with are inserted into her narrative which is equally but differently disapproving of Mrs Jellyby, and where Esther's own views are to be 'read' critically. Skimpole attacks feminism in his damning

Mrs Jellyby with faint praise – but he at least has the imagination to see the implications of her imperialism. Whether Skimpole's own African dream is imperialist (like an earlier version of Gaugin in Tahiti), or whether it critiques the Utilitarian dream within the imperialist drive (no wonder Dickens aroused John Stuart Mill's anger) is perhaps undecidable – because the text cannot take up a single position between so many voices, each of which is haunted by its own unconscious positions. What is apparent is that Skimpole may have to be excluded by that part of the text which has a drive towards narrative, cause and effect and closure. Skimpole's part is the perpetual present, the refusal of positions and the refusal to be put into a narrative (he gives his own) and the awareness that principle and property go together, so that, like Dickens, he stands for fictionalising the self (the self as fictional) and the world too.

Skimpole is only one side of the Victorian culture which is hinted at in this book. The presence of opium (also a subject of fascination to Baudelaire) in the book suggests another anti-bourgeois addictive element at work with power to undo and destabilise the subject, truly turning Nemo into no one. Mr Krook's disappearance as a subject is drink-related, and the young Alfred Pardiggle, aged five, son of the philanthropist Mrs Pardiggle, is made to join the 'Infant Bands of Joy' which will keep him away from tobacco for the rest of his life. Like the Irish refugees, these things are on the fringes of the book, but they suggest that even a double narrative is not enough for the plurality of attitudes and sympathies it holds – being both for interpretation and against it, and identifying it with the power of the police, being both for the single subject, and antagonistic towards the repression and discipline that produces it. Opium, of course, produces visions and hauntings. *Bleak House* both creates the single subject, and single identity, and dissolves it. Such a conflict in the text itself makes it romantic, haunted, unfamiliar – uncanny, if we recall that Freud's word for the 'uncanny', *unheimlich* (what is not at home) – is part of 'the romantic side of familiar things' that Dickens discusses in the Preface. The 'familiar things' would align the book with realism, but the whole is split between that, which is recognisably nineteenth century, and something else, which is much more decidedly of the modern, and which richly feeds the divisions of opinion about the book which are expressed in this New Casebook.

NOTES

All references in the Introduction are to the Penguin edition of *Bleak House* (1971).

1. An earlier version of Raymond Williams's essay – which comments on the earlier traditions of Dickens criticism – appears as 'Social Criticism in Dickens: Some Problems of Method and Approach', *Critical Quarterly*, 6 (1964), 214–27. Williams discusses his work on Dickens in *Politics and Letters: Interviews with New Left Review* (London, 1979), pp. 251–4. An anthology on Dickens in the 1970s would have been likely to find more Marxist criticism directed to questions of Dickens and social reform and revolution. The absence of such criticism now obviously deserves discussion: the D. A. Miller/LaCapra debate (essay 5) might be a starting point.

2. I have not included my own essay on the book, Jeremy Tambling, 'A Paralysed Dumb Witness: Allegory in *Bleak House*', in *Dickens, Violence and the Modern State* (London, 1995) but would refer readers to it. See Further Reading at the back of the book, and the notes to each chapter for further bibliographical help on *Bleak House*.

3. Philip Collins, 'Some Narrative Devices in *Bleak House*', *Dickens Studies Annual*, 19 (1990), 125–46, 126.

4. John Forster, *The Life of Charles Dickens* (1872), ed. J. W. T. Ley (London, 1928), 7.1.559.

5. Letter to George Smith, 11 March 1852, quoted in Robert Newsom, '*Villette* and *Bleak House*: Authorizing Women', *Nineteenth-Century Literature*, 46 (1991–2), 54–81, 55. See also Jean Frantz Blackall, 'A Suggestive Book for Charlotte Brontë?', *Journal of English and Germanic Philology*, 79 (1977), 363–83. Like all Dickens's novels, *Bleak House* was first published in serial form.

6. See Philip Collins, *Dickens: The Critical Heritage* (London, 1971), p. 95. The contemporary reviews of *Bleak House* are worth examining: Collins shows how they accused Dickens of lacking plot: the point is important for my discussion below.

7. See Jerome Meckier, 'Some Household Words: Two New Accounts of Dickens's Conversation', *Dickensian*, 71 (1975), 5–20, 5. Reference to the Gothic should also suggest Hawthorne, and *The Scarlet Letter* and *The House of the Seven Gables*: see Susan Shatto for this (in Further Reading) and Allan Pritchard, 'The Urban Gothic of *Bleak House*', *Nineteenth-Century Literature*, 45 (1991–2), 432–52.

8. George Eliot, 'The Natural History of German Life', *Westminster Review*, July 1856, reprinted in Thomas Pinney (ed.), *Essays of*

George Eliot (London, 1965), pp. 271–2. Emphases, save for the last, mine. Eugène Sue (1804–57) was the socialist author of the 10 volume *Mysteries of Paris* (1842–3). George Eliot met Dickens in 1852; I discuss Lewes's relationship with Dickens throughout my chapter on *Bleak House* (in *Dickens, Violence and the Modern State*).

9. On realism, see Lilian R. Furst, *Realism* (London, 1992); for Lukács, see G. H. R. Parkinson, *Georg Lukács* (London, 1977); for the issues of ideology and their use in Fredric Jameson, a use of Lukács which tries to accommodate him to poststructuralism, see his *The Political Unconscious: Narrative as a Socially Symbolic Act* (London, 1981), and William C. Dowling, *Jameson, Althusser, Marx: An Introduction to The Political Unconscious* (London, 1984). Barthes is best read through his *S/Z* (New York, 1980). See also Colin MacCabe, *James Joyce and the Revolution of the Word* (London, 1979). See also my *Narrative and Ideology* (Milton Keynes, 1991), ch. 7.

10. Catherine Belsey, *Critical Practice* (London, 1980), pp. 80, 81.

11. I comment more on Belsey's position in discussing *Oliver Twist* in *Yearbook of English Studies*, ed. Nicola Bradbury (Modern Humanities Research Association, 1996), pp. 43–53.

12. For an example of the psychoanalysis of cleanliness, we could look at Freud in one of his most famous cases, that of 'Dora', discussing Dora's mother (but there are problems here, as well, which feminist criticism has rightly picked up on): a woman 'who had concentrated all her interests upon domestic affairs, especially since her husband's illness [his syphilis] and the estrangements to which it led. She presented the picture, in fact, of what might be called "the housewife's psychosis". She had no understanding of her children's more active interests, and was occupied all day long in cleaning the house with its furniture and utensils and in keeping them clean – to such an extent as to make it almost impossible to use or enjoy them. This condition, traces of which are to be found often enough in normal housewives, inevitably reminds one of forms of obsessional washing and other kinds of obsessional cleanliness.' (Sigmund Freud: Case Histories: 8: *The Penguin Freud* [Harmondsworth, 1977] pp. 49–50.)

13. For Hillis Miller's work, see Robert Markley, '*Tristram Shandy* and "Narrative Middles": Hillis Miller and the Style of Deconstructive Criticism', in Robert Con Davis and Ronald Schliefer (eds), *Rhetoric and Form: Deconstruction at Yale* (Norman, 1985), and Donald Pease, 'J. Hillis Miller: The Other Victorian at Yale', in Jonathan Arac, Wlad Godzich and Wallace Martin (eds), *The Yale Critics: Deconstruction in America* (Minneapolis, 1983). There is an interesting interview with Hillis Miller in Imre Salusinsky (ed.), *Criticism in Society* (London, 1987).

14. Derrida's essay on Foucault, 'Cogito and the History and Madness', appeared in *Writing and Difference* (1967, trans. Alan Bass, Chicago, 1978). Foucault responded in the preface to the second edition of his book (*Histoire de la folie* in French) in 1972: the translation appears as 'My Body, This Paper, This Fire', trans. Geoff Bennington, *Oxford Literary Review*, 4: 1 (1979), 9–28. For an account of the debate, see John Frow, *Marxism and Literary Theory* (Cambridge, MA, 1986) ch. 8, and Roy Boyne, *Foucault and Derrida* (London, 1990).

15. D. A. Miller, *The Novel and the Police* (Berkeley, CA, 1988), p. viii.

16. Derrida's critique of Lacan, 'Le Facteur de la Vérité', appears in *The Post-Card: From Socrates to Freud and Beyond*, trans. Alan Bass (1980: Chicago, 1987). It was a response to Lacan's reading of Poe's 'The Purloined Letter' which is translated in *Yale French Studies*, 48 (1972), 39–72. The debate between psychoanalysis and deconstruction is, however, hardly to be resolved: see Barbara Johnson's 'The Frame of Reference: Poe, Lacan, Derrida', reprinted in *Untying the Text: A Post-Structuralist Reader*, ed. Robert Young (London, 1981). All these are put together in John P. Miller and William J. Richardson (eds), *The Purloined Poe* (Baltimore, MD, 1988).

17. Cumming's essay below refers in this context to Freud's 'Beyond the Pleasure Principle' (1920) which in its second section traces the child's response to the physical or psychic loss of the mother through the game of throwing away and retrieving a cotton-reel, while saying 'Fort' – Gone – and 'Da' – There – to accompany the actions. The child was Freud's grandson, and the mother, Sophie, Freud's daughter, had just died – a point Freud represses.

18. See Jacques Lacan, *Ecrits: A Selection* (London, 1977): the classic text on the subject's essential relation to the symbolic order is the 'Rome discourse' of 1953, 'The Function and Field of Speech and Language in Psychoanalysis', and for the 'name of the father' the essay 'On a Question Preliminary to Any Possible Treatment of Psychosis' (1958). The phallus in Lacan evokes completeness, the self-sufficiency of total meaning, and he does not identify it as something possessed by the male. The illusion that it can be possessed, however, underpins *patriarchy* as an ideology and produces an authoritative discourse which in Lacan and Derrida is variously called *logocentrism, phallocentrism* and *phallogocentrism* – terms which are used in this Casebook – names given to that single, monological discourse of power, which in feminist theory excludes as its other the feminine, a plural discourse which is outside power. These two types of discourse are not to be linked to the male/female distinction. Since neither gender possesses the phallus, power cannot so be distributed.

19. The law and deconstruction are discussed in Jack Balkin, 'Deconstructive Practice and Legal Theory', *Yale Law Journal*, 96

(1987), 743–86; see also the essays in Drucilla Cornell, Michel Rosenfeld and David Gray Carlson, *Deconstruction and the Possibility of Justice* (London, 1992). A conservative view of the novel appears in Richard A. Posner, *Law and Literature: A Misunderstood Relation* (Cambridge, MA, 1988), pp. 128–31.

20. The topic of philanthropy, obviously crucial for Dickens, and especially in relation to Carlyle, whose *Latter-Day Pamphlets* (1850) attack it fiercely (and are an important source for Dickens), could attract more research. It might begin with Lacan who relates it to problems in forming subjectivity and the ego, and refers to 'the aggressive motives that lie hidden in all so-called philanthropic activity' – Lacan, 'Aggressivity in Psychoanalysis', *Ecrits* (London, 1977), p. 13.

21. 'The distinction between *Verwerfung* [repudiation] and *Verdrängung* ('repression') is plain for both writers [Lacan and Freud]. Where foreclosure seeks to expel a given notion, thought, image, memory or signifier from the unconscious, repression seeks to confine it there. Where repression belongs to the ordinary functioning of the mind and in certain conditions may produce disabling neurotic effects, foreclosure is a violent refusal of symbolisation and its effects are catastrophic. It is an operation that gives psychosis a structure distinct from that of neurosis' – Malcolm Bowie, *Lacan* (Cambridge, MA, 1990), p. 107. In psychosis, the subject is 'objectified' by language, 'spoken rather than speaking' (*Ecrits*, p. 69). (Bowie's book is a fair introduction to Lacan; also useful as a starter is Jonathan Scott Lee, *Jacques Lacan* [Boston, 1990].)

It will be noticed that Audrey Jaffe's essay, (7, p. 166) speaks of Freud's term 'negation' (*Verneinung*). This term is associated with repression, and *Die Verneinung*, the paper of Freud of 1925 she refers to, is translated as 'Denial'. But Freud also uses another term, *Verleugnung*, which though sometimes translated 'denial' has the force of 'disavowal' and is discussed in Freud's essay 'Fetishism' (1923). These are different strategies for avoidance of internal and external realities, and both apply to the characters in *Bleak House*.

22. *Ecrits*, p. 217.

23. The *flâneur* is 'the term for the curious, idle, and ... seemingly omnipresent wanderer and observer of the Paris streets' (Jerrold Seigel, *Bohemian Paris: Culture, Politics and the Boundaries of Bourgeois Life, 1830–1930* [Harmondsworth, 1987, p. 29]). In 'The Painter of Modern Life' (trans. in *Baudelaire: Selected Writings on Art and Artists* by P. E. Charvet [Harmondsworth, 1972]) the word is rendered 'idler'. See Walter Benjamin, *Charles Baudelaire: A Lyric Poet in the Era of High Capitalism*, trans. Harry Zohn (London, 1973), pp. 34–66. (The section is relevant for Benjamin's discussion of the detective story: the *flâneur* also plays detective.) The *flâneur* is outside

the concerns of the crowd, watching it, but also 'abandoned in the crowd' (Benjamin, p. 55), like the child. (Skimpole compares himself to a child.)

24. Richard Maxwell, *The Mysteries of Paris and London* (Charlottesville, VA, 1992), p. 168.

25. Benjamin, *Baudelaire*, p. 134.

26. Gilles Deleuze and Felix Guattari discuss decoding in their *Anti-Oedipus*, vol. 1 of *Capitalism and Schizophrenia* (1968, trans. Robert Hurley, New York, 1977), pp. 33–5, 222–61. See Eugene W. Holland, *Baudelaire and Schizoanalysis: The Sociopoetics of Modernism* (Cambridge, 1993), Introduction, for a lucid account of schizoanalysis, which term – from Deleuze and Guattari – implies that the decodings in society produce schizophrenia, and they oppose the view of orthodox psychoanalysis that the family structure is the sufficient force which induces this.

27. Benjamin, *Baudelaire*, p. 132.

28. F. R. and Q. D. Leavis, *Dickens the Novelist* (London, 1970), p. 174. An informative, but equally negative essay about Skimpole comes from Donald E. Ericksen, 'Harold Skimpole: Dickens and the early "Art for Art's Sake" Movement', *Journal of English and Germanic Philology*, 72 (1973), 48–59.

29. Wilde is well written about in Ashis Nandy, *The Intimate Enemy: Loss and Recovery of Self under Colonialism* (Oxford, 1983), pp. 32–5. I discuss this in *Dickens, Violence and the Modern State* (pp. 157–8); see also the essay by Rustom Barucha, 'Forster's Friends' in Jeremy Tambling (ed.), *E. M. Forster*, New Casebook (London, 1995).

30. The issue of Dickens and feminism is also one of Dickens and imperialism. Mrs Jellyby seems to have been partly based on Caroline Chisholm, pioneer in sending emigrants to Australia, and in setting up the Family Colonisation Loan Society. On 14 August 1848, Dickens reviewed in *The Examiner* the book *Narrative of the Expedition Sent by Her Majesty's Government to the River Niger in 1841, under the Command of Captain H. D. Trotter, RN*. The expedition had been to introduce an improved system of agriculture, but it had succumbed to fever and to violence from the Africans. Dickens refers there to the 'king of Borrioboola'. Also, in 1852, *Uncle Tom's Cabin* appeared: Dickens spoke of this appreciatively in a review written with Henry Morley, 'North American Slavery' (*Household Words*, 18 September 1852), but despite being abolitionist, the attitudes to the slaves there are also equivocal, and there is evidence to suggest that Dickens was seen as guying Harriet Beecher Stowe in Mrs Jellyby. (A newer criticism has found Stowe's text itself both racist and anti-feminist.) See the Dickens *Letters*, vol. 6, 825 note, and 7.77 note (in Further Reading).

Behind Dickens is Carlyle with the *Occasional Discourse on the Nigger Question* published in *Fraser's Magazine*, November 1849 (reissued in 1853) and the *Latter-Day Pamphlets* of 1850: the black and the Irish are both treated in terms of inferiority.

31. In dialogism, there is the recognition that all speech uses, because they are addressed to another, are contaminated by the voice of the other, so that all speech becomes multi-voiced, polyphonic. Bakhtin carries this insight into the novel which he sees as a mixed genre, not sustaining a single voice or approach. See Mikhail Bahktin, *The Dialogic Imagination*, trans. Caryl Emerson and Michael Holquist (Austin, TX, 1981). Pam Morris reads Dickens using Bahktin: for her work, see Further Reading.

1

Interpretation in *Bleak House*

J. HILLIS MILLER

> forcing, adjusting, abbreviating, omitting, padding, inventing, falsifying, and whatever else is of the *essence* of interpreting
> (Nietzsche, *On the Genealogy of Morals*, III: 24)

Bleak House is a document about the interpretation of documents. Like many great works of literature it raises questions about its own status as a text. The novel doubles back on itself or turns itself inside out. The situation of characters within the novel corresponds to the situation of its reader or author.

In writing *Bleak House* Dickens constructed a model in little of English society in his time. In no other of his novels is the canvas broader, the sweep more inclusive, the linguistic and dramatic texture richer, the gallery of comic grotesques more extraordinary. As other critics have shown (most notably John Butt and Kathleen Tillotson in 'The Topicality of *Bleak House*' and Humphry House in '*Bleak House*: The Time Scale'[1]), the novel accurately reflects the social reality of Dickens' day, in part of the time of publication in 1851–3, in part of the time of Dickens' youth, in the late twenties, when he was a reporter in the Lord Chancellor's court. The scandal of the Court of Chancery, sanitary reform, slum clearance, orphans' schools, the recently formed detective branch of the Metropolitan Police Force, Puseyite philanthropists, the Niger expedition, female emancipation, the self-perpetuating procrastinations of Parliament and Government – each is represented in some character or scene. Every detail of topography or custom has its journalistic correspondence to the reality of Dickens' time. Everything mirrors some fact – from the exact references to street names and localities – mostly, it has been noted, within half a mile of Chancery Lane – to the 'copying' of Leigh Hunt and Walter Savage Landor in Skimpole and Boythorn, to such out-of-the-way details as the descriptions of a shooting gallery, a law stationer's shop, or the profession of 'follower'. Like Dickens' first book, *Sketches by Boz, Bleak House* is an imitation in words of the culture of a city.

The means of this mimesis is synecdoche. In *Bleak House* each character, scene, or situation stands for innumerable other examples of a given type. Mrs Pardiggle is the model of a Puseyite philanthropist; Mrs Jellyby of another sort of irresponsible do-gooder; Mr Vholes of the respectable solicitor battening on victims of Chancery; Tulkinghorn of the lawyer to great families; Gridley, Miss Flite, Ada and Richard of different sorts of Chancery suitors; Mr Chadband of the hypocritical Evangelical clergyman mouthing distorted Biblical language; Bucket of the detective policeman, one of the first great examples in literature; Jo of the homeless poor; Tom-all-Alone's of urban slums in general; Sir Leicester Dedlock of the conservative aristocracy; Chesney Wold of the country homes of such men. Nor is the reader left to identify the representative quality of these personages for himself. The narrator constantly calls the reader's attention to their generalising role. For each Chadband, Mrs Pardiggle, Jo, Chesney Wold or Gridley there are many more similar cases. Each example has its idiosyncrasies (who but Chadband could be just like Chadband?), but the essence of the type remains the same.

Bleak House is a model of English society in yet another way. The network of relations among the various characters is a miniature version of the interconnectedness of people in all levels of society. From Jo the crossing-sweeper to Sir Leicester Dedlock in his country estate, all Englishmen, in Dickens' view, are members of one family. The Dedlock mystery and the case of Jarndyce and Jarndyce bring all the characters together in unforeseen ways. This bringing together creates a web of connection from which no character is free. The narrator formulates the law of this interdependence in two questions, the first in reference to this particular story and the second in reference to all the stories of which this story is representative:

> What connexion can there be, between the place in Lincolnshire, the house in town, the Mercury in powder, and the whereabouts of Jo the outlaw with the broom, who had that distant ray of light upon him when he swept the churchyard-step? What connexion can there have

been between many people in the innumerable histories of this world, who, from opposite sides of great gulfs, have, nevertheless, been very curiously brought together!

(ch. 16)

In the emblematic quality of the characters and of their 'connexions' *Bleak House* is an interpretation of Victorian society. This is so in more than one sense. As a blueprint is an image in another form of the building for which it is the plan, so *Bleak House* transfers England into another realm, the realm of fictional language. This procedure of synecdochic transference, naming one thing in terms of another, is undertaken as a means of investigation. Dickens wants to define England exactly and to identify exactly the causes of its present state. As everyone knows, he finds England in a bad way. It is in a state dangerously close to ultimate disorder or decay. The energy which gave the social system its initial impetus seems about to run down. Entropy approaches a maximum. Emblems of this perilous condition abound in *Bleak House* – the fog and mud of its admirable opening, the constant rain at Chesney Wold, the spontaneous combustion of Krook, the ultimate consumption in costs of the Jarndyce estate, the deaths of so many characters in the course of the novel (I count nine).

With description goes explanation. Dickens wants to tell how things got as they are, to indict someone for the crime. Surely it cannot be, in the phrase he considered as a title for *Little Dorrit*, 'Nobody's Fault'. Someone must be to blame. There must be steps to take to save England before it blows up, like the springing of a mine, or catches fire, like Krook, or falls in fragments, like the houses in Tom-all-Alone's, or resolves into dust, which awaits all men and all social systems. It is not easy, however, to formulate briefly the results of Dickens' interpretative act. His two spokesmen, the narrators, are engaged in a search. This search brings a revelation of secrets and leads the reader to expect an explanation of their meaning. The novel as a whole is the narrators' reports on what they have seen, but these can only be understood by means of a further interpretation – the reader's.

Bleak House does not easily yield its meaning. Its significance is by no means transparent. Both narrators hide as much as they reveal. The habitual method of the novel is to present persons and scenes which are conspicuously enigmatic. The reader is invited in various ways to read the signs, to decipher the mystery. This invitation is made openly by the anonymous, present-tense narrator through rhetorical questions and other devices of language. The invitation to interpret is performed more covertly by Esther Summerson in her past-tense narrative. Her pretence not to understand the dishonesty, hypocrisy or self-deception of the people she encounters, though she gives the reader the information necessary to understand them, is such an invitation, as is her coy withholding of information which she has at the time she writes, but did not have at the time she has reached in her story: 'I did not understand it. Not for many and many a day' (ch. 17).

Moreover, the narrators offer here and there examples of the proper way to read the book. They encourage the reader to consider the names, gestures, and appearances of the characters as indications of some hidden truth about them. Esther, for example, in spite of her reluctance to read signs, says that Prince Turveydrop's 'little innocent, feminine manner' 'made this singular effect upon me: that I received the impression that he was like his mother, and that his mother had not been much considered or well used' (ch. 14). The anonymous narrator can tell from George Rouncewell's way of sitting, walking, and brushing his palm across his upper lip, as if there were a great moustache there, that he must 'have been a trooper once upon a time' (ch. 21).

The reader of *Bleak House* is confronted with a document which he must piece together, scrutinise, interrogate, at every turn – in short, interpret – in order to understand. Perhaps the most obvious way in which he is led to do this is the presentation, at the beginning of the novel, of a series of disconnected places and personages – the Court of the Chancery, Chesney Wold, Esther Summerson as a child, the Jellyby household and so on. Though the relations among these are withheld from the reader, he assumes that they will turn out to be connected. He makes this assumption according to his acceptance of a figure close to synecdoche, metonymy. Metonymy presupposes a similarity or causality between things presented as contiguous and thereby makes story-telling possible. The reader is encouraged to consider these contiguous items to be in one way or another analogous and to interrogate them for such analogies. Metaphor and metonymy together make up the deep grammatical armature by which the reader of *Bleak House* is led to make a whole out of discontinuous parts. At the beginning of the second chapter, for example, when the narrator shifts 'as the crow flies' from the Court of Chancery to Chesney Wold, he observes that both are alike in being 'things of precedent and usage', and the similarity between Krook and the Lord Chancellor is affirmed in detail by Krook himself:

> You see I have so many things here ... of so many kinds, and all, as the neighbours think (but *they* know nothing), wasting away and going to rack and ruin, that's why they have given me and my place a christening. And I have so many old parchmentses and papers in my stock. And I have a liking for rust and must and cobwebs. And all's fish that comes to my net. And I can't abear to part with anything I once lay hold of ... or to alter anything, or to have any sweeping, nor scouring, nor cleaning, nor repairing going on about me. That's the way I've got the ill name of Chancery.
>
> (ch. 5)

Such passages give the reader hints as to the right way to read *Bleak House*. The novel must be understood according to correspondences within the text between one character and another, one scene and another, one figurative expression and another. If Krook is like the Lord Chancellor, the various Chancery suitors – Miss Flite, Gridley, Tom Jarndyce and Richard Carstone – are all alike; there are similarities between Tulkinghorn, Conversation Kenge and Vholes; Tom-all-Alone's and Bleak House were both in Chancery; Esther's doll is duplicated with a difference by the brickmaker's baby, by the keeper's child at Chesney Wold and by Esther herself. Once the reader has been alerted to look for such relationships she discovers that the novel is a complex fabric of recurrences. Characters, scenes, themes and metaphors return in proliferating resemblances. Each character serves as an emblem of other similar characters. Each is to be understood in terms of his reference to others like him. The reader is invited to perform a constant interpretative dance or lateral movement of cross-reference as she makes her way through the text. Each scene or character shimmers before her eyes as she makes these connections. Think, for example, how many orphans or neglected children there are in *Bleak House*, and how many bad parents. The Lord Chancellor himself may be included, figuratively, among the latter, since his court was charged in part to administer equity to widows and orphans, those especially unable to take care of themselves. The Chancellor stands *in loco parentis* to Ada and Richard, the 'Wards in Chancery'.

In this system of reference and counter-reference the differences are, it is important to see, as essential as the similarities. Each lawyer in the novel is different from all the others. Esther did not die, like the brickmaker's baby, though her mother was told that she was dead. The relation between George Rouncewell and his mother is an inverse variant of the theme of bad parents and neglected children. Krook is not the Lord Chancellor. He is only a sign for him. The man himself is kindly enough, though certainly a bit eccentric. The Lord Chancellor is a kindly man too, as he shows in his private interview with Ada and Richard. They are sinister only in their representative capacities, Krook as a symbol of the disorder, avarice and waste of Chancery, the Lord Chancellor as the sign of the authority of his court. An emblem is always to some extent incompatible with its referent. A sign with ominous or deadly meaning may be an innocent enough old weather-beaten board with marks on it when it is seen close up, or it may be the absurd painting of 'one impossible Roman upside down', as in the case of the 'pointing Allegory' on Mr Tulkinghorn's ceiling (ch. 16). The power of a sign lies not in itself but in what it indicates. *Bleak House* is made up of a multitude of such indications.

Though many of the connections in this elaborate structure of analogies are made explicitly in the text, many are left for the reader to see for himself. One valuable bit of evidence that Dickens took conscious pains to prepare these correspondences is given in his plan for Chapter 16.[2] In this chapter Lady Dedlock gets Jo to take her to see the paupers' graveyard where her lover lies buried. Jo points through the iron gate at the spot, and Lady Dedlock asks if it is 'consecrated ground'. Dickens' notes show that he was aware, and perhaps intended the reader to be aware, of the similarity between Jo's gesture of pointing and the gesture of the pointing Allegory on Mr Tulkinghorn's ceiling. The latter is mentioned in passing earlier in the chapter and of course is made much of at the time of Tulkinghorn's murder. 'Jo – ,' says the note for this chapter, 'shadowing forth of Lady Dedlock in the churchyard. / Pointing hand of allegory – consecrated ground / "Is it Blessed?"' The two gestures of pointing are alike, as is suggested by the similarity of pose in the illustrations of both by 'Phiz' for the first edition: 'Consecrated ground' and 'A new meaning in the Roman'. Both are examples of that procedure of indication which is the basic structural principle of *Bleak House*. This procedure is 'allegorical' in the strict sense. It speaks of one thing by speaking of another, as Dickens defines the Court of Chancery by talking about a rag and bottle shop. Everywhere in *Bleak House* the reader encounters examples of this technique of 'pointing' whereby one thing stands for another, is a sign for another, indicates another, can be understood only in terms of another, or named only by the name of another. The reader must thread her way through the labyrinth of such connections in order to succeed in her interpretation and solve the mystery of *Bleak House*.

The situation of many characters in the novel is exactly like that of its writer or reader. So many people in this novel are engaged in writing or in studying documents, in attempting to decipher what one chapter-title calls 'Signs and Tokens', in learning to read or write, in hiding documents or in seeking them out, there are so many references to letters, wills, parchments and scraps of paper, that the interpretation of signs or of texts may be said to be the fundamental theme of the novel. Krook's shop is full of old law papers – one of them, it turns out, perhaps the authentic will for resolving the case of Jarndyce and Jarndyce. Krook is obsessed, rightly enough, with the idea that he possesses documents of value, but he does not trust anyone to read them or to teach him to read. He tries to teach himself, forming laboriously with chalk on his wall the letters that spell out 'Jarndyce', rubbing out each letter in turn as he makes it. Miss Flite carries everywhere her reticule full of documents. Richard broods day and night over the papers in his case, as he is drawn deeper and deeper into Chancery. Gridley too pores over documents. Much essential business in this novel, as, to be sure, in many novels, is carried on by means of letters. Tulkinghorn finds out Lady Dedlock's secret by the law writing in her lover's hand which matches the note of instructions Trooper George has from his old officer, Captain Hawdon. Esther teaches her little maid, Charley, how to read and write. Mrs Jellyby's irresponsibility is signified in the way she sits all day writing or dictating letters about Borrioboola-Gha instead of caring for her family. Poor Caddy Jellyby, her mother's amanuensis, is bespattered with ink, and Lawyer Tulkinghorn is a fathomless repository of secrets, all inscribed on the family papers in his strong-boxes.

Some of the most dreamlike and grotesque episodes in the novel involve documents, for example, the chapter in which Grandfather Smallweed, after Krook's death, rummages among the possessions of the deceased, surrounded, in his chair, with great piles of paper, or the chilling scene of the end of Jarndyce and Jarndyce. The latter moves beyond 'realism' in the usual sense toward what Baudelaire in 'The Essence of Laughter' calls the 'dizzy hyperbole' of the 'absolute comic':

It appeared to be something that made the professional gentlemen very merry, for there were several young counsellors in wigs and whiskers on the outside of the crowd, and when one of them told the others about it, they put their hands in their pockets, and quite doubled themselves up with laughter, and went stamping about the pavement of the Hall. ... [P]resently great bundles of papers began to be carried out – bundles in bags, bundles too large to be got into any bags, immense masses of papers of all shapes and no shapes, which the bearers staggered under, and threw down for the time being, anyhow, on the Hall pavement, while they went back to bring out more. Even these clerks were laughing.

(ch. 65)

Not to put too fine a point upon it, as Mr Snagsby would say, what is the meaning of all this hermeneutical and archival activity? The reader of the novel must go beyond surface appearances to the deeper coherence of which these surfaces are the dispersed signs. In the same way, many of the characters are cryptographers. They attempt to fit details together to make a pattern revealing some hidden secret. Like Krook they must put 'J' and 'a' and so on together to spell 'Jarndyce'. They want to identify the buried truth which is the substance behind all the shadowy signs with which they are surrounded, as Richard Carstone believes that there 'is – is – must be somewhere' 'truth and justice' in the case of Jarndyce and Jarndyce (ch. 37). Two motives impel these readers of signs. Like Richard, Gridley or even, in spite of herself, Esther, they may want to find out secrets about themselves. Each seeks his un-revealed place in the system of which he is a part. To find out how I am related to others will be to find out who I am, for I am defined by my connections, familial or legal. Esther *is* the illegitimate daughter of Lady Dedlock and Captain Hawdon. Richard *is*, or perhaps is not, a rightful heir to the Jarndyce fortune. Other charac-ters – Mr Tulkinghorn, Guppy, Grandfather Smallweed, Hortense, Mrs Snagsby or Inspector Bucket – want to find out secrets about others. Their motive is the search for power. To find out the hidden place of another in the system is to be able to manipulate him, to dominate him, and of course to make money out of him.

These two versions of the theme of interpretation echo through the novel in melodramatic and parodic forms. Many characters find themselves surrounded by mysterious indications, sinister, threat-ening or soliciting. Poor Snagsby says, 'I find myself wrapped round with secrecy and mystery, till my life is a burden to me' (ch. 47). He is 'a party to some dangerous secret, without knowing what it is.

And it is the fearful peculiarity of this condition that, at any hour of his daily life, ... the secret may take air and fire, explode, and blow up' (ch. 25). Most of the characters are more aggressive than Mr Snagsby in their relation to secrets. Mr Tulkinghorn's 'calling is the acquisition of secrets, and the holding possession of such power as they give him, with no sharer or opponent in it' (ch. 36). Guppy slowly puts together the evidence of Lady Dedlock's guilt and Esther's parentage. 'It's going on', he says of his 'case', and I shall gather it up closer and closer as it goes on' (ch. 29). In the same way, Hortense, Lady Dedlock's maid, is 'maliciously watchful ... of everyone and everything' (ch. 18), and the 'one occupation' of Mrs Snagsby's jealous life 'has been ... to follow Mr Snagsby to and fro, and up and down, and to piece suspicious circumstances together' (ch. 54). She has, says Mr Bucket, 'done a deal more harm in bringing odds and ends together than if she had meant it' (ch. 54). Just as Gridley, Richard and Miss Flite are obsessed with the documents in their 'cases', so the Smallweeds carry on Krook's search for valuable papers after his death, 'rummaging and searching, digging, delving, and diving among the treasures of the late lamented' (ch. 39). Tom Jarndyce, the original owner of Bleak House, who finally blew out his brains in despair, lived there, 'shut up: day and night poring over the wicked heaps of papers in the suit, and hoping against hope to disentangle it from its mystification and bring it to a close' (ch. 8). Even Sir Leicester, when he hears the story of a noble lady unfaithful to her husband, 'arranges a sequence of events on a plan of his own' (ch. 40), and Esther, though she makes no detective effort to uncover the facts about her birth, nevertheless finds Lady Dedlock's face, 'in a confused way, like a broken glass to me, in which I saw scraps of old remembrances' (ch. 18). She is, in spite of herself, led to put these broken pieces together to mirror the truth about herself, just as, in relation to another secret, she says, 'I observed it in many slight particulars, which were nothing in themselves, and only became something when they were pieced together' (ch. 50).

The remarkable fact is that these interpreters for the most part are failures. Sometimes their interpretations are false, fictional patterns thrown over the surface of things like a mirage without relation to any deeper truth. Sometimes authentic secrets are discovered but are found out too late or in the wrong way to be of any use to their discoverers. *Bleak House* is full of unsuccessful detectives. The 'plan of his own' which Sir Leicester constructs does not save him from the revelation that will shatter his proud complacency. Mrs Snagsby is ludicrously mistaken in her idea that her husband has been unfaithful and is the father of Jo. Krook dies before he finds anything of value in his papers, and even Grandfather Smallweed makes little out of his discovery. Guppy finds out Lady Dedlock's secret, but it does not win him Esther's hand. Gridley dies without resolving his suit. The case of Jarndyce and Jarndyce is used up in costs before the revelation of the newly-discovered will which might have brought it to a close. Even Tulkinghorn and Bucket, the two most clairvoyant and persistent detectives in the novel, are failures. Tulkinghorn is murdered just before he is going to make use of the secret he has discovered about Lady Dedlock. Bucket, in spite of the fact that 'the velocity and certainty of [his] interpretation ... is little short of miraculous' (ch. 56), does not save Lady Dedlock. The masterly intuition which leads him to see that she has changed clothes with the brickmaker's wife (another lateral displacement) gets Esther to her mother just too late. They find her 'cold and dead' on the steps of Nemo's graveyard. Moreover, the novel is deliberately constructed by Dickens in a way calculated to make the reader a bad detective. Carefully placed clues are designed to lead the reader to believe that either George Rouncewell or Lady Dedlock has murdered Tulkinghorn. Even now, when Dickens' strewing of false clues may seem amateur in comparison with the sophisticated puzzles in modern mystery stories, some readers, one may imagine, are inveigled into thinking that Lady Dedlock is a murderess.

A clue to the meaning of this emphasis on false or fruitless interpretation may be given by what appears to be a fault in the novel. The most salient case of an apparent loose end or inconsistency is the failure to integrate perfectly the two major plots. '[T]he plan, so logical and complete', says Angus Wilson in his recent lively study of Dickens,

> by which the Jarndyce lawsuit corrupts all who touch it (save Mr Jarndyce, a nonesuch) is quite upset when we discover that Lady Dedlock's fall from virtue has nothing to do with her being a claimant in the case. The fault is the more glaring because Miss Flite, the little, mad suitor at law, specifically tells how her own sister went to the bad as a result of the misery brought to the family by their legal involvement.[3]

This fissure in the novel, a conspicuous rift in its web, seems all the more inexplicable when we consider Dickens' obvious care in other parts of the book to tie together apparently unrelated details. This is done, for example, by the use of a pattern of figurative language which runs throughout the text. One case of this is the apparently trivial metaphor which Dickens uses in the second chapter to describe Lady Dedlock's icy boredom by saying that, unlike Alexander, 'having conquered *her* world, [she] fell, not into the melting but rather into the freezing mood' (ch. 2). This is picked up in the climatic scenes of her death in the melting snow which lies everywhere and which matches the break in her frigid restraint leading to her death. Surely, the reader supposes, Dickens could have related Lady Dedlock's 'crime' more closely to the corrupting effect of Chancery if he had wanted to do so. Perhaps he did not want to. Perhaps he wanted to mislead the reader into thinking that the revelation of Lady Dedlock's secret is at the same time an explanation of the real mystery in the novel – that is, the question of why English society is in such a sad state. At the same time he may have wanted, by leaving the loose end in the open, to invite the reader to investigate further before he takes the revelation of the one mystery as a sufficient explanation of the other. The larger mystery, the mystery of Chancery or of the degeneration of England, is in fact not explained, or if it is explained this is done in so obscure a manner as to leave things at the end of the novel almost as dark, as mud-soaked and fog-drenched, as they are in the opening pages.

The sombre suggestion toward which many elements of the novel lead, like points converging from different directions on a single spot, is that the guilty party is not any person or persons, not correctable evil in any institution. The villain is the act of interpretation itself, the naming which assimilates the particular into a system, giving it a definition and a value, incorporating it into a whole. If this is the case, then in spite of Dickens' generous rage against injustice, selfishness and procrastination, the evil he so brilliantly identifies is irremediable. It is inseparable from language and from the organisation of men into society. All proper names, as linguists and ethnologists have recognised, are metaphors. They alienate the person named from his unspeakable individuality and assimilate him into a system of language. They label him in terms of something other than himself, in one form of the differentiating or stepping aside which is the essence of language. To name someone is to alienate him from himself by making him part of a family. Even the orphans or the illegitimate characters in *Bleak House* – Jo,

Guster or Esther Summerson – are not free from this alienation. Institutions like Chancery, the workhouse or the Tooting baby-farm where Guster 'grew', or persons like Mrs Pardiggle and the Reverend Chadband, act in place of proper parents for such people and force them into social moulds. Everyone in *Bleak House* is, like Jo, made to 'move on', in one form or another of the displacement which separates so many of the characters of *Bleak House* from themselves.

It is no accident that the names of so many characters in the novel are either openly metaphorical (Dedlock, Bucket, Guppy, Vholes, Smallweed, Summerson, Badger, Clare, Boythorn, Krook, Swills, Flite, Volumnia) or seem tantalisingly to contain some covert metaphor lying almost on the surface of the word (Tulkinghorn, Turveydrop, Chadband, Pardiggle, Jellyby, Rouncewell, Squod, Bagnet, Snagsby, Skimpole). Each of these names, especially those in the last group, seems to shimmer with multiple meanings drawn from various contexts, like the portmanteau words of 'Jabberwocky'. They invite etymological interpretation or 'explication' in the root sense of an unfolding. Turveydrop? Turf? Turd? Curve? Drop of turf? 'Turvey, turvey, clothed in black', as in the children's singing game? An essay could be written exploring the implications of these names. The meaning of names and of naming is, as in Proust's *Remembrance of Things Past*, an important theme in *Bleak House*, though Dickens, unlike Proust, seems to remain in that realm of fiction where names truly correspond to the essence of what they name. He does not appear to move on to the stage of disillusion where the incommensurability of name and person or of name and place appears.[4] Dickens' version of this disillusionment, however, is the implicit recognition that the characters to which he gives such emblematic names are linguistic fictions. The metaphors in their names reveal the fact that they are not real people or even copies of real people. They exist only in language. This overt fictionality is Dickens' way of demystifying the belief, affirmed in Plato's *Cratylus*, that the right name gives the essence of the thing. Along with this goes the recognition throughout *Bleak House* that a man's name is a primary way in which he is separated from his privacy and incorporated into society. 'Lady Dedlock', says Tulkinghorn in a reproachful reminder of her crime and of her responsibility to the name she has wrongly taken, 'here is a family name compromised' (ch. 48). Just as Dickens names his characters and helps them do their duty as emblems by borrowing labels for

them from other contexts, and just as Miss Flite gives her birds allegorical names which juxtapose the victims of Chancery (Hope, Joy,
Youth and so on), its effects (Dust, Ashes, Waste, Want, Ruin, etc.),
and its qualities or the instruments of its deadly fictions (Folly,
Words, Wigs, Rags, Sheepskin, Plunder, Precedent, Jargon,
Gammon and Spinach), so the characters have been appropriated
by society, named members of it, and cannot escape its coercion.

If the metaphors in the names in *Bleak House* are functional, it is
also significant that so many characters have more than one name –
nicknames, aliases or occupational names. The effect of these
nominal displacements, as the reader shifts from one to another, is
to mime in the permutations of language that movement within the
social system which prevents each person from being himself and
puts him beside himself into some other role. Young Bartholomew
Smallweed is 'metaphorically called Small and eke Chick Weed, as
it were jocularly to express a fledgling' (ch. 20). Captain Hawdon
takes the alias of 'Nemo', 'nobody', as if he were trying to escape
the involvement in society inevitable if one has any name at all.
Gridley is known in the court he haunts as 'The man from
Shropshire'. Tony Jobling takes the alias of Mr Weevle. Jo is called
'Toughey' or 'the Tough Subject', names pathetically inappropriate. George Rouncewell is 'Trooper George'. Mr Bagnet is 'Lignum
Vitae', and Mr Kenge the lawyer has been given the splendid name
of 'Conversation Kenge'. Ada and Richard are 'the Wards in
Jarndyce', and Miss Flite calls Esther 'Fitz-Jarndyce', suggesting
thereby not only her relationship to her guardian, John Jarndyce,
but also the figurative similarity between her situation as an illegitimate child and the situation of Ada and Richard as wards of the
court.

In the context of the sinister connotation of multiple naming in
Bleak House there is something a little disquieting, in spite of its
loving intent, in the way Mr Jarndyce gives Esther a multitude of
nursery rhyme and legendary pseudonyms, including the name of a
fifteenth-century witch: 'Old Woman', 'Little Old Woman',
'Cobweb', 'Mrs Shipton', 'Mother Hubbard', 'Dame Durden'. To
give someone a nickname is to force on her a metaphorical translation and to appropriate her especially to oneself. This is precisely
Jarndyce's selfishness in planning to make Esther his wife, which
after all would be another form of renaming. Nor can he protect
Esther from her involvement in society by way of her birth. Perhaps
her first experience of this is her receipt of a letter from Kenge and

Carboy which takes her, as so many characters in the novel are taken, into the legal language which turns her into an object: 'We have arranged for your being forded, carriage free, pʳ eight o'clock coach from Reading ... ' (ch. 3). A fit emblem for the violence exercised over the individual by language and other social institutions is that terrifying form of helplessness Esther endures when she lies ill with the smallpox caught from Jo, who caught it from Tom-all-Alone's, the Jarndyce property ruined because it is in Chancery, or perhaps from the place where her unknown father lies buried, 'sown in corruption' (ch. 11). 'Dare I hint', asks Esther, 'at that worse time when, strung together somewhere in great black space, there was a flaming necklace, or ring, or starry circle of some kind, of which I was one of the beads! And when my only prayer was to be taken off from the rest, and when it was such inexplicable agony and misery to be a part of the dreadful thing?' (ch. 35).

Perfect image of the alienation the characters of *Bleak House* suffer by being named members of society! The figure of a moving ring of substitution, in which each person is not himself but part of a system or the sign for some other thing, is used throughout the novel to define those aspects of society Dickens attacks. The evil of Mrs Jellyby's 'telescopic philanthropy' or of Mrs Pardiggle's 'rapacious benevolence' is that they treat people not as individuals but as elements in a system of abstract do-gooding. Mrs Pardiggle has 'a mechanical way of taking possession of people', 'a show ... of doing charity by wholesale, and of dealing in it to a large extent', and a voice 'much too business-like and systematic' (ch. 8). The world of aristocratic fashion is a 'brilliant and distinguished circle' (ch. 12), 'tremendous orb, nearly five miles round' (ch. 48), just as London as a whole is a 'great tee-totum ... set up for its daily spin and whirl' (ch. 16). Within her circle Lady Dedlock lives imprisoned 'in the desolation of Boredom and the clutch of Giant Despair': substituting one place for another in a perpetually unsuccessful attempt to escape from her consciousness of the false self she has assumed. 'Weariness of soul lies before her, as it lies behind ... but the imperfect remedy is always to fly, from the last place where it has been experienced' (ch. 12).

A similar metaphor is used in the satire of representative government. It underlies that brilliant chapter in which the ruling classes gather at Chesney Wold to discuss the dissolution of Parliament and the formation of a new Government. (John Butt and Kathleen Tillotson in the article cited above discuss the references here to

Disraeli, Russell and the Parliamentary crisis of the early fifties.) Representative government is another form of delegation. Each Member of Parliament acts as the synecdochic sign for his constituents. Dickens, as is well known, had little faith in this form of government. The relation between representative and represented is always indirect. Any authentic correspondence between sign and signified is lost in the process of mediation. When Sir Thomas Doodle undertakes to form a new ministry he 'throw[s] himself upon the country', but this throwing is only figurative, 'chiefly in the form of sovereigns and beer'. This has the advantage over direct appeal to the voters that 'in this metamorphosed state he is available in a good many places simultaneously, and can throw himself upon a considerable portion of the country at one time' (ch. 40). In the practice of Parliamentary government the People are no more than 'a certain large number of supernumeraries, who are to be occasionally addressed, and relied upon for shouts and choruses, as on the theatrical stage' (ch. 12). The actual business of governing is carried on by a small group of leaders of the two parties, Lord Coodle, Sir Thomas Doodle and so on down to Poodle and Quoodle on one side, Buffy, Cuffy, Duffy, Fuffy, Guffy and so on on the other. The comic names admirably suggest not only the anonymity of these men but the fact that each may replace any of the others. They exist, like the letters of the alphabet which Krook or Charlie Neckett so painfully learn, as the possibility of an inexhaustible set of permutations and combinations in which Noodle would replace Moodle; Puffy, Muffy; Puffy, Poodle; or Nuffy, Noodle, and nothing would be changed at all. Government is a circular game of substitutions like the nursery rhyme based on the letters of the alphabet beginning 'A was an apple-pie'.

This nursery rhyme, incorporated into another reference to the basic elements of language and to naming as the absorption of the particular into a system, is referred to in John Jarndyce's analysis of the Court of Chancery. Chancery, he says, is a dance or round. It proceeds through interminable linguistic substitutions replacing one declaration by another and never getting closer to any end. People, once they are named parties to a suit, are swept into the ring, as Esther is caught in her dream necklace, and can never hope to escape. No other text identifies so well the structure of *Bleak House* as a work of literature and also the structure of the society it describes. 'It's about a Will, and the trusts under a Will – or it was, once', says Jarndyce.

It's about nothing but Costs, now. We are always appearing, and dis-
appearing, and swearing, and interrogating, and filing, and cross-filing,
and arguing, and sealing, and motioning, and referring, and reporting,
and revolving about the Lord Chancellor and all his satellites, and
equitably waltzing ourselves off to dusty death, about Costs. ... Law
finds it can't do this, Equity finds it can't do that; neither can so much
as say it can't do anything, without this solicitor instructing and this
counsel appearing for A, and that solicitor instructing and that counsel
appearing for B; and so on through the whole alphabet, like the
history of the Apple Pie. And thus, through years and years, and lives
and lives, everything goes on, constantly beginning over and over
again, and nothing ever ends. And we can't get out of the suit on any
terms, for we are made parties to it, and *must be* parties to it, whether
we like it or not.

(ch. 8)

'Nothing ever ends' – an important thematic stand of the novel is
the special mode of temporal existence in an unjust society, or
perhaps under any social order. Such an order has replaced realities
by signs, substances by shadows. Each sign, in such a 'system',
refers not to a reality but to another sign which precedes it and
which is pure anteriority in the sense that it refers back in its turn to
another sign. A sign by definition designates what is absent, something which may exist but which at present is not here, as the cross
on the top of St Paul's Cathedral, 'so golden, so high up, so far out
of his reach', is a 'sacred emblem' indicating the apparent absence
of God from Jo's life (ch. 19). A sign which refers back to another
sign designates what is in its turn another absence. Gridley, the
'Man from Shropshire', protests against the explanation of his suffering that blames it all on that code of equity which Conversation
Kenge calls 'a very great system, a very great system' (ch. 62).
'There again!' says Gridley.

The system! I am told, on all hand, it's the system. I mustn't look to
individuals. It's the system. I mustn't go into Court, and say, 'My
Lord, I beg to know this from you – is this right or wrong? Have you
the face to tell me I have received justice, and therefore am dismissed?'
My Lord knows nothing of it. He sits there, to administer the system.

(ch. 15)

In spite of Dickens' sympathy for Gridley's indignant outrage, the
whole bent of *Bleak House* is toward indicating that it is in fact the
systematic quality of organised society which causes Gridley's suffering – not a bad system of law, but any system, not a bad repre-

sentative government, but the institution itself, not the special evil of aristocratic family pride, but any social organisation based on membership in a family. As soon as a man becomes in one way or another part of such a system, born into it or made a party to it, he enters into a strange kind of time. He loses any possibility of ever having a present self or a present satisfaction, loses any possibility of ever going back to find the origin of his present plight, loses the possibility of ever escaping from his present restless state or of making any end to it other than 'dusty death'. This intolerable experience of time is dramatised with admirable explicitness, not only in the Chancery suit which can never end except in its consumption in costs, but also in the unhappy life of Richard Carstone. If no proper 'Will' or explicable origin of Jarndyce and Jarndyce can ever be found (there are in fact three wills in the case), Richard as a result lives in perpetual deferring or postponement, never able to settle down to a profession or to commit himself to a present project. He dwells in a continual expectation of a settlement which can never come: 'Everything postponed to that imaginary time! Everything held in confusion and indecision until then!' (ch. 37). 'The uncertainties and delays of the Chancery suit' have made him unlike his natural self and have 'imparted to his nature something of the careless spirit of a gamester, who [feels] that he [is] part of a great gaming system' (ch. 17). 'Now?' asks Richard. 'There's no now for us suitors' (ch. 37). If there is no now there is also no past or future for people who have been forced to accept their membership in a pattern of signs without substance. Each element in such a game refers to other elements in it, in a perpetually frustrated movement which can hope for no end. The other nightmare of Esther's dream expresses this perfectly: 'I laboured up colossal staircases, ever striving to reach the top, and ever turned, as I have seen a worm in a garden path, by some obstruction, and labouring again' (ch. 35).

Miss Flite, mad as she is, is close to the truth about Chancery when she says, 'I expect a Judgment. On the day of Judgment. And shall then confer estates' (ch. 14). The only escape from the circle of signs would be the end of the world or death, that 'beginning the world' which Richard undertakes at the moment he dies, but 'Not this world, O not this! The world that sets this right' (ch. 65). Dickens here, as in his work throughout, suggests an absolute incompatibility between this world and the far-off supernatural world. The many deaths in *Bleak House* have a significance somewhat different from that in many novels. In fiction generally, according to Walter Benjamin, the reader enjoys vicariously a finality he can never experience directly in his own life, my death being on principle an end I shall never be able to view in retrospect. In a novel, says Benjamin, the 'meaning' of each character's life 'is revealed only in his death', and 'what draws the reader to the novel is the hope of warming his shivering life with a death he reads about'.[5] Certainly there are in *Bleak House* many deaths to read about. Their peculiarity is that they are not satisfactory ends for the lives of those who die. Each character who dies passes suddenly from one world to another, leaving his affairs in the world as unsettled and as unfinished as ever. Krook dies without discovering the secrets in his papers. Gridley dies without resolving his suit, as Richard is killed by the final frustration of his hopes for an end to this case. Tulkinghorn dies without being able to use the power he has gained over Lady Dedlock. Jo's death is elaborately portrayed as the final example of his 'moving on'. The deaths in *Bleak House* constitute only in a paradoxical way 'ends' which establish the destinies of those who die. Their deaths define them once and for all as people whose lives were unfinished, as people who never achieved the peace of a settlement. Their lives had meaning only in reference to the perpetually unsettled system of which they were part.

Bleak House itself has exactly the same structure as the society it exposes. It too assimilates everything it touches into a system of meaning. In the novel each phrase is alienated from itself and made into a sign of some other phrase. If the case of Jarndyce and Jarndyce is a 'masterly fiction' (chs 3, 65), and if many characters in the novel spend their time reading or writing, *Bleak House* is a masterly fiction too, and Dickens too spent his time, like Mrs Jellyby, covering paper with ink, his eye fixed not on his immediate surroundings but on an imaginary world. The novel too has a temporal structure without proper origin, present, or end. It too is made up of an incessant movement of reference in which each element leads to other elements in a constant displacement of meaning. *Bleak House* is properly allegorical, according to a definition of allegory as a temporal system of cross-references among signs rather than as a spatial pattern of correspondence between signs and referents. Most people in the novel live without understanding their plight. The novel, on the other hand, gives the reader the information necessary to understand why the characters suffer, and at the same time the power to understand that the novel is fiction rather than mimesis. The novel calls attention to its own procedures and confesses to its own rhetoric, not only, for example, in the onomastic system of metaphorical names already discussed, but also in the insistent metaphors employed throughout.

Each character in *Bleak House* is not only named in metaphor but speaks according to his own private system of metaphors. Moreover, he is spoken of by the narrators in metaphors which recur. Nor are these metaphors allowed to remain 'buried'. In one way or another they are brought into the open. Their figurative quality is insisted upon. In this way the reader has constantly before him one version of the interpretative act whereby nothing is separately itself, but can be named only in its relation to some other thing. Dickens is master of an artificial style which makes its artifice obvious. Among the innumerable examples of this the following contains the linguistic texture of the novel in miniature: 'The Mercuries, exhausted by looking out of the window, are reposing in the hall; and hang their heavy heads, the gorgeous creatures, like overblown sun-flowers. Like them too, they seem to run to a deal of seed in their tags and trimmings' (ch. 48). The nominal metaphor (Mercuries) has been used throughout to label the Dedlock footmen. To this is here added a second figure, a metaphor of a metaphor. These Mercuries are like gorgeous sunflowers. To name them in this way has a double effect. It invites the reader to think of real footmen being described by the narrator in ornately witty language. This language names them as something other than themselves, but it also calls attention to its own wit, uncovers it by playing with it and extending it. The reader knows it is 'just a figure of speech'. The footmen are not Mercuries, nor are they sunflowers. These are ways of talking about them which bring them vividly before the reader and express the narrator's ironic scorn for aristocratic display. At the same time, the figures and figures within figures remind the reader that there are no real footmen in the novel. The Mercuries have only a linguistic existence. They exist as metaphors, and the reader can reach them only through Dickens' figurative language. This is true for all the characters and events in the novel. The fabric of Dickens' style is woven of words in which each takes its meaning not from something outside words, but from other words. The footmen are to be understood only in terms of Mercury, Mercury only in terms of sunflowers. This way of establishing fictional reality matches the kind of existence the characters in the novel have. They too are helpless parts of a structure based on words.

Does the novel propose any escape from this situation, or is it a wholly negative work? How might one step outside the ring? Esther Summerson and John Jarndyce are the chief examples in *Bleak House* of Dickens' commitment to a Christian humanism compounded of belief in 'the natural feelings of the heart' (ch. 55), in unselfish engagement in duty and industrious work, in spontaneous charity toward those immediately within one's circle, and of faith that Providence secretly governs all in this lower world. This Providence will reward the good with another existence not cursed by the shadow of indefinite postponement. John Jarndyce has 'resolutely kept himself outside the circle' of Chancery (ch. 37), holding himself free of its false hopes in an heroic effort of detachment. 'Trust in nothing but in Providence and your own efforts' (ch. 13), he tells Richard. He uses his apparently inexhaustible money to do good quietly to those around him, loving all, asking nothing in return, and purging himself ultimately from his one selfishness, the desire to take Esther as his wife. He is Dickens' most successful version of that recurrent personage in his fiction, the benevolent father-figure.

Esther has been much maligned by critics for her coy revelations of how good she is, how much she is loved, and for her incorrigible habit of crying for joy. Nevertheless, she is in fact a plausible characterisation, more palatable perhaps if one recognises the degree to which the other narrator is an ironic commentary on her language, her personality, and her way of seeing things. She has reacted to the harsh teaching of her godmother's 'distorted religion' (ch. 17) ('It would have been far better, little Esther, that you had had no birthday; that you had never been born!' [ch. 3]) by resolving 'to be industrious, contented and kind-hearted, and to do some good to some one, and win some love to myself' (ch. 3). The emotional logic of this reaction is well known by now, and it is acutely rendered by Dickens, though we would perhaps be less inclined than he to admire its indirections. As opposed to Mrs Pardiggle's abstract and wholesale philanthropy, Esther thinks it best 'to be as useful as I [can], and to render what kind services I [can], to those immediately about me' (ch. 8). She is conspicuously unwilling to engage in that form of the will to power which infects so many others in the book, the desire to decipher signs and to ferret out secrets. 'Duty, duty, Esther' (ch. 38) is her motto. She strikes out 'a natural, wholesome, loving course of industry and perseverance' (ch. 38), ringing herself into her household tasks with a merry peal of her bundle of keys. These are the symbol of her power to 'sweep the cobwebs out of the sky', like the little old woman in the nursery rhyme, and to bring order everywhere she goes.

Even so, the interpretation of Jarndyce and Esther cannot be so straightforward. Perplexing puzzles and inconsistencies remain. What is the source of Jarndyce's money? It must come by inheritance and through his membership in the Jarndyce family, since he is never shown lifting a finger to earn any of it. This kind of inheritance, however, is shown throughout the novel to involve a man, in spite of himself, in the evils of 'system'. Moreover, there are many ways to exercise power over others. Not the least effective of these is self-abnegation. There is a kind of coercion in Jarndyce's goodness. He gives Esther to Allan Woodcourt without consulting her in the matter, and there is something a little unsettling about the fact that the new Bleak House, exact duplicate of the old, built secretly by Jarndyce for Esther and Allan, is another example of that theme of doubling which has such dark implications elsewhere in the novel. The patterns created by the lives of the good characters correspond rigorously to the patterns in the lives of the bad. This is as true for Esther as for Jarndyce. If Chancery is a 'system' which sweeps everything it encounters into its dance, Esther, in another disquieting detail, is said by Harold Skimpole to be 'intent upon the perfect working of the whole little orderly system of which [she is] the centre' (ch. 37). If old Mr Turveydrop's falseness is expressed by the fact that he forms himself after the Prince Regent and is a 'Model of Deportment', Bucket praises Esther's courage when they are tracking down her mother by saying, 'You're a pattern, you know, that's what you are, ... you're a pattern' (ch. 59).

Bleak House is a powerful book, an extraordinary work of Dickens' creative power. It is also to some degree a painful book. The pain lies partly in its prevailing darkness or bleakness, its presentation of so many admirably comic creations who are at the same time distorted, grotesque, twisted (Krook, Grandfather Smallweed, Mrs Jellyby, Chadband, Guppy, Miss Flite – what a crew!). It is painful also because of its self-contradictions. Like the case of Jarndyce and Jarndyce it remains unfinished at its end, a tissue of loose ends and questions rather than of neatly resolved patterns. As in all Dickens' work, there is at the centre of *Bleak House* a tension between belief in some extra-human source of value, a stable centre outside the shadows of the human game, and on the other hand the shade of a suspicion that there may be no such centre, that all systems of interpretation may be fictions.

In *Bleak House* this tension is dramatised in a way appropriate for a novel which focuses on the theme of interpretation. It lies in the contrast between Esther's way of seeing the world and that of the anonymous narrator. Skimpole, Chadband, Mrs Jellyby and the rest each dwell hermetically sealed within an idiosyncratic system of language. In particular, Skimpole's light-hearted reading of the world as designed for his delectation and amusement, expressed with great verve by Dickens, is a frighteningly plausible reversal of Esther's commitment to duty and responsibility. Esther's language too is a special perspective, perhaps a distorting one, as is the view of the other narrator. Each has his characteristic rhetoric, a rhetoric which interprets the world along certain lines. To Esther the course of her life seems secretly governed by a divine Providence. She sees this most concretely in the benign presences she glimpses in the landscape around Chesney Wold: 'O, the solemn woods over which the light and shadow travelled swiftly, as if Heavenly wings were sweeping on benignant errands through the summer air' (ch. 18). To the other narrator no such presences are visible. He sees a world darkening toward death, a world in which it is always foggy or raining. His vision, for example in the description of Tom-all-Alone's in chapter 46, may be defined as nihilistic:

> Darkness rests upon Tom-all-Alone's. Dilating and dilating since the sun went down last night, it has gradually swelled until it fills every void in the place. ... The blackest nightmare in the infernal stables grazes on Tom-all-Alone's, and Tom is fast asleep.
>
> (ch. 46)

Which of these is a misinterpretation? Perhaps both are? Though the happy ending of *Bleak House* may beguile the reader into accepting Esther's view as the true one, the novel does not resolve the incompatibility between her vision and what the other narrator sees. The meaning of the novel lies in this irresolution.

Like many other nineteenth-century writers Dickens was caught between his desire to reject what he found morally objectionable or false about Christianity, in particular its doctrine of original sin, and his desire to retain some form of Christian morality. This retention was for Dickens, as for others in his time, the only protection against nihilism. *Bleak House* presents the reader with a sick, decaying, moribund society. It locates with profound insight the causes of that sickness in the sign-making power, in the ineradicable human tendency to take the sign for the substance, and in the instinctive habit of interpretation, assimilating others into a private or collective system of meaning. At the same time the novel itself performs a large-scale act of interpretation. If there were no interpretation there would be no novel. It frees itself from the guilt of this only by giving the reader, not least in its inconsistencies, the evidence necessary to see that it is an interpretation.

On the one hand the distorted Christianity of Esther's aunt is firmly repudiated. Against her, 'Watch ye therefore! lest coming suddenly he find you sleeping', is set Jesus' forgiveness of the woman caught in adultery: 'He that is without sin among you, let him first cast a stone at her!' (ch. 3). On the other hand, the novel apparently sustains Lady Dedlock in her remorse, in her somewhat narrowly Christian interpretation of what from another point of view, abundantly suggested in the novel, is her natural and good love of Captain Hawdon. A later generation might see marriage as one of the perfidious legalities distorting the natural feelings of the heart. In fact in Dickens' own day Ludwig Feuerbach in *The Essence of Christianity*, George Eliot in her liaison with George Henry Lewes, perhaps even in her fiction, and Anthony Trollope in such a novel as *Dr Wortle's School* saw individual acts of love as sanctifying the legal institution of marriage rather than the other way around. Lady Dedlock's mystery and the mystery of Chancery are so closely intertwined that the reader may be enticed into thinking that the solution of the one is the solution of the other. Some 'illicit' act like fornication must lie at the origin of Jarndyce and Jarndyce and be the explanation of the suffering it causes, visiting the sins of the fathers on the children, generation after generation. The novel persuasively shows, however, that nothing lies at the origin of Jarndyce and Jarndyce but man's ability to create and administer systems of law. Such systems give actions and documents a meaning. It would seem, nevertheless, that the Ten Commandments fit this definition of evil as well as the laws and precedents governing Chancery. Both the particular commandments against which Lady Dedlock has sinned and the system of Chancery have jurisdiction over the relations of man to woman, parent to child. Between its commitment to a traditional interpretation of these relations and a tendency to put all interpretation in question as the original evil *Bleak House* remains poised.

From J. Hillis Miller, *Victorian Subjects* (Brighton and Durham, NC, 1991), pp. 179–99.

NOTES

[The Introduction suggested the historical importance of Hillis Miller's essay. Many themes influential for current Dickens commentary have come from it: discussions of allegory; the notion of interpreting some only partially recoverable dark secret in the past; the importance of names in Dickens, and people's relationship to simple proper or improper names, or else to things, or objects; the importance of pointing (signifying). Inspiration from Barthes and from semiotics, too, provides the question, which is applied to Dickens criticism, whether words and signs indicate something beyond themselves, or are merely signifiers linked to each other in an endless metonymy (where one signifier is linked to another and replaceable by another, in an endless succession which offers, but does not fulfil, the suggestion of complete meaning residing in the complete chain). Where the relation between signifier and signified is taken to be unstable, with no passing beyond the signifier to the level of the signified – the realm of clear meaning – this approach, as with Hillis Miller's earlier work on Dickens, *Charles Dickens, The World of His Novels* (1958), argues that the text is no more than 'a huge structure based on words' – the creation of a fictional reality, analogous to the indecipherable lawsuit of *Jarndyce* v. *Jarndyce*. But even to solve the lawsuit produces no enlightenment: nor does the unveiling of an analogous mystery, Lady Dedlock's secret. While Hillis Miller follows Nietzsche in taking the act of interpretation to be violent, the *primary* act of violence is that interpretation tries to get outside the signifier, by forgetting the existence of the text and of textuality, in the dream of escaping from a system which is linguistic and self-referential, into the space of the real. Names, for instance, invite the possibility of interpretation: names such as Tulkinghorn and Turveydrop imply a meaning, even if this cannot be quite specified: but interpretation only covers over the *aporia* (the impassable gap) involved in stepping from the text to anything beyond it.

This approach which rests upon Derrida and his argument that there is 'nothing outside the text' – *il n'y a pas de hors-texte* (*Of Grammatology*, trans. Gayatri Chakravorty Spivak [Baltimore, MD, 1976], p. 158) – is questionable since the reader must ask about the place of history and politics that it seems to leave out. Can Hillis Miller's essay explain the historical existence of the system it points to? For Hillis Miller, 'nothing lies at the origin of Jarndyce and Jarndyce but man's ability to create and administer systems of law' (p. 57). It might be possible to inflect 'law' psychoanalytically, as the next essay does; it is possible to wonder whether this creativity in making law is not a residual humanism in Hillis Miller's approach which is unLacanian, and out of keeping with the idea, basic to deconstruction, of language as that which speaks and hence creates the subject. And while Hillis Miller's essay denies, as does deconstruction, and Nietzsche, in *The Genealogy of Morals*, the importance of origins, and thus puts the existence of a plot in *Bleak House* into question, it remains to be asked whether the system described in this criticism is not wholly abstract, separated from history. Other essays will return to this theme. Ed.]

1. In *Dickens at Work* (1957), and *The Dickens World* (1941), respectively.

2. See p. 940, Penguin edition.

3. *The World of Charles Dickens* (1970), p. 234.

4. See Roland Barthes, 'Proust et les noms', *To Honor Roman Jakobson* (The Hague, 1967), pp. 150–8.

5. *Illuminations* (New York, 1969), p. 101.

2

'The Universe Makes an Indifferent Parent': *Bleak House* and the Victorian Family Romance

CHRISTINE VAN BOHEEMEN-SAAF

[Two extracts are included from this essay, which begins with the loss of historic and pre-historic origins, as this was becoming more evident with the nineteenth century's new attention to geology and to other, almost infinitely other, forms of life, and which suggests that the condition of modernity is that of being an orphan, where – as Chancery, suggesting the absence of God the father proves – 'the universe makes an indifferent parent' (*Bleak House*, ch. 6, p. 122). The first extract has to do with Esther's 'confrontation with the otherness of her origin'.]

I

Looking back over Esther's development as a character, one notices that the ambivalence of the final symbol of selfhood has been present in Dickens' portrayal of her all along, and reflects an underlying ambivalence in the novel's notion of human identity. From Esther's earliest moments of conscious reflection, her awareness is structured by the tension between her true but unmentionable natural identity and the necessity to ensure a place and role in the patriarchal social system to which she is an outsider. As she gathers from her godmother's unrelenting insistence that she had better not have been born at all, the anniversary of her birth is a day of evil and sinful disgrace to those sharing the secret surrounding her birth. Esther's manner of coping with the social and emotional isolation of her position is to deny that deepest, most natural part of herself, which in her childish understanding merely seems to keep the 'wound' of the day of her birth open. This 'natural' self, on which her own generativity and full womanhood depend, she projects upon her doll, the only one to whom she opens her heart. But this child had better never been born at all: departing for school, Esther buries her doll in the garden. Simultaneously, she sets out to win social approval with the vow 'to repair the fault I had been born with (of which I confessedly felt guilty and yet innocent) ... and [to] strive as I grew up to be industrious, contented and kindhearted, and to do some good to some one, and win some love to myself if I could' (ch. 3). From the very beginning, then, Esther's 'self' is split into two halves, one 'buried' and unmentionable, one obsessively concerned with conformity to patriarchal views of feminine identity. We might say that Esther's struggle for selfhood takes place at two levels simultaneously, one questing for an identification with the (m)other in order to achieve sexual identity, the other for substitute fatherhood and a place in society.[1]

Initially, the attempts to earn a place in society and the protection of a father figure occupy the foreground of the narrative. At the Miss Donnys', and then at Bleak House, Esther persistently attempts to blot out the shame of her birth by trying to become an 'original' herself. As everyone agrees, she is a model of deportment – a 'pattern young lady', as detective Bucket praises her – obsessively creating order out of disorder and stalling the disintegration of society at large (domestically reflected in the state of Mrs Jellyby's closets) by her unrelenting diligence and the protection of her household keys, which she jingles to the refrain of 'Esther, duty, my dear.' Indeed, Esther's attempt to lock out the 'original sin' leads her farther and farther away from selfhood to the perfection of an imaginary, obsessive role, and to speaking to herself in the third person; when her substitute father and guardian finally offers to marry her, it momentarily seems as if Esther will become, like her biblical namesake, 'a queen' of starry purity.[2]

For all Esther's exertions to earn an unfallen status, at moments of emotional crisis the repressed image of the doll revives in her memory, bringing with it softer sensations. When the young lawyer

Guppy proposes marriage in the chapter entitled 'Signs and Tokens', her own refusal leaves her perturbed: 'I surprised myself by beginning to laugh about it, and then surprised myself still more by beginning to cry about it. … I was in a flutter for a little while; and felt as if an old chord had been more coarsely touched than it ever had been since the days of the dear old doll, long buried in the garden' (ch. 9). A similar reaction marks Esther's first meeting with her mother, whom she has never known and who is still a mere stranger to her: 'And, very strangely, there was something quickened within me, associated with the lonely days at my godmother's; yes, away even to the days when I had stood on tiptoe to dress myself at my little glass, after dressing my doll' (ch. 18).

Thus, underneath the narrative strand which moves toward Esther's social rootedness, there is the concern with the buried but stirring insistence of the original 'wound' or 'sin', which must be confronted to be cured or appeased. This confrontation happens, always at the level of implication, in stages. The first begins on the crucially important evening of Esther's contact with Jo, who will transmit the mysterious and highly contagious disease that originates from a rat scurrying from Captain Nemo's pauper grave in Tom-all-Alone's. At that moment, though Esther has not yet learned the identity of her mother – or even of her existence – she has the 'undefinable impression' of 'being something different from what I then was' (ch. 3). As Mark Spilka and Taylor Stoehr have suggested, this disease, never given a name in the novel, is on a symbolic level related to the unbridled sexuality of Esther's parents; and 'smallpox' is indeed close enough to 'pox' to assume a sexual connotation.[3]

In addition, smallpox, a disease which leaves pockmarks on the face, suggests the 'wound' of castration of non-phallic origin. The imagery in which Esther describes the experience of her illness is suggestive of an archetypal and successful quest for identity – she recalls the sensation of crossing a dark lake and of labouring, like a worm, up colossal staircases; however, this confrontation with the uncanny taboo – the return of the repressed – does not lead to the blinding insight of a figure like Oedipus (though it strikes her with temporary blindness). Here is the *anagnorisis* when Esther looks at the pockmarks on her face:

> My hair had not been cut off. … It was long and thick. I let it down, and shook it out, and went up to the glass upon the dressing-table.

There was a little muslin curtain drawn across it. I drew it back; and stood for a moment looking through such a veil of my own hair, that I could see nothing else. Then I put my hair aside, and looked at the reflection in the mirror. ... I was very much changed – O very, very much. At first my face was so strange to me, that I think I should have put my hands before it and started back. ... Very soon it became more familiar, and then I knew the extent of the alteration in it better than I had done at first. It was not like what I had expected; but I had expected nothing definite, and I dare say anything definite would have surprised me.

(ch. 36)

In this revelation, in which Esther's social self finds her true self fearsomely *unfamiliar*, we recognise the same gesture of moving aside the hair to look at the face which marks the revelatory moment of Esther's later identification of and with her mother. Indeed, the frightening face surrounded by copious hair is an image of the Medusa's head, as Freud has told us, the visual representation of castrated female sexuality that turns the beholder into stone.[4] At one level, then, as a suggestive foreshadowing of the later event, this passage seems to imply Esther's acceptance of the biological truth of her origin without so much as touching the hem of Victorian respectability. However, in the evasiveness of the final phrases, refusing to accept loss or otherness in denying the existence of a previous expectation, her repression of the reality of her biological self is renewed.

Consequently, her illness results in an increased need to maintain the separateness of the split-off image of the doll rather than its integration. This shows itself in Esther's relationship to Ada Clare, who – like Charley, Esther's little maid – is a reincarnation of the long-buried doll. Charley's wide-eyed tininess suggests the child-hood confidante, but Ada has its 'beautiful complexion' and 'rosy lips', and is, moreover, an idealised alter ego: contrary to the sex-lessness indicated by Esther's nicknames (Mother Hubbard, Dame Durden, Mrs Shipton), Ada represents feminine sexuality, as indi-cated by her betrothal to Richard; in contrast to Esther's sense of her own unworthiness, Ada seems bright, beautiful, good, and unblemished. No wonder that Esther seems to love Ada almost more than herself. When Ada marries Richard, Esther hopes to live with them; keeping 'the keys of their house', she will be made 'happy for ever and a day' (ch. 14). When her longing to reconsti-tute the triangle of family romance in this manner is not fulfilled,

Esther is wild with grief. At night she steals to Ada's house and listens to the sounds within! During her illness, it is Ada's pure beauty which must be protected from the disease at all cost. Ada's perfection, the token that she has had no contact with the blight of natural female origin clinging to Esther, is 'the light' in Esther's blindness. During her illness Esther seems to feel that without preserving this idealised version of herself uncontaminated and intact, she cannot continue to live: if Ada is allowed to look upon her marked face for only one moment, Esther will die.

Esther's continued fear of revealing her face to Ada marks her unchanged refusal to accept herself as her mother's daughter. From this point of view, it is highly significant that the chapter that has as its central event the relatively restrained recognition of the kinship between Esther and her mother should end in a climax of much greater emotional intensity with the reunion of Esther and Ada. Here we see Ada play the mother role, accepting Esther's face, 'bathing it with tears and kisses, rocking [her] to and fro like a child, calling [her] by every tender name that she could think of' (ch. 36). Only after Esther has truly accepted the familiarity of her mother's 'sin' will she change positions with Ada: whereas Esther has a romance and starts her own family, the widowed Ada moves back to Bleak House to take care of her guardian.

This moment of acceptance comes after another confrontation with the 'sin' from which all corruption in *Bleak House* has started, after another archetypal descent, which, unlike Esther's illness, is a confrontation with real death. It is the death of Lady Dedlock, who has completed her own circuitous return to the reality of the past and lies dead at the grave of the man 'who should have been her husband', in the spot from which all corruption in the world of this novel takes its origin. This final image of Tom-all-Alone's is the 'primal scene' of the motivation of the narrative. From here the subversive threat of the levelling of hierarchical distinctions – of a breakdown of the walls of subjectivity that ensure the operative power of such concepts as race, class, sex, and age – has arisen, the threat of which the narrator asserts that 'His Grace shall not be able to say Nay to the infamous alliance' (ch. 46). Esther's journey toward this heart of London's darkness, undertaken to 'save' her mother from the final deed, leads her through a 'labyrinth of streets', in between darkness and dawn, into a mental state between waking and dreaming in which the reality she had always known seems so changed that 'great water-gates seemed to be opening and closing in my head, or in the air; and ... the unreal things were more substantial than the real' (ch. 59). Directly preceding this, she has confessed that it seemed as if the 'stained house-fronts put on human shapes and looked at' her; in the light of the house symbolism of the novel, this seems a hallucinatory realisation that the stain of Tom-all-Alone's is also her own but cannot yet be admitted into consciousness. Thus, when she arrives at the entrance to this enclosed place – the curiously Victorian version of the *hortus conclusus* – she still cannot relate its otherness to herself:

> The gate was closed. Beyond it, was a burial-ground – a dreadful spot in which the night was very slowly stirring; but where I could dimly see ... houses ... on whose walls a thick humidity broke out like a disease. On the step at the gate, drenched in the fearful wet of such a place, which oozed and splashed down everywhere, I saw, with a cry of pity and horror, a woman lying – Jenny, the mother of the dead child.
>
> (ch. 59)

But this last phrase is not final; it is to be revised into the 'dead mother of the living child'. The truth about her own face will come home after a gesture we remember from Esther's illness: 'I lifted the heavy head, put the long dank hair aside, and turned the face. And it was my mother, cold and dead' (ch. 59). At last, then, the unfortunate girl has owned her mother, has looked the evil of her birth in the face and accepted it as her own; from this moment on the taboo on her sexuality is lifted. Avoiding the mistakes of her mother, Esther does not marry the elderly Jarndyce, who calls her 'my child', but confesses her hitherto unacknowledged attraction to Alan Woodcourt.

[The second extract comes after Christine van Boheemen-Saaf's discussion of the various 'fathers' in the text, and it leads into a discussion of two novelistic plot types the text works between – the older 'family romance', which involves the hero/heroine's discovery of ideal parents, beyond the parents they thought they had, and the newer form of the detective novel.]

II

Though *Bleak House* has many features of the older family romance, the moment which resolves the original blight, the discovery of the dead mother at the entrance to Tom-all-Alone's, is reached only after a deliberate, organised search, directed by a trained professional. Unlike the popular family romance, which assumes that identity is there merely waiting to be discovered, *Bleak House* is notable for its fairly early revelation of origin (in itself a reconstitution) and its lengthy process of bringing Lady Dedlock, the criminal, to what is in terms of Victorian narrative logic her justly deserved end. But this logic is Victorian not only because of the emphasis on the process of excommunication rather than mere discovery: the nature of what is communicated is of equal importance. Thus, in the light of psychoanalytic theories of the detective story, it is curiously appropriate that the moment at Tom-all-Alone's, while not a revelation of the crime of murder, should be both the revelation of a moment of pathetic death, and a displaced version of the primal scene. In her analysis of Poe's 'The Murders in the Rue Morgue', Marie Bonaparte writes: 'The unconscious source of our interest in narratives of this type lies, as Freud first led us to recognise, in the fact that the researches conducted by the detective reproduce, by displacement onto subjects of a quite different nature, our infantile investigations into matters of sex.'[5] In other words, the detective story, displacing the primal scene onto a scene of violence, offers the reader an opportunity to allay his fear and curiosity without having to acknowledge it.

But what is 'primal scene' but another term for the moment of biological origin? And if it is true that biological origin as a problem is characteristic of the Victorian age, can we not, in turn, explain the origin and popularity of the detective story as the fictional reflection of the deeper, unconscious concerns of the age? However, unconscious concern with origin can account for only one aspect of the mystery story, its fascination with violence. As a fiction privileging organised investigation, rational detection rather than accidental discovery, the detective novel is the fictional form of an epoch which has committed itself to a belief in the liberating efficacy of scientific research. As Hartman writes, 'It explains the irrational ... by the latest rational system'.[6] The 'whodunit' is the poor, or less prestigious, stepsister of a scientific treatise like the *Origin of Species*, and Darwin's injunction that we 'possess no pedigrees or armorial bearings' [i.e., fixed origin], and 'we have to *discover* and *trace* the many diverging lines of descent in our natural genealogies' (my emphasis), conforms to what the detective novel, in its characteristically displaced form, does.

Probably because of its experimental searching for an adequate form *Bleak House* is both more primitive and less displaced than the more sophisticated work of Dickens' friend Wilkie Collins and his acquaintance Poe, though the indebtedness to 'The Purloined Letter' (1845) seems especially great.[7] Thus, what Hartman calls the 'scene of suffering' is displaced by a scene of recognition both more clearly sexual and more ambivalent than the central event in the crime mystery. I say more ambivalent, because in the detective novel the 'parent for whom the reader (the child) has negative oedipal feelings' is represented as the pitiful victim, whereas Lady Dedlock, the dead mother, is both victim and criminal at once.[8] *Bleak House* shows us in the moment at Tom-all-Alone's a 'whodunit' off guard as a 'Hawdon-it', and this lesser depth of its 'buried life' seems to provide unique insight into the generic moment of transformation from (family) romance into detective novel.

With this realisation we have arrived at a better position from which to judge the validity of the initial assumption of this essay – that Dickens' concern with orphanhood in *Bleak House* and other writings, and the revisionary tactics with which he excommunicates the threat of otherness from the surface level of his novel, should not be seen as merely reflecting a personal psychological need or the artistic credo that 'in all familiar things, even in those which are repellent on the surface, there is Romance enough, if we will find it out'.[9] Dickens, as the strategist of his narrative, is an analogue of the energetic detective Bucket, searching and finding out with his pen – guided by his pointed forefinger – the (dis)closure of Esther's illegitimate origin;[10] and just as Bucket's mysterious powers dissolve the anxiety of his world, Dickens' narrative magic wipes the cobwebs of doubt from the Victorian sky, giving his audience on an unconscious level what it needs to pull through, *the reassuring message of the familiar myth*.

From *Interpreting Lacan*, ed. Joseph H. Smith and William Kerrigan (New Haven, CT, 1983), pp. 225–57.

NOTES

Christine van Boheemen-Saaf's essay, represented only by these extracts, deals, like Hillis Miller's essay, with a universe with no grounding origin (showing this through an account of the mud and fog of the first chapter).

The idea of the 'origin' is associated with the father: this reading of the text is Lacanian, suggesting that the father, as the centring 'phallic' principle, is missing. This, which in Lacan would be productive of psychosis in the children, if it were to be the case, is, however, linked in this essay to a new emphasis on the mother. Darwinian ideology, the essay argues, foregrounds female Nature, and so brings back the mother-figure. The text is read in terms of Esther's coming to terms with the sexuality of the mother.

Yet *Bleak House*, according to this essay, does not remain content with the power of the female: rather the 'disruptive heterogeneity' it implies is contained by a replacement of old fathers by new, exemplified by the move from Tulkinghorn to Bucket, who, it may be noted, in contrast to other essays in this New Casebook, is read positively for his energy. And the new detective novel form, which is fascinated by origins, particularly those of the impossible and putative 'primal scene' (the fantasised 'locked room' setting where the child becomes aware of the scene of his own conception) and the mysteries of which it tries to solve, is the ideological form which accords with nineteenth-century anxieties about loss of a privileged origin (the sense that everything comes out of the mud). The popularity of the 'family romance' that Freud discusses – the child's wish to construct some ideal origins for itself, superior to its actual parents – is an ideological desire created in a moment which is obsessed with the fear that there is no other origin than a non-differentiating Nature. In this argument, the detective novel is born in order to legitimate the priority of the patriarchal family. Ed.]

1. The critical view of Esther as a flawed character has lately superseded the earlier indictment of her character as insignificant, hypocritical, or falsely sweet. Alex Zwerdling argues in 'Esther Summerson Rehabilitated', *PMLA*, 88 (1973), 429–39, that 'Dickens' interest in Esther is fundamentally clinical: to observe and describe a certain kind of psychic debility. The psychological subject matter of Dickens' later novels demanded a new narrative technique, in which the character could present himself directly. ... Esther Summerson is Dickens' most ambitious attempt to allow a character who does not fully understand herself to tell her own story' (p. 432). Though I do not disagree with Zwerdling, I am not here concerned with psychological realism. I focus instead on Esther as a function in a narrative strategy, an 'actant' in a story, to use Greimas' term. From this analytical point of view the dualism of Esther's character is related to Taylor Stoehr's findings in *Dickens: The Dreamer's Stance* (Ithaca, NY, 1965), which point to the many instances of doubling in this novel. Apart from the two voices and their contrary visions of the world, doubling has led to the creation of many pairs of characters which are 'projections onto separate characters of the conflicting impulses of the dreamer. Through them Dickens conveys the ambivalence and complexity of his dream meaning without expressly stating it' (p. 167). Stoehr sees the function of the double plot as keeping social and sexual problems from intermingling.

My interpretation differs in that I try to show that on a deeper level, they are concerned with the same ontological problems of identity, but that only the private confrontation leads to the suggestion of resolution.

2. The biblical Esther, a Jewish orphan and the ward of Mordecai, was chosen by the Babylonian King Ahasuerus to replace his wife Vashti, who had refused to appear dressed in nothing but the royal crown at a banquet held for the princes of the realm. Queen Esther was noted for a feminine diplomacy and manipulative respect for authority which allowed her to save her people from the extinction planned by Haman.

3. M. Spilka, *Dickens and Kafka: A Mutual Interpretation* (Bloomington, IN, 1963), p. 214; Stoehr, *Dickens*, pp. 143–4.

4. S. Freud, 'Medusa's Head' (1922), *Standard Edition* (London, 1955), vol. 18.

5. M. Bonaparte, 'The Murders in Rue Morgue', *Psychoanalytic Quarterly*, 4 (1935), 259–93, 292. The connection between detective story and 'primal scene' was first brought to my attention by Geoffrey H. Hartman's 'Literature High and Low: The Case of the Mystery Story', in *The Fate of Reading: And Other Essays* (Chicago, 1975). Hartman speaks of 'one definitively visualised scene to which everything else might be referred', a 'scene of suffering' or a '*tò pathos*' (p. 207). [The 'scene of suffering' translates the Greek term, which is derived from Greek tragedy, which of course involves 'scenes'. – Ed.] His argument also refers to the work of Charles Rycroft, 'The Analysis of a Detective Story', in *Imagination and Reality: Psychoanalytical Essays 1951–61* (London 1968), and of Geraldine Pedersen-Krag, 'Detective Stories and the Primal Scene', *Psychoanalytic Quarterly*, 18 (1949), 207–14. I have relied on all these works in reaching my conclusions.

6. Hartman, 'Literature High and Low', p. 209.

7. Thus we know from the very beginning who the criminal is: a woman whose prominent social position places her in the public eye. Moreover, the 'crime' relates to a piece of writing, a personal letter, suggesting illicit personal relations. Apart from the gusty autumn weather of the setting, the analogy extends to the similarity in character of Tulkinghorn and Mr. D—, who hoard the secret, and their replacement in the plot by the detectives Bucket and Dupin. An interesting psychoanalytic interpretation of Poe's story, which confirms by analogy this reading of *Bleak House*, is in J. Lacan, 'The Seminar on *The Purloined Letter*', trans. J. Mehlman, *French Freud, Yale French Studies*, 48 (1972). Lacan's interpretation has been criticised by Jacques Derrida in 'Le Facteur de la Verité', *Poetique*, 21 (1975), 96–147. For an exposition of Lacan's analysis, see S. Felman, 'On

Reading Poetry: Reflections on the Limits and Possibilities of Psycho-analytic Approaches', in J. H. Smith (ed.), *The Literary Freud: Mechanisms of Defense and the Poetic Will*, vol. 4 of *Psychiatry and the Humanities* (New Haven, CT, 1980).

Dickens had met Poe in Philadelphia during his American tour of 1842, and had promised to find an English publisher for *Tales of the Grotesque and Arabesque*. Though publication of 'The Purloined Letter' postdates their meeting, it seems unlikely that Dickens, who had kept in touch with Poe, would not have read this *Tale*.

8. Pedersen-Krag, 'Detective Stories', p. 209.

9. From 'A Preliminary Word', in the first number of *Household Words*, 30 March 1850, when Dickens was writing *David Copperfield*.

10. Dickens had originally pictured his authorial persona for *Household Words* as a 'certain SHADOW, which may go into any place, by sun-light, moonlight, starlight ... and be supposed to be cognizant of everything'. This reminds one rather suggestively of Bucket's omnipresent omniscience. See E. Johnson, *Charles Dickens: His Tragedy and Triumph* (New York, 1952: rev. edn 1977), pp. 356 ff.

3

Double Vision and the Double Standard in *Bleak House:* A Feminist Perspective

VIRGINIA BLAIN

The device of dual narration has often been taken to be the key to interpreting *Bleak House*, but I should like to suggest that previous discussions have overlooked an important aspect of Dickens's use of this device. It seems to me that the juxtaposition of the two narrative voices sets up a submerged dialectic between male and female viewpoints, and that once we are aware of the operation of this dialectic, other features of the novel take on a new significance.[1] John Carey has drawn attention to the way in which suppressed violence can give rise to sexual conflict in Dickens's novels.[2] Such conflict, I would suggest, informs not only the vision of violence in familial and personal relationships in *Bleak House*, but also the vision of hidden violence in the legal system. I draw on the work of René Girard[3] in support of my perception of the significance of this link between the legal and the social/sexual bases of society as portrayed in *Bleak House*. The proposition Girard puts to us about the hidden connections in a modern society between violence and sexuality[4] appears to be unconsciously sensed by Dickens. Dickens's perception of the gender division into 'separate spheres' for men and women affords him the opportunity for a dual viewpoint on societal corruption, both public and private. But through its articulation as a dialectic the narrative structure does more than this, in my view. Its workings produce a novel which probes deeply at the roots of this corruption and strongly suggests that they are at least partly embedded in the violence of hidden sexual hostilities. The text thus carries inscribed within it a significance for a late twentieth-century female reader, in particular, which it did not reveal to earlier critics or to the author himself.

In Part I of the discussion which follows, I aim to give an understanding of the importance of the male/female dialectic both to the structure of the novel and, more particularly, to the characterisation of Esther. In Parts II and III, where the focus shifts onto Esther's mother, I shall point to some hitherto unrecognised aspects of Lady Dedlock's pivotal role in the novel. I also offer a new interpretation of her relationship with the legally established patriarchy (especially Mr Tulkinghorn) on the one hand, and with her illegitimate daughter, Esther, on the other. Finally, in Part IV, I shall suggest that her chase and death take on a new significance when they are read as part of a purification rite for a whole diseased society.

I

Dickens's use in *Bleak House* of the unusual strategy of dual narration has drawn from his commentators no mean portion of the critical debate which surrounds this novel. The role of Esther Summerson has long been a major focus for controversy, and in recent years a great deal of energy has been expended on what one critic has called 'the rehabilitation of Esther Summerson'.[5] The case for the psychological 'truth' of her presentation as a young woman of some emotional retardation, springing from an early childhood deprived of love and esteem, and warped by her inturned sense of social guilt, has been sufficiently well-documented to need no further elaboration here.[6] The omniscient narrator, in his turn, has been subjected to various modes of critical investigation, though not under quite the same cloud of controversy that has shadowed discussion of Esther. Although few since E. M. Forster (in *Aspects of the Novel*) have wanted to argue that this narrative voice is that of Dickens himself, equally few have dared to follow Grahame Smith's example, in his monograph of *Bleak House* (London, 1974), in proffering a full identikit portrait of this protean figure:

> The narrator of *Bleak House* is an educated man, but not one who feels the need to make a display of his learning, and this is part of a general pattern of characteristics that I would suggest make the narrator a coherent figure. ... I see the third-person narrator of *Bleak House* as urbane, witty, cultured; in short a man of the world, but a man of the world whose poise never degenerates into cynicism.
>
> (pp. 12–13)

None the less, even among those who take up neither of these extreme positions, there is one point of unspoken agreement: that of the omniscient narrator's gender. He is unquestionably male. Even if he is nothing but a voice, it is a male voice. This seems to me to be one of those points which are so obvious that their significance is in danger of being missed; but when we remind ourselves on whose vision the idea of omniscience is ultimately based ('Our *Father*' of Jo's dying prayer) we perceive afresh some of the assumptions we have been used to making about Victorian literature. An omniscient narrator was masculine almost by definition.[7] To my knowledge, there was no model of female omniscience available to Victorian novelists, either in literature or in Heaven.

I want to argue that it has a profound significance for the meaning of *Bleak House* as a whole when we read it as a novel told half from a male standpoint and half from a female. In earlier studies, the differences between the two narrating voices in *Bleak House* have been accounted for in different ways by different critics. Esther's is the 'inner' voice, his the 'outer' voice: hers is the subjective voice, his the objective; hers is personal, his impersonal. Each of these qualities can of course be seen as glosses on the basic premise that one voice is feminine and one is masculine. The inner perspective, the subjective viewpoint, the interest bounded by personal limits, these are all qualities typically, even archetypically, associated with the feminine principle, while objectivity, impersonality and largeness of vision all belong to the masculine realm.

The full significance of Esther Summerson's 'femaleness', in her narrator's role and in the action, has yet to be charted.[8] Ellen Moers has called it 'the single "woman question" novel in the Dickens canon',[9] and it certainly seems clear that in this novel Dickens had a great many things he wanted to say about women and their social and sexual roles. In order to say them convincingly, he hit upon the brilliant idea of presenting one woman's experience of herself and of womanhood as part of the reader's very means of vision, part of the experience of reading the novel. Twentieth-century readers might wish to object that Esther, as 'female eunuch' *par excellence*, is disqualified from speaking authoritatively of or from female experience. But this argument can be reversed very easily when we remember how pervasive in the middle classes was the notion of women as 'relative creatures' at this period in Queen Victoria's reign:[10] creatures destined solely to be a man's helpmate, as daughter, wife, or mother, for whom any separate individual identity was seen to be a burden. Thus Esther, far from being an unrepresentative woman, might well be seen as archetypically representative of the Victorian middle-class woman who has been shaped by her adoption of the values of the patriarchal society she inhabits, and whose own selfhood is very much in question as a result.

It is important to emphasise the structural significance of Dickens's choice of a female narrative voice as a counterbalance to the masculine omniscient narrator. Each has been given almost exactly half the space of the novel. While the masculine, all-knowing voice offers us the analytical overview of the novel's world, the viewpoint (to adapt Hillis Miller's definition of the omniscient narrator's role) of the middle-class male community mind become aware of itself,[11] the female, limited voice, by contrast, gives us the private, personal viewpoint. Esther cannot tell about either the working of the law in Chancery, or the making of the Law in Parliament; as a woman, she is shut out from these two patriarchal structures, and as an illegitimate woman she is placed at an even further remove from the centre of legal power. Thus, paradoxically her 'inner' view of characters and events is really that of an outsider in society, while the other narrator's 'outer' view springs very much from an inside vantage point.

Although many of the same characters appear in each, the two narratives are not alternative accounts of the same events. Of course, by choosing Esther to offset his omniscient narrator, Dickens is able to reinforce not only the separation between the male and female viewpoint, by allowing to each a particular sphere of comment, but also their difference, which he exploits by using each as a purveyor of criticism of the other's domain. Some of this criticism is explicit (and can therefore be read as consciously intended), but a more subversive criticism is inscribed implicitly within the text. In making what might at first seem a perverse allocation of material, and giving the telling of the story of Richard Carstone's battle with Chancery to the female narrative voice and the story of Lady Dedlock's guilty secret to the male narrative voice, the novel is opening a pathway for a commentary on the male preserve of legal inheritance from a female standpoint, and on the female 'preserve' of illicit sexuality (Lady Dedlock) or illegal inheritance (Esther herself) – from a male. For Esther's narration gives no glow of feminine (or sentimental) sympathy to Richard's story; as Taylor Stoehr rightly points out,[12] she in fact makes a less than sympathetic narrator of this tale of failure and suffering. Equally or even more surely, the detached voice of the omniscient narrator, with his relentlessly rhetorical insistence on the allegory of the Ghost's Walk, succeeds in achieving an almost total alienation of the most sympathetic reader from the plight of the unhappy Lady Dedlock.

II

Lady Dedlock's melodramatic tale of woe has indeed often been regarded as an unfortunate intrusion in the novel, an instance of Dickens's inability to sustain a wholly unified concept of the novel as artistic structure. In my reading however, Lady Dedlock is vital to the balance of the whole novel, and at least as crucial a figure as the Lord Chancellor himself (in both his manifestations). Dickens points similarities between the latter's Court of Chancery and Lady Dedlock's world of fashion (both 'things of precedent and usage') as early as chapter 2, and it is clear that she is as powerful a figurehead in the hierarchy of the female world as he is in the male. Further, both are dependent finally upon the power of parliamentary law, resting at this time largely in the hands of the aristocracy, represented in the novel by Sir Leicester Dedlock. To Sir Leicester's fellows and their hereditary power, the Lord Chancellor owes his position, and to Sir Leicester himself, and the hereditary station he occupies, Lady Dedlock owes hers. 'Indeed, he married her for love. A whisper still goes about, that she had not even family' (ch. 2, p. 12).[13]

The comparison between the structural function of these two pivotal figures can be carried further and by implication can be seen to mirror the structural function of the two narrative voices. The Lord Chancellor's Quilpish double, 'lord chancellor' Krook, subsumes into himself all the smouldering violence which can find no outlet in the real Court of Chancery, thus freeing the true Lord Chancellor to appear 'both courtly and kind' (Esther's words in ch. 3, p. 31). Similarly, Lady Dedlock has a double or surrogate, no less sinister in kind than Krook. This of course is the Frenchwoman Hortense, perceived in a striking passage in chapter 18 as deliberately walking shoeless through the wet grass 'as if through blood' (p. 231), and who, like Krook, has the function of drawing to herself much of the passionate violence that one might have expected to accrue to a woman in Lady Dedlock's increasingly beseiged position as she engages more and more fully in her secret and deadly duel with Tulkinghorn.

Then again, there is a strong parallel between the Lord Chancellor and Lady Dedlock in their relative positions as parent-figures: 'The Lord High Chancellor, at his best, appeared so poor a substitute for the love and pride of parents', muses Esther (ch. 3, p. 31), but does she convince us that she holds any better an opinion of her own mother? 'I told her ... [t]hat it was not for me, then resting *for the first time*, on my mother's bosom, to take her to account for having given me life' (ch. 36 p. 449, my italics).[14] Both the Lord Chancellor, *in loco parentis* to Richard and Ada, and Lady Dedlock, aided to ignorance of her child's need by her barbarous sister, are well-intentioned in theory but profoundly damaging in practice towards their children. It is no accident that we are shown mad Miss Flite deluded into inventing an unhappy marriage between Lady Dedlock and the Lord Chancellor: '"... in *my* opinion ... she's the Lord Chancellor's wife. He's married, you know. And I understand she leads him a terrible life"' (ch. 35, p. 439).

It is surely not surprising that we can trace such parallels as these in *Bleak House*. That the novel achieves its effects largely by the exploitation of parallels and hidden connections has long been recognised. What *is* perhaps surprising is that critics have continued to puzzle over what has been called the 'problem' of the novel's having two 'centres', the Chancery centre and the Lady Dedlock centre. Even Hillis Miller, who assures us in his introduction to the Penguin edition (1971) that:

> Metaphor and metonymy together make up the deep grammatical armature by which the reader of *Bleak House* is led to make a whole out of discontinuous parts
>
> [p. 32, above]

is obliged to admit the possibility that Angus Wilson was right in seeing the double centre as a fault in the novel. Miller writes:

The most salient case of an apparent loose end or inconsistency is the failure to integrate perfectly the two major plots. This fissure in the novel, a conspicuous reft in its web, seems all the more inexplicable when we consider Dickens's obvious care in other parts of the book to tie together apparently unrelated details ... Surely, the reader supposes, Dickens could have related Lady Dedlock's 'crime' more closely to the corrupting effect of Chancery if he had wanted to do so. Perhaps he did not want to. Perhaps he wanted to mislead the reader into thinking that the revelation of Lady Dedlock's secret is at the same time an explanation of the real mystery of the novel – that is, the question of why English society is in such a sad state?

[p. 39, above]

'Mislead' Hillis Miller might think it does, but is this not a twentieth-century critic's misreading of what Dickens would have seen merely as a question of 'leading'? He has so often been accused of unconscious sexism (as though a man of his time and background could *not* have been sexist – unless or even if he were John Stuart Mill) that we may have blinded ourselves to the possibility that by the very fact of his being *more* aware of the distinction between male and female roles in society, his 'sexism' was at least less unconscious than that of his twentieth-century critics. Miller is pursuing other goals in his essay, and ignores what perhaps seems to him too simple an interpretation to be a key to the connection between Lady Dedlock and her secret life, and the world of the Lord High Chancellor. Yet surely there are grounds for suggesting that one is a symptomatic representative of the novel's women, and the other, of the novel's men? A reading along these lines would put the vexed question of the division between the sexes near the heart of the novel's meaning.

Despite the recognition critics like Butt and Tillotson have given to the importance of the satire of women in the novel,[15] despite the recognition that half the novel has been 'handed over' to a female narrator, it is remarkable that no one has argued that the key to the relationship between the 'two centres' is precisely the relationship between the sexes. That Dickens should have chosen Lady Dedlock and her illegitimate daughter as representative examples of the female sex is both extraordinary and profoundly significant; and it is equally significant, though less immediately extraordinary, that he chose lawyers for his 'representative' males. For the whole legal system sustaining Chancery is in its very essence a man's preserve, where lawyers inherit causes from their fathers, where the male mystique is as powerful as, if more sinister than, that surrounding a privileged gentlemen's club. Not only do Chancery lawyers inherit causes through the male line; they also control the pattern of property inheritance within a whole society, ensuring the continuance of a patriarchy.[16]

If it is true, as has often been claimed, that Chancery acts as a moral yardstick for characters in the novel, then Dickens must be assumed to be aware that it effectively excludes almost all the female characters from its particular challenge, since they have little or no place in the struggle over inherited property which, by the law itself, generally belonged to their 'legal' representative, man. Lady Dedlock, ironically enough, has brought as her only 'dowry' to Sir Leicester her interest in the Jarndyce case; Ada forfeits her property rights to Richard upon marriage (and indeed he then spends – or borrows against – her expectations as well as his own); only the unattached Miss Flite finds a regular (or irregular) place in court entirely on her own account; and of course, it sends her mad. But the fact that Chancery is an inapposite moral testing device for women in the novel does not mean that Dickens has left them unprovided for. Their touchstone is the highly charged symbol of the hearth and home. Just as it is lamentably easy for men to make a Bleak House of the Court of Chancery or of Tom All-Alone's, so it is all too easy for women to make a Bleak House of a home (only Esther being supremely gifted with the opposite ability). I want now to examine some of the ways in which the novel develops this theme.

Lady Dedlock is the paradigm for all the failed home-makers in the novel. We are early forewarned of her 'hearth-rending' propensities,[17] and she is indeed the stereotype of the fallen woman, for whom redemption within a Victorian novel was next to impossible. But in developing links of identity between Lady Dedlock and other female characters such as Hortense, Jenny (whose clothes she dons for death), and of course Esther herself (whose *alter ego* she increasingly becomes), the novel gives credence to the notion of a secret community among women, and further contrives to hint that a society which tolerates such a woman as Lady Dedlock as one of its chief representatives of womanhood will find her taint spreading to all members of the sex, just as the taint of Chancery defiles all men who touch it. In one sense, Dickens was certainly concerned to keep the two plots separate. Like Ruskin, for whom *Bleak House* might well have stood as a source, Dickens apparently believed in the separate realms of 'Kings' Treasuries' and 'Queens' Gardens', and he could never have intended, as one of his recent critics argues, that Esther should be regarded, not as a woman, but as a 'sexually undifferentiated hero'.[18]

There is no evidence in this novel to show that Dickens wanted any real integration of man's and woman's worlds. Even those female characters who exhibit 'manly' qualities of leadership and strength without apparently forfeiting authorial approval (Mrs Bagnet, Mrs Bucket, Mrs Rouncewell) are still shown to be putting the interests of husband or son before their own. Woman, ideally at least, is the upholder of the private inner world of the family, the keeper of the sanctity of the hearth and, most importantly of all, the guardian of chastity; while man is the upholder of the public outer world of the 'family' of England, and governor and the guardian of the law. Dickens sets up numerous analogies and parallels between these roles or spheres and between the corruptions each is heir to, but there seems little point in criticising him for 'failure' to integrate the Chancery and Lady Dedlock plots when one of his chief objects appears to be to keep them apart, both in theory and in practice, the better to serve as comments on, and parallels to, each other. For the gender division as Dickens saw it offered an opportunity for a split viewpoint not only on society's rotting superstructure of legal, aristocratic, hereditary privilege, but also on the hidden source of this corruption – the underlying propensity to violence.

III

Every community in so-called civilised societies contains repressed violence. After all, it is the fear of community hostility and disorder breaking into open acts of violence which has led to the establishment of judicial systems to control man's litigious nature. Under a judicial system, as René Girard argues in his seminal work *Violence and the Sacred*, vengeance is rationalised, and unlike the individual, this system 'never hesitates to confront violence head on, because it possesses a monopoly on the means of revenge' (p. 23). In this regard, as Girard makes plain, modern societies are not so far removed as they might like to think from primitive communities where the ritual sacrifice of a surrogate victim or scapegoat serves as a purgation of violence by metamorphosing the very real (though often hidden) hostilities that all members of a community feel for one another into a common hostilility against an object chosen precisely because of its inability to avenge itself. Like the primitive urge to find a sacrificial victim, the law contains in its own ritualised actions the violence it seeks to quell.

This is why there is so much mythic resonance to be found in the placing of Chancery and the figure of Lady Dedlock within the same novel. Sexuality, as Girard reminds us, 'is a permanent source of disorder even within the most harmonious of communities ... [it] leads to quarrels, jealous rages, mortal combats' (p. 35). Social guilt and social violence are openly examined in the novel; sexual guilt and sexual violence run like a hidden stream beneath. John Carey is surely right to insist that 'violence and destruction were the most powerful stimulants to [Dickens's] imagination'.[19] One of Dickens's great achievements in *Bleak House*, it seems to me, lies in giving such evocative expression to a fear that society's controls over violence in the community are breaking down so that the very institutions designed to offer most protection to individuals – Chancery or the Law[20] on the one hand, the Family on the other, and underpinning both, Religion itself – are being subverted into instruments of the very violence which is such a threat to social order.

The attention that has been directed by so many critics to the platitudinous side of the novel, to the notion that Dickens recommended as solution to the corrupt state of England a more thorough and dutiful housekeeping, so that the cosy warmth of Esther in Bleak House might be writ large throughout the commonwealth, has drawn notice away from those parts of the book which speak to us so much more profoundly because they are animated by so much more creative energy. In allowing the character of Lady Dedlock to serve as scapegoat for the sexual and ultimately, I would contend, the social ills of society, Dickens not only shows us how a male-dominated system will always find a way to let its men both eat their cake and have it – indulge sexual appetite while condemning it – but also reveals, albeit unwittingly, something of the same propensity in himself as author. How else do we account for the submerged or guilty celebration of sexual violence which lurks about the figure of the rascally Krook and his mysterious feline companion, Lady Jane?

The telling symbol of the 'marriage' imagined by mad Miss Flite as connecting the Lord Chancellor and Lady Dedlock is daringly echoed in the highly suggestive portrayal of the relationship between the bottle shop Lord Chancellor Krook, with his 'three sacks of ladies' hair below' (p. 51), and Lady Jane.

'Hi, Lady Jane!'
A large grey cat leapt ... on his shoulder and startled us all.
'Hi! show 'em how you scratch, Hi! Tear, my lady!' said her master.
The cat leaped down, and ripped at a bundle of rags with her tigerish
claws, with a sound that it set my teeth on edge to hear.

(ch. 5, p. 51)

Compare this to the description of Hortense mastered by Bucket in
Chapter 54

'I would like to kiss her!' exclaims Mademoiselle Hortense panting
tigress-like.
'You'd bite her, I suspect,' says Mr Bucket.
'I would!' making her eyes very large. 'I would love to tear her, limb
from limb.'

(p. 652)

I cannot believe it an accident that Krook's sinister cat, with her
witch-like propensity for feasting on corpses (after being ejected
from the dead Nemo's room, 'she goes furtively downstairs winding
her lithe tail and licking her lips') and with her association by
imagery with the tigerish Hortense, should have been given an
aristocratic name that allows Krook to address her as 'My Lady'.
These associations link her immediately with Lady Dedlock, and
suggest further, a titillating combination of childlike purity and
corrupt sexuality. Being a grey cat, she was probably named after
the unfortunate Lady Jane Grey, described by Dickens in his *Child's
History* as: 'amiable, learned, and clever', 'young ... innocent and
fair', who only accepted the crown 'in obedience to her father and
mother'.[21] At the same time, the vulgar sense of 'Lady Jane' as a
name for the female genitals familiar to the modern reader from
Lawrence's *Lady Chatterley's Lover*,[22] is recorded in Partridge as
being in popular use from at least 1850. Thus Lady Jane offers, by
her very name, a fitting double image of the female sex, and reinforces the suggestion, already implicit in Hortense, that beneath
Lady Dedlock's frozen surface lurk fiendish powers of destruction,
if once 'the floodgates were opened', to use Sir Leicester's own
words.

It is very fitting, too, that it is Krook and Lady Jane who unwittingly harbour the secrets of inheritance that have been locked up
by their counterparts, the Lord Chancellor and Lady Dedlock and,
implicitly, by the author in his two narrators. The true Jarndyce
will is finally discovered – ironically too late to save Richard –

among Krook's rubbish. Lady Dedlock, as a woman, of course has
the hidden key to the secret of Esther's illegitimate 'inheritance',
namely, the knowledge of Esther's true parentage; and it is her own
tell-tale love letters to Captain Hawdon which are finally discovered, again too late, in the symbolically resonant hiding place of
Lady Jane's bed (ch. 54, p. 642). The splendid parodic death of
Chancery in Krook's transmogrification by combustion into a
'cinder of a small charred and broken log of wood sprinkled with
white ashes' and 'a dark grey coating on the walls and ceiling'
(ch. 32, p. 402) significally leaves the equivalently parodic embodiment of female sexuality, Krook's cat, alive and snarling at what
little remains of her master.

It is the dark and sinisterly masculine figure of Mr Tulkinghorn
which manages to arouse the enmity of both feline females, the
cat (who 'expands her wicked mouth, and snarls at him' (ch. 10,
p. 124) or 'spits at his rusty legs ... swearing wrathfully' (ch. 39,
p. 493), and Hortense, 'That feline personage, with her lips tightly
shut, and her eyes looking at him sideways' (ch. 42, p. 517); the
latter, of course, eventually justifying his hostility by unleashing her
innate violence and shooting him. Various motives have been suggested for Tulkinghorn's vendetta against Lady Dedlock, but the
chief complaint has been about lack of motive. Critics don't seem to
want to see the motive that Dickens openly supplies him with – his
irrational hatred of the female sex – let alone admit its adequacy.
Yet Dickens provides in Tulkinghorn a powerful illustration of the
threat misogyny poses to a humanistic vision.

> There are women enough in the world, Mr Tulkinghorn thinks – too
> many; they are at the bottom of all that goes wrong in it, though, for
> the matter of that, they create business for lawyers. What would it be
> to see a woman going by, even though she were going secretly? They
> are all secret. Mr Tulkinghorn knows that, very well.
>
> (ch. 16, p. 200)

Again, he says to himself:

> 'These women were created to give trouble, the whole earth over. The
> Mistress not being enough to deal with, here's the maid now! But I
> will be short with *this* jade at least!'
>
> (ch. 42, p. 517)

Marriage, too, arouses his particular scorn, especially the Dedlock
marriage, where it is almost as though he is jealous of Sir Leicester's

love for Lady Dedlock, with whom he is a rival for her husband's trust.

> My experience teaches me, Lady Dedlock, that most of the people I know would do far better to leave marriage alone. It is at the bottom of three-fourths of their troubles. So I thought when Sir Leicester married, and so I always have thought since.
>
> (ch. 41, p. 512)

Nice as it is that the nasty old gentleman meets his Nemesis through the irrational vengeance of Lady Dedlock's surrogate self, it does not in fact do that beleaguered lady much good. For his is no sacrificial death, since he has an avenger at the ready in the shape of the irrepressible and aggressively masculine Inspector Bucket.[23] '"Duty is duty, and friendship is friendship. I never want the two to clash, if I can help it"', he says, as he cheerfully arrests his friend, honest George, for murder (ch. 49, p. 597), thus showing his unhesitating allegiance to the tough masculine ethic of the law, which has its face of vengeance hidden under rationalisation. However, Lady Dedlock has by now realised that if she is to save her daughter she must destroy herself; to legitimise Esther she must take upon herself society's hostility towards the illegitimate, and accept a view of herself as guilty Woman, a role of high melodrama that she proceeds to act out with a certain masochistic flair.

A society which denies the legitimacy of female sexuality is virtually denying legitimacy to women. This is why it is such a powerful part of the novel's meaning that Esther is illegitimate. The purgation of the taint of illegitimacy becomes, in a sense, the purgation of the taint of female sexuality. Lady Dedlock is a scapegoat insofar as she represents the secret 'guilt' of sexuality in every woman that must be driven out of the community so that it can be purged from the threat of its own consuming violence. According to Girard, the sacrificial victim or scapegoat for a community must always be someone who is both in a respected position and at the same time, an outsider who will have no avenger. This double role Lady Dedlock fulfils perfectly. She is at the pinnacle of fashionable female society, yet she is an imposter in the ranks of the Dedlocks. Joined with her in the role of outsider are Hortense (a foreigner), Jenny (a social outcast) and Esther (illegitimate). The novel deliberately merges the identities of these women, so that when the climactic chase comes, it draws part of its power from the feeling that Lady Dedlock has taken upon herself the sacrificial role demanded of all women but carried in her case to its extreme. Esther, we remember, is told in early childhood by her aunt Barbary, in words that echo through the book:

> Your mother, Esther, is your disgrace, and you were hers. The time will come – and soon enough – when you will understand this better, and will feel it too, *as no one save a woman can.*
>
> (ch. 3, p. 19, my italics)

It is of course women, who already bear the labour of birth itself, who also bear the brunt of the man-made sin of giving 'illegitimate' birth. This explains the portent of the aunt's words, which fully recognise sexual transgression as a distinctively female guilt. Once again it seems that Dickens was far more aware than his liberal-minded twentieth-century critics of the extra burden such notions of illegitimacy placed upon a female bastard. Those who claim that Esther's 'femaleness' is unimportant, that what matters to Dickens in her portrayal is the study of a *child*,[24] are missing a crucial point: that an illegitimate girl has an inherited slur against her own sexual purity that would never adhere to a boy in the same position.[25] Similarly, when Gordon Hirsch argues that 'it is too restrictive to see [Esther] exclusively as a woman. Rather, she is a child of inde-terminate sex, as perhaps even the sexual ambiguity of her surname, Summer-son, implies' (pp. 138–9), he reveals more of his own outlook than of Dickens's. The point about her surname 'Sum-merson' that I would wish to stress is that it is an adopted name, not her real one. Her real name – Esther Hawdon (whore; hoyden) – carries with it the awful implication of exactly what role would have awaited Esther had she been thrown into the streets as a young girl by the sanctimonious Mrs Rachael. It is again Mrs Rachael who, later in the novel (as Mrs Chadband), informs Mr Guppy that Esther is not Esther Summerson, but Esther Hawdon (ch. 29, p. 362). Esther's status in the book as one of the narrators has deflected attention from the particular brand of sexual guilt she bears. Modern readers have perhaps been too ready to accept her low self-esteem as a neurotic symptom and to under-estimate the extent of her plight as an illegitimate female. In the eyes of her society, she bears a sexual taint by inheritance on the distaff side. There are many hints in the novel of the sexual stigma that she has inherited from her mother: her scarring from disease contracted through no fault of her own; the humiliation inflicted on her by Mr Guppy and Mrs Woodcourt; her Aunt's prophecy ('you will feel it, as none save a woman can').[26] Esther's battle to establish a respectable identity ought properly to be seen in the context of a battle against unspoken imputations against her sexual purity. This, surely, underlies the otherwise inexplicable cat-and-mouse game Jarndyce plays at the end of the novel, with the object of proving to the sceptical world (represented by Mrs Woodcourt) Esther's 'true legitimacy' (ch. 64, p. 753), viz. her ability to sacrifice her own sexuality (linked with her mother) to a sense of duty to her 'father'. Her 'father', in this instance, is Jarndyce himself, but the wider implications of her duty extend to the whole patriarchal system.

IV

The sexual taint on Esther (as Dickens shows) is bestowed on her not by her mother's act so much as by the hostility to women endemic in a patriarchal society. It is this taint which sets her invisibly apart from other women and yet at the same time makes them their archetypal representative. This is because she bears within her as a deeply-buried wound the guilt and shame that the position of women in such a society inflicts on all females to some degree. None the less, her 'inheritance of shame' as she aptly terms it (ch. 44, p. 538), can only be expunged at the cost of her joining with the patriarchy, the world of men, of male legality and legitimacy, and to do this effectively she has to cast off her mother. And this is precisely what she does, in my reading, by joining forces with Mr Bucket in the death-chase of Lady Dedlock. Readers have long felt the power of this climactic chase, while being at the same time rather at a loss to account for its resonance in a novel about Chancery. I want now to offer a reading which suggests that Dickens's unerring dramatic instincts have here a deeper basis than has hitherto been suspected. This part of the novel takes on a wider significance when we realise the importance of the submerged tensions of sexual repression and vengeance which underpin it.

That Tulkinghorn and his avenger Bucket are both agents of a judicial system which has been exposed in the novel as an instrument of vengeance, and are both at the same time so strongly identified with the masculine ethic of the society, makes them fitting accomplices in the purgation of 'illicit' female sexuality through the sacrifice of Lady Dedlock along with her surrogate, Hortense.

Taylor Stoehr has argued that the chief weakness of the split point of view in *Bleak House* is that the two themes (Esther's sexual-social dilemma and Richard's vocational one) are never brought into meaningful contact with each other.[27] But in my view the ultimate effect of the split narrative is, on the contrary, finally to enforce a connection, by pressing the analogy between the separate male and female spheres until they achieve climactic union in the expulsion of Lady Dedlock, who is used very precisely, in Girard's terms, as a ritual sacrificial victim or scapegoat for the transferred hostilities within a patriarchal society.

It has often been remarked that it is in the pursuit of Lady Dedlock that the two narratives draw together. Esther in her role as female voice has always been time-bound in her narration;[28] it is the male narrator who can command the 'timeless' present tense. But now for the first time, the two narratives 'coincide in their focusing of time and space at the end of Chapter 56' as Stoehr reminds us (p. 148). He continues.

> Bucket, who has appeared in Esther's narrative only once, is now taken into her story completely, as he and Esther rush through the countryside in pursuit of Lady Dedlock. This chapter (57) and the next but one, both told from Esther's point of view, bring us to the gates of the burial ground, which also figures in Esther's narrative now for the first time, and Lady Dedlock is thus brought into her daughter's story, and out of the present-tense narrative, for good and all. The whole sequence, in which *single* chapters from the two narratives alternate for the first time in the novel, is constructed as a joining of the points of view *in order to bring Esther and her mother together.*
>
> (p. 149, my italics)

It is this conclusion that I feel constrained to question, yet it is the conclusion most commonly drawn from this part of the novel. John Lucas spells it out even more clearly in his book on Dickens, *The Melancholy Man* (London, 1970), where he writes:

> Esther's narrative ... has to do with what seem to be entirely different matters and yet all the while is moving closer to the other narrative, until there is a total fusion of the two in the *girl's reunion with the mother who has denied her.*
>
> (p. 208, my italics)

What kind of a 'reunion' can Esther possibly have with a dead body? The mother is not only 'cold and dead' when discovered by her daughter, but also in one of those disguises which is perhaps not so much a disguise as a revelation of true identity, the clothes of that more obvious social outcast, that other 'distressed, unsheltered' creature, Jenny, the brickmaker's wife, whom Esther now tellingly 'recognises' as 'the mother of the dead child' (ch. 59, p. 713). For surely it is the childish Esther herself who has now 'died' to her mother, in order to live again – to live 'legitimately' – as a woman in that very society which has made of her mother a scapegoat to purge its own sins of violence, both sexual and social. Esther, in a sense, has to 'kill' her mother within herself, in order to escape her contagion. The chase by Bucket, with the passive collusion of Esther, ostensibly to 'save' Lady Dedlock, has in fact resulted in her death – since the more relentless their pursuit, the more desperate her flight, and the more inevitable her end. In fulfilling the role of surrogate victim for society's guilty violence, Lady Dedlock beautifully illustrates by her melodramatic death what Girard observes in his book to be the 'fundamental identity' of 'vengeance, sacrifice and legal punishment' (p. 25).

As Girard cogently argues, the whole notion of legitimacy has grown up in our society linked with religion as a means of containing violent impulses. Sexuality is 'impure' because it has to do with violence, not the other way about, and Girard notes the possibility of 'some half-suppressed desire in men to place the blame for all forms of violence on women'.[29] Sir Leicester may forgive his wife her sexual transgression (once he is paralysed, and she at the point of death[30]); none the less it is deeply necessary to the mythic shape of the novel that Lady Dedlock suffer and die, cast out from society. Her punishment must exceed her 'crime' for her function as ritual victim, or scapegoat, to be fulfilled. It is only by virtue of the relative innocence of a scapegoat that it can take on the burden of others' guilts. The expulsion of the scapegoat is not only part of a purification ritual, but vital in preventing violence from escalating through reciprocated acts of vengeance.

By the very act of showing Lady Dedlock as a scapegoat figure, Dickens indicates what lay just as deep and hidden in him as any horror of female power or female sexuality: a knowledge that woman was being punished for the sins of a patriarchal society. For one of the points that the novel makes about Lady Dedlock is that, as a scapegoat, she must be far *less* guilty than the society which expurgates its own violence and purifies its shrines by encouraging her death. At some level Dickens *knows* about suppressed sexual violence, and it is this knowledge, working through the dual view-point of the two narrators, that provides the impetus for the expulsion of Lady Dedlock when the double narrative is brought together. By implication, it is fear of the destructive power of this violence which reinforces the 'separate spheres' policy of this society and which gives such a fierce edge to the novel's satire of women like Mrs Jellyby, Mrs Pardiggle and Mrs Snagsby, who try to usurp male prerogatives.

In the same way, the dialectic of the dual narrative paradoxically offers both an enactment and a critique of the sexual division into separate spheres. At one level, it enacts it by leading to a conventionally happy ending for the heroine narrator Esther, which comes to her as a reward for proper 'womanly' behaviour. But at another level it deconstructs itself by signally failing to contain the violence it apparently seeks to repress but in fact covertly fosters. This violence, simmering underground throughout the novel, erupts at intervals until it is finally appeased by the cathartic end of Lady Dedlock. Thus Esther's reward can only come at the expense of the destruction of her mother, who takes on all the 'sins' of illicit female sexuality which so threaten the fabric of a patrilineal society. Surely this is what still sticks in the throat about the character of Esther, after all the psychological explanations have been accepted: she is rewarded for having purged her mother's sexual taint, and by so doing, for having connived at what amounts to her own clitoridectomy.[31]

From *Literature and History* 2 (1985), 31–46.

NOTES

[This is a feminist essay on *Bleak House*, inviting comparison with another, later one, Katherine Cummings's (no. 8). Virginia Blain sees a male/female distinction inflecting the two narratives of the text, and while not freeing Dickens necessarily from the charge of sexism, she shows how the text engages with female sexuality, which it both highlights and then discards. Using the critic and anthropologist René Girard's study *Violence and the Sacred* (1971), she shows how the legalities of society legitimise revenge – which in this novel means the destruction of Lady Dedlock, who is treated as a scapegoat for her society. Girard's emphasis on violence at work in the normal processes of society, and which easily becomes state-violence, may be compared with the work of Foucault, whose theme is precisely that. Blain illustrates the division in the text between the legal and the non-legal as a gender-split; in the novel, the men are lawyers and the women outside the law; Esther, for example, being obviously illegitimate is definitionally, therefore, outside the law. The essay suggests that the tie-up in the text's two voices is over the question of Lady Dedlock: here she disagrees with Hillis Miller. The reader will judge between the two positions, but it may be that the text deliberately fails to connect the Dedlock case and the Jarndyce case because this is an aspect of its plotlessness – where the concept of 'plot' would entail the possibility of making final connections and of finding a complete interpretation. Since Virginia Blain engages with a specific issue of the text, its handling of women and the way in which in male ideology violence and sexuality are always linked (so that violence is justified implicitly because it is tied to women and to their 'irrationality' and 'passion'), her essay takes a different turn altogether from Hillis Miller's, and is important in attempting to relate the text to history and to specific realities. Ed.]

An earlier version of this paper was presented at a conference of the Australasian Victorian Studies Association held at Massey University, New Zealand, in 1982 and appeared in the Proceedings of the Association (Christchurch, NZ. 1983).

1. After this article was written, Carol A. Senf's article, entitled '*Bleak House*, Dickens, Esther, and the Androgynous Mind', appeared in *The Victorian Newsletter*, 64 (Fall, 1983) 21–7. Senf shares my view that Dickens meant *Bleak House* to be read as a dialectic between male and female narrative viewpoints, but her article deals primarily with Dickens's intention to contribute to the 'separate spheres' debate by inviting his readers to resolve the dialectic androgynously in their own minds. My article has no quarrel with this view, but is concerned instead to explore some of the implications of this narrative dialectic which are more devious and less overtly willed than anything we might label as Dickens's conscious 'intention'.

2. John Carey. *The Violent Effigy: A Study of Dickens's Imagination* (London, 1973; repr. 1979).

3. *Violence and the Sacred*, trans. Patrick Gregory (Baltimore, MD, 1977).

4. 'In refusing to admit an association between sexuality and violence – an association readily acknowledged [by primitive peoples] – modern thinkers are attempting to prove their broadmindedness and liberality. Their stance has led to numerous misconceptions.' *Violence and the Sacred*, p. 35.

5. Alex Zwerdling, 'Esther Summerson Rehabilitated', *PMLA*, 88 (1973), 429–39.

6. For a recent summary of significant critical views of Esther, see Michael Slater, *Dickens and Women* (London, 1983), pp. 255–6, p. 431.

7. See, for instance, the argument conducted by S. Gilbert and S. Gubar, in Part One of *The Madwoman in the Attic: The Woman Writer and the Nineteenth-Century Literary Imagination* (New Haven, CT, 1979).

8. Valerie Kennedy's argument in '*Bleak House*: More Trouble with Esther?', *Journal of Women's Studies in Literature* (1979) 330–47, goes some way towards rectifying this position, but still leaves much to be said.

9. '*Bleak House*: the Agitating Women', *The Dickensian*, 69 (1973), 13.

10. See Françoise Basch, *Relative Creatures: Victorian Women in Society and the Novel 1837–67*, trans. Anthony Rudolf (London, 1974).

11. J. Hillis Miller, *The Form of Victorian Fiction* (Notre Dame, 1968), p. 78. His definition omits the qualifier 'male'.

12. *The Dreamer's Stance* (New York, 1965), p. 159.

13. Page references throughout are to the Norton Critical Edition, edited by George Ford and Sylvere Monod (New York, 1977).

14. I am indebted to Lawrence Frank's article. '"Through A Glass Darkly": Esther Summerson and *Bleak House*', *Dickens Studies Annual*, 4 (1975), 91–112, for drawing this point to my attention. Frank claims that Esther's 'forgiveness of her mother is a terrible rebuke' (p. 102).

15. *Dickens at Work* (London, 1957).

16. For an enlightening discussion of the disabilities of women as owners of property in the nineteenth century, see Lee Holcombe's essay on 'Victorian Wives and Property' in *A Widening Sphere: Changing Roles of Victorian Women*, ed. Martha Vicinus (London, 1980), pp. 3–28.

17. 'Athwart the picture of my Lady, over the great chimney-piece, [the sunshine] throws a broad bend-sinister of light that strikes down crookedly into the hearth, and seems to rend it' (ch. 12, p. 138).

18. Gordon D. Hirsch, 'The Mysteries in *Bleak House*', *Dickens Studies Annual*, 4 (1975), 16.

19. *The Violent Effigy*, p. 16.

20. The useful 'Introductory Note on Law Courts and Colleges' in the Norton edition points out that 'as originally established in earlier centuries, the Court of Chancery served to protect the rights of individuals and to compensate for the rigidities of the Law. By Dickens' time, however, what had once been a humane and flexible institution had developed rigidities of its own' (p. xvii).

21. *A Child's History of England*, III (London, 1854), pp. 74 ff.

22. The second and earlier version of this novel was titled *John Thomas and Lady Jane*.

23. According to Girard, the point about sacrificial victims is that they must be chosen from those who have no avengers, since only then can their death break the chain of escalating violence: 'Sacrifice is primarily an act of violence without risk of vengeance' (p. 13). Bucket's peculiar maleness is noted by Carey, who comments on the telling scene where he rummages in Lady Dedlock's boudoir chest of drawers: 'Inspector Bucket's masculine paw disembowelling the little female hideout approaches nearer to sexual union than any of the loving couples in the book' (*The Violent Effigy*, p. 168).

24. See for instance Zwerdling's article (cited n. 5 above).

25. The history of society's stigmatisation of the illegitimate child beginning in the late sixteenth century and peaking in the nineteenth, is told in I. Pinchbeck and M. Hewitt, *Children in English Society* (London, 1969–73). At law, of course, there was no difference in the treatment of male and female bastards: each was deemed *filius nullius*, child of nobody, and none could inherit property. But the popular nineteenth-century belief that 'children begotten in sin would naturally inherit their parents' weakness' (p. 584), would of course have operated more severely against female illegitimates under the double standard, as Miss Barbary's words to Esther make clear.

26. As Gail Cunningham notes, 'The loss of female virtue [in *Bleak House*] ... is apparently contagious'. See her discussion of Lady Dedlock in *The New Woman and the Victorian Novel* (London, 1978), pp. 25–7.

27. *The Dreamer's Stance*, pp. 147 ff.

28. It could, indeed, be argued that the real 'secret' of *Bleak House* is the one kept by Esther from the reader until the very end – that at the time when she is telling her story, she is no longer an outsider, but a happy and respectable wife and mother.

29. *Violence and the Sacred*, p. 36.

30. See Gail Cunningham's argument that 'Only ... when it is a matter of life or death, does Sir Leicester divulge his feelings, because only then can they be appropriately heartrending and safely ineffectual. To forgive Lady Dedlock to her face would make nonsense of the preceding action ... This sort of sin can only be forgiven on the point of death' (*The New Woman and the Victorian Novel*, pp. 26–7).

31. Cf. the more generalised comments on the social and legal significance of symbolic clitoridectomy made by Gayatri Chakravorty Spivak:

    In legally defining woman as object of exchange, passage, or possession in terms of reproduction, it is not only the womb that is literally 'appropriated': it is the clitoris as the signifier of the sexed subject that is effaced. All historical and theoretical investigation into the definition of woman as legal *object* – in or out of marriage; or as politico-economic passageway for property and legitimacy would fall within the investigation of the varieties of the effacement of the clitoris.

(*French Feminism in an International Frame,*
Yale French Studies, 62 (1981), p. 181.

4

Discipline in Different Voices: Bureaucracy, Police, Family, and *Bleak House*

D. A. MILLER

I

The Court of Chancery in *Bleak House* (1852–53) makes a certain difference in Dickens's representation of social discipline. This representation had hitherto been restricted to places of confinement that, as much as they referred to a disciplinary society committed to the manufacture and diffusion of such enclosures, carried an even more emphatic allusion to the space between them: a space of freedom or domestic tranquillity that was their 'other'. The often ferocious architecture that immured the inmates of a carceral institution seemed to immure the operations practised on them there as well, and the thick, spiked walls, the multiple gateways, the attendants and the administrators that assured the confinement of those within seemed equally to provide for the protectedness of those without, including most pertinently the novelist and his readers. Embodied in the prison, the workhouse, the factory, the school, discipline became, quite precisely, a *topic* of Dickensian representation: a site whose redoubtable but all the more easily identified boundaries allowed it to be the target of criticism to the same extent that they isolated it from other, better sites. The topic of the carceral in Dickens – better, the carceral as topic – thus worked to secure the effect of difference between, on the one hand, a confined, institutional space in which power is violently exercised on collectivised

87

subjects, and on the other, a space of 'liberal society', generally determined as a free, private, and individual domain and practically specified as the family. Yet clear though the lines of demarcation were, it was alarmingly easy to cross them. After all, what brought carceral institutions into being in the first place were lapses in the proper management of the family: in its failure to constitute itself (the problem of illegitimate or orphaned children and the institutional solution of foundling hospitals and baby farms) or in its failure to sustain itself by means of a self-sufficient domestic economy (the problem of poverty and debt and the institutional responses of workhouses and debtor's prisons). And in the portrayal of its hero in the workhouse, *Oliver Twist* (1838) dramatised the shameful facility with which such institutions might mistakenly seize upon what were middle-class subjects to begin with. Still, if to witness the horror of the carceral was always to incur a debt of gratitude for the immunities of middle-class life, then to sense the danger from the carceral was already to learn how this debt had to be acquitted. When Oliver Twist, enchanted by the difference between his previous experience and his life at Mr Brownlow's, begged the latter not to send him back to 'the wretched place I came from', Brownlow declared: 'You need not be afraid of my deserting you, unless you give me cause.' Earlier he had promised Oliver access to the culture represented by the books in his library on similar conditions: 'You shall read them, if you behave well.'[1] The price of Oliver's deliverance from the carceral (either as the workhouse or as Fagin's gang) would be his absolute submission to the norms, protocols, and regulations of the middle-class family, in which he received tuition not just from Brownlow but from the Maylies as well. Liberal society and the family were kept free from the carceral institutions that were set up to remedy their failures only by assuming the burden of an immense internal regulation. If discipline was confined to the carceral, then, this was so in order that it might ultimately be extended – in the mode of what was experientially its opposite – to the space outside it.

The Court of Chancery in *Bleak House* forces upon this representation the necessity of a certain readjustment. In the first place, an essential characteristic of the court is that its operations far exceed the architecture in which it is apparently circumscribed. The distinctive gesture of the carceral – that of locking up – makes little sense here when, at the end of the day, what is locked up is only 'the empty court' and not 'all the misery it has caused'.[2] Though the court is affirmed to be situated 'at the very heart of the fog' (p. 2), this literally nebulous information only restates the difficulty of locating it substantially, since there is 'fog everywhere' (p. 1). The ultimate unlocalisability of its operations permits them to be in all places at once. 'How many people out of the suit, Jarndyce and Jarndyce has stretched forth its unwholesome hand to spoil and corrupt, would be a very wide question' (p. 5), but it would perhaps also be a moot one, since nearly all the characters we meet in the novel are in the cause, either as parties to it or administrators of it, even those such as Esther who seem to have nothing to do with it. And the suit is as long as it is wide, the spatial extension of its filiations being matched by the temporal duration that unfolds under its 'eternal heading' (p. 5). Dickens's satire on the inefficiency of the court begins to seem a feeble, even desperate act of whistling in the dark, for the power organised under the name of Chancery is repeatedly demonstrated to be all too effective. Like the fog and dirt that are its first symbols, this power insinuates itself by virtue of its quasi-alchemical subtlety. To violent acts of penetration it prefers the milder modes of permeation, and instead of being densely consolidated into a force prepared to encounter a certain resistance, it is so finely vaporised – sublimated, we should say, thinking of alchemy and psychoanalysis together – that every surface it needs to attack is already porously welcoming it. Unlike, say, the power that keeps order in Dotheboys Hall in *Nicholas Nickleby* (1839), this power does not impose itself by physical co-ercion (though, as the case of Gridley reminds us, it does dispose of carceral sanctions for those who hold it in contempt). Rather, it relies on being voluntarily assumed by its subjects, who, seduced by it, addicted to it, internalise the requirements for maintaining its hold. 'Fog everywhere.' What Chancery produces, or threatens to produce, is an organisation of power that, ceasing entirely to be a *topic*, has become topography itself: a system of control that can be all-encompassing because it cannot be compassed in turn. Writing in the nineteenth century, John Forster would not be the last critic of *Bleak House* to notice how 'the great Chancery suit, on which the plot hinges, on incidents connected with which, important or trivial, all the passion and suffering turns, is worked into every part of the book'.[3] Yet though we see nothing but the effects of Jarndyce and Jarndyce, everywhere present, affecting everyone, everything, we never come close to seeing what the suit is all about, as though this were merely the pretext that allowed for the disposition and deployment of the elaborate channels, targets, and techniques of a state bureaucracy. The interminable process of interpretation to which the original will gives rise, literally maddening to those who bring to it the demand that it issue in final truths and last judgments, is abandoned rather than adjudicated. If Chancery thus names an organisation of power that is total but not totalisable, total *because* it is not totalisable, then what is most radically the matter with being 'in Chancery' is not that there may be no way out of it (a dilemma belonging to the problematic of the carceral), but, more seriously, that the binarisms of inside/outside, here/elsewhere become meaningless and the ideological effects they ground impossible.

Furthermore, the nature of Chancery necessarily affects the nature of the resistance to it. Whereas the topic of the carceral, localising disciplinary practices that thereby seemed to require only local remedies, always implied a feasible politics of reformism, the total social reticulation of Chancery finds its corresponding oppositional practice in the equally total social negation of anarchism. Repeatedly, the court induces in the narration a wish for its wholesale destruction by fire: 'If all the injustice it has committed, and all the misery it has caused, could only be locked up with it, and the whole burnt away in a great funeral pyre – why, so much the better for other parties than the parties in Jarndyce and Jarndyce!' (p. 7). Even the elision of agency managed by the passive voice (who, exactly, would burn the court?), stopping short of any subjective assumption of the action, mirrors perfectly the court whose operations are in no one's control. The wish, moreover, may be considered fulfilled (albeit also displaced) when Mr Krook, who has personified the Chancellor and Chancery from the first, dies of spontaneous combustion. It is as though apocalyptic suddenness were the only conceivable way to put an end to Chancery's meanderings, violent spontaneity the only means to abridge its elaborate procedures, and mere combustion the only response to its accumulation of paperwork. One of the least welcome implications of an all-inclusive system, such as Chancery appears to be, is that even opposition to it, limited to the specular forms of reflection and inversion, merely intensifies our attachment to the perceptual grid constructed by its practices.

To say so much, of course, is to treat Chancery, if not more radically, then certainly more single-mindedly, than Dickens is ever willing to do. For while a major effort of *Bleak House* is to establish Chancery as an all-pervasive system of domination, another is to refute the fact of this system and recontain the court within a larger spatial organisation that would once again permit an elsewhere along with all the ideological effects attaching to it. If Krook's death, for instance, illustrates the apocalyptically antisocial kinds of retribution that are the only adequate responses to Chancery remaining, it can also be seen to reinstate precisely those social and political possibilities that Chancery, as a total order, ought to have made impossible. For insofar as Krook dies, as in certain modern aetiologies of cancer, of his own internal repressions, then Chancery can be safely trusted to collapse from its own refusal to release what is unhealthily accumulating in its system. Alternatively, insofar as Krook's violent end is meant to foreshadow what is in store for the institution he figures, then his death carries a warning to the court to amend its ways or else. In either case, we are reinstalled within the reformist perspectives that Chancery had, we thought, in principle annulled.

Even the omnipresence of the Chancery suit that Forster rightly noted is frequently neutralised by a certain inconsequentiality. John Jarndyce, Ada Clare, and Esther Summerson are all in the suit without being spoiled or corrupted by it – indeed, they constitute the domestic retreat to which the institutional, social space of the court can then be contrasted. Richard Carstone, whose aimlessness internalises the procedural protractions of the court, makes a better example of Chancery's power to spoil and corrupt. Yet it is also possible to argue, as did an early critic of the novel, under the impression that he was exposing its deficiency, that Richard 'is not made reckless and unsteady by his interest in the great suit, but simply expends his recklessness and unsteadiness on it, as he would on something else if it were non-existent'.[4] It is, of course, Dickens's own text that opens up the possibility of this moral explanation in its reluctance to commit itself to social determination:

> 'How much of this indecision of character,' Mr Jarndyce said to me, 'is chargeable on that incomprehensible heap of uncertainty and procrastination on which he has been thrown from his birth, I don't pretend to say; but that Chancery, among its other sins, is responsible for some of it, I can plainly see. It has engendered or confirmed in him a habit of putting off – and trusting to this, that, and the other chance, without knowing what chance – and dismissing everything as unsettled, uncertain, and confused. The character of much older and steadier people may be even changed by the circumstances surrounding them. It would

be too much to expect that a boy's, in its formation, should be the subject of such influences, and escape them.'

(p. 167)

Jarndyce kindheartedly proposes the sociological key to Richard's character in the same breath as he admits its insufficiency. And what is at stake in his hesitation between 'engendered' and 'confirmed', between the court as cause and the court as occasion, goes beyond the double view of Richard. Ultimately, the text oscillates between two seemingly incompatible sets of assumptions about the nature of Chancery's power – one deriving from the perception of total domination, the other still attached to the topic of the carceral. Thus, just as the satire on the inefficiency of the court contradicts the demonstrated power of such inefficiency, so too the anachronism of Chancery, upheld as 'a slow, expensive, British, constitutional sort of thing' (p. 13) by such fossils as Sir Leicester, counters the newness of the phenomenon that Dickens is describing under that name: the expanded development of the Victorian state bureaucracy that is at least as current as the novel's official exhibit of modernity in the Detective Police.[5]

All the evidence of Chancery's totalising effects – of its productivity as an all-englobing system of power – is equivocal in such ways, as the text at once claims that this system is and isn't efficient, is and isn't everywhere, can and can't be reformed. In the literal sense of giving utterance to a double discourse, *Bleak House* is a contradictory text. Yet as we continue to consider the operation of such 'contradiction' in the text, we should be wary of prejudging it, in a certain Marxist manner, as the 'symptom' of an ideological bind, obligingly betrayed to our notice in the text's taken-for-granted 'distanciation' from its own programme.[6] We need rather to be prepared to find in the source of 'incoherence', the very resource on which the text draws for its consistency; in the ideological 'conflict', a precise means of addressing and solving it; in the 'failure' of intention on the part of the text, a positively advantageous *strategy*.

II

Of all the mysteries that will crop up in *Bleak House*, not the least instructive concerns the curious formal torsion whereby a novel dealing with a civil suit becomes a murder mystery, and whereby the themes of power and social control are passed accordingly from the abyssal filiations of the law into the capable hands of the detective police. By what kinds of logic or necessity is the law thus turned over to the police, and the civil suit turned into the criminal case? For if Jarndyce and Jarndyce provides the ground from which mysteries and the consequent detections originate, it is certainly not because the suit is itself a mystery. In one way, it is so illegible that we don't even have a sense, as we should with a mystery, of what needs to be explained or, more important, of what might constitute either the clues or the cruxes of such an explanation. In another, the suit may be read fully and at leisure: in the reams of dusty warrants, in the tens of thousands of Chancery-folio pages, in the battery of blue bags with their heavy charges of paper – in all the archival litter that has accumulated over the dead letter of the original will. Dickens's presentation offers either too little or else too much to amount to mystery. Besides, nothing about the suit is secret or hidden, unless we count the second will found late in the novel, and this hardly brings us closer to a judgment. All that is ever unavailable is the dead legator's intentions.

It would be seriously misleading, however, on the basis of this exception, to deconstruct the suit into an allegory of interpretation as that which, confronting the absence of an immediate meaning effected by the very nature of the sign or text, must unfold as an interminable proliferation of readings.[7] For one thing, if the suit can be thought to give expression to such difficulties of interpretation, this is because, more than merely finding them acceptable, it goes out of its way to manufacture them; and no response would serve Chancery or the logic of its law better than to see this manufacture as inhering in the nature of 'textuality' rather than belonging to an institutional practice that seeks to implant and sanction its own technical procedures. For another, it seems wilful to see the work of interpretation occurring in what is far more obviously and actually the profitable business of deferring it indefinitely. With its endless referrals, relays, remands, its ecologically terrifying production of papers, minutes, memoranda, Dickens's bureaucracy works positively to elude the project of interpretation that nominally guides it. (And by the time that the Circumlocution Office in *Little Dorrit* [1857] avows the principle 'HOW NOT TO DO IT', even the nominal commitment seems abandoned.[8]) Esther properly recognises how 'ridiculous' it is to speak of a Chancery suit as 'in progress', since the term implies a linear directedness that, while fully suitable to the project that subtends Esther's own narration (indicatively begun under the title of 'A Progress'), must be wholly absent from a case that, typically, 'seemed to die out of its own vapidity, without coming, or being by anybody expected to come, to any result' (p. 345). Moreover, to see that, in Chancery, the process of decision and interpretation is diverted is also to see that it is diverted *into* Chancery, as an apparatus. It is diverted, in other words, into the work of establishing the very channels for its diversion: channels by means of which a legal establishment is ramified, its points of contact multiplied, and routes of circulation organised for the subjects who are thus recruited under its power.[9]

Yet Chancery can never dispense with the judgments that it also never dispenses. Though the project of interpretation is virtually annulled in the workings of its formalism ('the lantern that has no light in it'), the *promise* of interpretation, as that which initiates and facilitates this formalism, remains absolutely necessary. At the theoretical level of ideology, the promise functions to confer legitimacy on Chancery proceedings: as even poor crazed Miss Flite, in her confusion of the Last Judgment with the long-delayed judgment in her own case, is capable of revealing, the legal system must appeal for its legitimacy to transcendent concepts of truth, justice, meaning, and ending, even when its actual work will be to hold these concepts in profitable abeyance or to redefine and contain them as functions of its own operations. And at the practical and technical level of such operations, the promise of judgment becomes the lure of advertising, extended by venalities such as Vholes to promote the purchase and exercise of their services.

Perhaps the most interesting effect of all produced by the promise, however, considerably exceeds these theoretical and practical functions. If Chancery exploits the logic of a promise by perpetually maintaining it as *no more than such*, then the suit must obviously produce as much frustration as hopefulness. Accordingly, one consequence of a system that, as it engenders an interpretative project, deprives it of all the requirements for its accomplishment is the desire for an interpretative project that would *not* be so balked. This desire is called into being from within the ground of a system that, it bears repeating, resists interpretation on two counts: because it cannot be localised as an object of interpretation, and because it is never willing to become the agency or subject of interpretation. What such a desire effectively seeks, therefore, is a reduced model of the untotalisable system and a legible version of the undecidable suit. What such a desire calls for, in short, both as a concept and as a fact, is the detective story.

The detective story gives obscurity a name and a local habitation: in that highly specific 'mystery' whose ultimate uncovering motivates an equally specific programme of detection. If the Chancery system includes everything but settles nothing, then one way in which it differs from the detective story is that the latter is, precisely, a *story*: sufficiently selective to allow for the emergence of a narrative and properly committed, once one has emerged, to bringing it to completion. In relation to an organisation so complex that it often tempts its subjects to misunderstand it as chaos, the detective story realises the possibility of an easily comprehensible version of order. And in the face – or facelessness – of a system where it is generally impossible to assign responsibility for its workings to any single person or group of persons, where even the process of victimisation seems capricious, the detective story performs a drastic simplification of power as well. For unlike Chancery, the detective story is fully prepared to affirm the efficacy and priority of personal agency, be it that of the criminal figures who do the work of concealment or that of the detective figures who undo it. It is not at all surprising, therefore, that the desire for the detective story first emerges from within the legal community itself, in Tulkinghorn and Guppy, since lawyers, having charge of the system, are most likely to be aware of the extent to which they merely convey a power which is theirs only to hold and not to have. It is entirely suitable that those who continually *exercise* this power – in the root sense, that is, of driving it on – should be the first to dream of *possessing* it, so that the calling of Mr Tulkinghorn, for instance, 'eke solicitor of the High Court of Chancery' (p. 11), becomes 'the acquisition of secrets and the holding possession of such power as they give him, with no sharer or opponent in it' (p. 511). At the other end of the legal hierarchy (though not, one may be sure, for long), Mr Guppy prepares for a similar vocation: 'Mr Guppy suspects everybody who enters on the occupation of a stool in Kenge and Carboy's office, of entertaining, as a matter of course, sinister designs upon him. He is clear that every such person wants to depose him. If he be ever asked how, why, when, or wherefore, he shuts up one eye and shakes his head. On the strength of these profound views, he in the most ingenious manner takes infinite pains to counter-plot, when there is no plot; and plays the deepest games of chess without any adversary' (p. 272). Guppy's counter-plotting 'when there is no plot' may be seen as the usefully paranoid attempt of an ambitious clerk to grasp the power of the legal system over him by turning everybody in it into his personal enemy. It may also be seen as the desperately fanciful effort of an otherwise bored office worker to overwrite the impersonal and inconsequential tedium of his tasks with lively dramas centred on himself. In either case, it suggests precisely the sense in which the non-narrative system of Chancery generates narratives both to grasp its evasiveness and to evade its grasp.

Yet within this perspective, one must register the general failure of the amateur detectives in *Bleak House* to impose a will to truth and power. Anecdotally, their stories all reach a final point of checkmate. Guppy's chance to lay his hands on the decisive evidence goes up in smoke with Krook; Tulkinghorn is murdered before he has quite decided how to make use of his discovery; and even Mrs Snagsby is still 'on the great high road that is to terminate in Mr Snagsby's full exposure' (p. 734) when Mr Bucket is obliged to set her straight. These abortive endings, which effectively place the stories under the paradigm of the interminable Chancery suit, also carry 'political' rebukes, as the detectives are denied the power to which their knowledge seemed to entitle them. Tulkinghorn's violent death at the hands of a woman over whom he had flaunted his control is the most dramatic example of such chastisement; but another is Guppy's rejection by Esther, the woman who initially inspired his detective work and who he hoped might reward it with her hand; and still another is the gentle but public reprimand that Mrs Snagsby receives from Mr Bucket. The profound reason for the anecdotal failure of these stories is that they are undertaken as individual projects. That individuality not only must debilitate the power of the will-to-power, but also qualifies the general validity of the production of truth. Even when the stories have more to go on than does Mrs Snagsby's – exemplary in its forced, false, but flawless coherence – they are marred by an egocentricity that confers on them the epistemologically suspect tautology of wish-fulfilments. Just as Guppy's detection is part and parcel of his *arrivisime*, an ambitious attempt to ennoble the woman of his choice and to win her gratitude for doing so, similarly, Tulkinghorn, who holds that women 'are at the bottom of all that goes wrong in [the world]' (p. 222), finds his sexual resentment justified in a story of female error and deceit. Even Mrs Snagsby's fantasy that Jo has been illegitimately sired by her husband likewise satisfies her need to see herself as wronged, and so consolidates the basis of her domestic tyranny. It is not enough to say that, if the detective story is meant to be an individual rendition of an order and a power that are social and institutional in nature, then a great deal must be lost in the translation. For that loss to be registered as *its* loss, in its formal incompletion, its cognitive inadequacy, and its political failure, what must also be asserted is the priority assumed by social and institutional categories over the individual projects that they will ultimately reabsorb.

Even as a failure, however, the project of detection enjoys a certain dangerous efficacy. For it fails in every respect except that of catching on. Its weakness as an individual enterprise becomes a demonstrable strength as the number of individuals undertaking it increases and it thereby acquires a certain social distribution and consistency. As a *common* individual project, detection poses a threat to the social and institutional orders that continue to doom it to failure as a single undertaking. From beginning to end, the project sanctions the deviate erotic desire that inspires it and that it releases into action. The unsavoury sexual secrets that ultimately gratify this desire are themselves subversive of socially given arrangements. Regularly involving a double transgression, of class as well as conjugal boundaries, they give scandal to the twin unities that Dickens puts at the basis of a decent social order, family and station. To disclose these secrets, moreover, exacerbates their scandalous effects, as when what Mrs Snagsby thinks she knows leads her to seek a marital separation, and what Tulkinghorn tells Lady Dedlock prompts her public flight. In a context where home and family are the chief bulwarks against drifting into the interminable circulations of Chancery, the kind of individuality implied and exfoliating in the project of detection must seem ultimately anarchic. Born, as Tulkinghorn's case makes particularly clear, when the law is taken into one's own hands, it gives birth to the familiar rivalrous, self-seeking world of which the tension between Tulkinghorn and Guppy is an early symptom, and in which the murderous personal arrogations of Mademoiselle Hortense are, though shocking, perfectly proper.

We begin to see why the detective narratives require to come under the management of a master-agency charged with the task both of suppressing their successes (in fostering extreme threats to social order) and of supplying their failures (to provide a widely available, consoling simplification of this order). We begin to understand, in other words, the profound necessity of the police in *Bleak House*. Though the Court of Chancery, to make itself tolerable, produces a desire for the detective story, as for that which will confer on it the legibility of a traditionally patterned meaning, this desire, far from issuing in an order that can be comfortingly proffered and consumed as the essence of the chaos that is Chancery's appearance, threatens to reduplicate such chaos in the yet more explicit form of social disaggregation. What keeps the production of this desire from being dangerously excessive – what in fact turns the dangerous excess back into profit – is that the detective story, following the same logic whereby it was produced among the effects of Chancery, produces among *its* effects the desire for its own authoritative version and regulatory agency. Out of control to the point that, at Tulkinghorn's murder, the very principle of sense-making appears to have gone 'stark mad' (p. 665), the detective story eventually asks to be arrested by the Detective Police.

Such regulation should not be seen purely as a repressive practice, involving, for instance, the capture of a murderer like Mademoiselle Hortense or a runaway like Lady Dedlock. The police not only repress but also, profoundly, satisfy the desire to which Chancery gives rise. For in addition to doing the negative work of correcting for the socially undesirable consequences of amateur projects of detection, they perform the positive work of discharging for society as a whole the function that these amateur projects had assumed unsuccessfully: that of providing, within the elusive organisation of Chancery, a simplified representation of order and power. The novel's shift in focus from the Court of Chancery to the Detective Police encompasses a number of concomitant shifts, which all operate in the direction of this simplification: from civil law and questions of liability to criminal law and less merely legal questions of guilt; from trivial legal hairsplitting to the urgency of the fact, beyond such disputing, of murder; from a cause with countless parties represented by countless attorneys in an anonymous system, to a case essentially reduced to two personal duels, between the criminal and his victim and between the criminal and the detective; from long, slow, to all appearances utterly inefficient procedures to swift and productive ones; and finally, from an institution that cannot justify its power to one that, for all the above reasons, quite persuasively can. It is as though every complaint that could be made about the one institution had been redressed in the organisation of the other, so that one might even argue, on the basis of Dickens's notorious willingness to serve as a propagandist for the New Police, that the excruciating *longueurs* of Chancery existed mainly to create the market for Mr Bucket's expeditious *coups*.[10] Along these lines, one might even want to read, in the police activity that develops over the dead body of the law ('or Mr Tulkinghorn, one of its trustiest representatives' [p. 305]), Dickens's exhilarated announcement of the agencies and practices of social discipline that, claiming to be merely supplementing the law, will come in large part to supplant it.[11] Yet to the extent that we stress, in the evident archaism of Chancery, the emergence of a new kind of bureaucratic organisation, and in the blatantly modern Detective Police (instituted only ten years before the novel began to appear), a harkening back to a traditional and familiar model of power, then we need to retain the possibility that Dickens's New Police still polices, substantively as well as nominally, *for* the law, for the Chancery system, and that, as a representation, it serves a particular ideological function within this system, and not against it. Made so desirable as a sort of institutional 'alternative' to Chancery, the police derive their ideological efficacy from providing, within a total system of power, *a representation of the containment of power*. The shift from Chancery to the police dramatically localises the field, exercise, and agents of power, as well as, of course, justifies such power, which, confined to a case of murder and contained in a Mr Bucket, occupies what we can now think of as the right side. And when the novel passes from adulatory wonder at the efficiency of the police to sad, resigned acknowledgement of their limits (such as emerges in Hortense's last exchange with Bucket), the circumscription of power, reaching the end to which it always tended, has merely come full circle.

III

The police thus allow for the existence of a field outside the dynamic of power and free from its effects. Once installed in this realmless realm, one could cease to internalise – as the desperate, hopeful psychology of compulsion – the lures of the Chancery system; from within it, one could bear witness to the possibility of a criticism of that system that would no longer be merely the sign of the impossibility of withdrawing from it. Shifting focus from the Court of Chancery to the Detective Police, the novel works toward the recovery of this place elsewhere, in a two-pronged strategy whose other line of attack lies in Esther's absolute refusal to be touched by the suit and in the constitution of Bleak House that her refusal enables. For in point of fact the 'outside' of power is specified as a domestic space, occupied by an ideal of the family. Not the least evil of the Chancery system in this respect was that, in it, police and family blurred into one another. As an apparatus of power concerned to impose, protect, and extend itself, Chancery naturally included a policing function, but it had the aspect of a family as well, not only because the suits that came before it arose from family disputes, but also because (as when it put its wards Ada and Richard under the guardianship of John Jarndyce) it sanctioned families of its own. In effect, the emergence of Bleak House on the one hand and of Mr Bucket (who, though Mrs Bucket is as fond of children as himself, has none) on the other achieves the extrication of the family from the police, a disarticulation into separate domains of what it was a trick of Chancery's domination to have knitted seamlessly together.

We mustn't be surprised, however, if there is a trick to this new arrangement too – and perhaps a far better one. When Mr Bucket escorts Mr Snagsby through Tom-all-Alone's (much as Inspector Field took Dickens with him on his tours of duty), the detective's thoroughgoing knowledge of the place as well as the extreme deference shown to him by its inhabitants (who call him 'master') indicate the degree to which the police have saturated the delinquent milieu. If the saturation doesn't appear to have much curtailed delinquency, or even, strangely, to have prevented Tom-all-Alone's from continuing to serve as a refuge for those wanted by the police, these perhaps were never the ends of police penetration. What such penetration apparently does secure is a containment of crime and power together, which both become visible mainly in a peripheral place, 'avoided by all decent people' (p. 220).[12] The raison d'être of Tom-all-Alone's is that it *be* all alone, as the text is prepared to admit when it speculates 'whether the traditional title is a comprehensive name for a retreat cut off from honest company' (p. 220). Yet the marginal localisation of the police thus achieved is subjected to a dramatic ambiguity as soon as, beyond ensuring the circulation of vagrants like Jo or the apprehension of murderers who, doubly exotic, come both from foreign parts and from the servant class, the police pass into the fashionable upper-class world of Chesney Wold or even the just barely respectable shooting gallery of Mr George. Though disturbed by Bucket's night-time visit, heralded only by the glare of his bull's-eye, the denizens of Tom-all-Alone's are neither surprised nor shamed by what is evidently a very familiar occurrence. Compare their dull acceptance to Sir Leicester's appalled imagination: 'Heaven knows what he sees. The green, green woods of Chesney Wold, the noble house, the pictures of his forefathers, strangers defacing them, officers of police coarsely handling his most precious heirlooms, thousands of fingers pointing at him, thousands of faces sneering at him' (pp. 743–4). Compare it even to Mr George's sharp mortification: 'You see ... I have been handcuffed and taken into custody, and brought here. I am a marked and disgraced man, and here I am. My shooting-gallery is rummaged, high and low, by Bucket; such property as I have – 'tis small – is turned this way and that, till it don't know itself' (p. 705). The sense of scandal that informs both passages, even as it acknowledges that the police can break out of their limits to become a total, all-pervasive institution like Chancery, reinforces our perception of the boundaries that ordinarily keep them in their place. It qualifies the police intervention in either case as an exceptional state of affairs, warranted only by the exceptional circumstances that call it into being.

The representation of the police, then, is not just organised by a comforting principle of localisation; it is also organised within the fear-inspiring prospect of *the possible suspension of this principle.* One may read the resulting ambiguity in the very character of Mr Bucket. The fact that the representation of the police is virtually entirely confined to the portrayal of this one character is of course revealing of the strategy of containment taken toward the police. The Court of Chancery required dozens of lawyers in the attempt to represent it, and even then the attempt had always to remain unequal to a system whose essential anonymity resisted its being seized as character. The police, however, can be adequately rendered in the character of a single one of their agents, and this fact, among others, makes them a superior institution. Whereas the law is impersonal and anonymous, the law enforcement is capable of showing a human face – if that is the word for the mechanically recurring tics and character traits that caused Inspector Bucket to be received at the time of the novel's publication as one of Dickens's most 'delightful' creations.[13] Yet if police power is contained in Bucket, Bucket himself is *not* contained in the way that characters ordinarily are. A master of disguise, who makes himself appear in as 'ghostly' a manner as, with a touch of his stick, he makes others 'instantly evaporate' (pp. 308, 310), Bucket seems superhuman and his powers magical. To Mr Snagsby, confused and impressed, he appears 'to possess an unlimited number of eyes' (p. 315); and Jo, in his ignorance and delirium, believes him 'to be everywhere, and cognizant of everything' (p. 639). With ironic reservations that only refine the ambiguity, the narration even offers its own language in support of these baffled perceptions: 'Time and place cannot bind Mr Bucket' (p. 712), it tells us, and 'Nothing escapes him' (p. 713).

Another way to bring out the ambiguity that invests the established limits of the police is to ask: on behalf of whom or what does the Detective Police do its policing? Answers in the text, accurately reflecting a historical ambiguity, are various. Bucket works now in the capacity of a private detective employed by individuals such as Tulkinghorn; now as the public official of a state apparatus that enjoins him, for instance, to secure Gridley for contempt of court; and now in some obscure combination of the two functions, as when, at the end, he seems to police simultaneously on behalf of society at large and at the behest of Sir Leicester Dedlock. In a sense, the progress toward the legitimacy of power that we read in the focal shift from Chancery to the Detective Police occurs within the representation of the police itself, which, at the beginning, acting as the agent of an arbitrary system or an equally arbitrary individual will, acquires in the end – via murder and a missing person – the means of legitimising the exercise of its power, even though this is still nominally in the hire of Sir Leicester. Yet this effort of the narrative sequence to legitimise the power of the police leaves looking all the more unresolved the question of their whereabouts, which are established in so many places, as so many indistinct, overlapping, competing jurisdictions, that they cease to seem established at all.

All the ambiguities about the police serve to establish a radical uncertainty about the nature of private, familial space. 'As [Mr Bucket] says himself, what is public life without private ties? He is in his humble way a public man, but it is not in that sphere that he finds happiness. No, it must be sought within the confines of domestic bliss' (pp. 675–6). But as we know, Bucket here maintains the difference between public (institutional) and private (domestic) spheres as part of a successful attempt to neutralise it. The difference on which he affably insists allows him to be welcomed into the Bagnet household, where at the proper moment – no longer as a new friend of the family, but now a public official – he can arrest their friend and guest Mr George. Is the private sphere autonomous or not? The representation of the police in *Bleak House* permits us to answer the question either way: to insist, when this is necessary, on the elsewhere opened up by the localisation of the police (who considerately police, among other things, their own limits); or to suggest, when this is desirable, the extent to which this elsewhere is constantly liable to being transgressed by the police. The police simultaneously produce and permeate (produce as permeable) the space they leave to be 'free'.

If, therefore, we need to say that, in its representation of bureaucracy and the police, *Bleak House* regularly produces a difference between these institutions and the domestic space outside them, we must also recognise that it no less regularly produces this difference *as a question*, in the mode of the 'problematic'. The bar of separation and even opposition that it draws between the public and private spheres is now buttressed, now breached, firm and fragile by turns. On one hand, Chancery is a total system of domination, engendering resistances whose mere inversions or duplications of its injunctions only entrench its power more deeply. On the other hand, Chancery's domination seems to cease precisely at the points where one elects to erect bulwarks against it such as Esther's Bleak House. Or again: if the police represent a reduction of the domination of Chancery, and thus permit a domestic autonomy, it is also suggested that the police, as all-encompassing as Chancery, can at any moment abolish that autonomy. Or still again: the police are other, better than Chancery, but they are also the organ that polices on its behalf and thus works to preserve it. We cannot too strongly insist that these 'paradoxes' are not merely confusions or historical contradictions that tug and pull at a text helpless to regulate them, but rather productive ambiguities that facilitate the disposition, functioning, and promotion of certain ideological effects, some of which we have already suggested. Neither, however, should '*Bleak House*, by Charles Dickens' be denounced – or congratulated – as the ultimate strategist of these effects, as though one could allow such effects their broad cultural resonance without also recognising their broad cultural production and distribution. Yet if the novel no more 'manipulates' the equivocations we have traced than 'succumbs' to them, perhaps the most pertinent reason is that it lacks the distance from them required to do either. We shall see how, in the first place, these equivocations *are its own*, always already borne in the novel as a form; and also how, in the last instance, these equivocations *come to be its own*, as the novel reproduces in the relationship between form and content the dialectic that occurs within each of its terms.

IV

It would certainly appear as though the existence of that sheltered space which the novelistic representation labours to produce – but with, we have seen, such dubious results – is unconditionally taken for granted in the novel form, whose unfolding or consumption has not ceased to occur in such a space all along. Since the novel counts among the conditions for this consumption the consumer's leisured withdrawal to the private, domestic sphere, then every novel-reading subject is constituted – willy-nilly and almost before he has read a word – within the categories of the individual, the inward, the domestic. There is no doubt that the shift in the dominant literary form from the drama to the novel at the end of the seventeenth century had to do with the latter's superior efficacy in producing and providing for privatised subjects. The only significant attempt to transcend the individualism projected by the novel took place precisely in Victorian England as the practice of the *family reading*, which may be understood as an effort to mitigate the possible excesses of the novel written for individuals by changing the locus of reading from the study – or worse, the boudoir – to the hearth, enlivened but also consolidated as a *foyer d'intrigue*. A Victorian novel such as *Bleak House* speaks not merely for the hearth, in its prudent care to avoid materials or levels of explicitness about them unsuitable for family entertainment, but from the hearth as well, implicitly grounding its critical perspective on the world within a domesticity that is more or less protected against mundane contamination.

Yet if only by virtue of the characteristic length that prevents it from being read in a single sitting, the novel inevitably enjoins not one, but several withdrawals to the private sphere. Poe, who first raised the issue of the effects of this length, considered the discontinuousness of novel reading to be one of the liabilities of the form, which thereby had to forego 'the immense benefit of *totality*'. In the novel state, Poe thought, the autonomy of 'literary concerns' was always being frustrated by the foreign intervention of 'worldly interests'.[14] If, however, novel reading presupposes so many disparate withdrawals to the private sphere, by the same token it equally presupposes so many matching returns to the public, institutional one. An important dimension of what reading a novel entails, then, would lie – outside the moment and situation of actual perusal – in the times and places that interrupt this perusal and render it in the plural, as a series. Just as we read the novel in the awareness that we must put it down before finishing it, so even when we are not reading it, we continue to 'live' the form in the mode of *having to get back to it*. Phenomenologically, the novel form includes the interruptions that fracture the process of reading it. And the technical equivalent of this phenomenological interpenetration of literary and worldly interests would be the practice of various realisms, which, despite their manifold differences, all ensure that the novel is always centrally about the world one has left behind to read it and that the world to which one will be recalled has been reduced to attesting the truth (or falsehood) of the novel. It is not quite true, therefore, that the novel is simply concerned to attach us to individuality and domesticity, to privacy and leisure. What the form really secures is a close *imbrication* of individual and social, domestic and institutional, private and public, leisure and work. A drill in the rhythms of bourgeois industrial culture, the novel generates a nostalgic desire to get home (where the novel can be resumed) in the same degree as it inures its readers to the necessity of periodically renouncing home (for the world where the novel finds its justification and its truth). In reading the novel, one is made to rehearse how to live a problematic – always surrendered, but then again always recovered – privacy.

V

The same opposition – or at least the question of one – between private-domestic and social-institutional domains that is produced in the representation and consumed as the form occurs again in the relationship between the representation and the form. For though the form projects itself as a kind of home, what is housed in this home, as its contents, is not merely or even mainly comfortable domestic quarters, but also the social-institutional world at large. If the novel is substantially to allege its otherness in relation to this world, and thus to vouch for its competence to survey, judge, and understand it, then far from seeking to be adequate or isomorphic to its contents (when these are carceral, disciplinary, institutional), it is instead obliged to defend itself against them by differentiating the practices of the world from the practices of representing it. The current critical fondness for assimilating form and content (via homologies, thematisations, *mises-en-abyme*) becomes no more than a facile sleight-of-hand if it does not face the complication it in fact encounters in the question of the difference between the two that the novel regularly raises.[15] Specifically, as I hope to show in a moment, *Bleak House* is involved in an effort to distinguish its own enormous length from the protractedness of the Chancery suit, and also its own closure from the closed case of the Detective Police. But even remaining at a general and fundamental level, we can see the difference in the fact that, for instance, while the world of *Bleak House* is dreary enough, yet were the novel itself ever to become as dreary, were it ever to cease *making itself desirable*, it would also by the same token cease to be read. Pleasurably, at our leisure and in our homes, we read the novel of suffering, the serious business of life, and the world out-of-doors. Moreover, the critical and often indignant attitude that *Bleak House*, by no means untypically, takes toward its social world reinforces this 'erotic' difference with a cognitive one: the novel views the world in better, more clear-sighted and disinterested ways than the world views itself.

The suit in *Bleak House* has only to be mentioned for its monstrous length to be observed and censured. 'Jarndyce and Jarndyce still drags its dreary length before the Court, perennially hopeless' (p. 4). The suit is not merely long, but – here lies the affront – excessively so, longer than it is felt it ought to be. Yet what Dickens calls the 'protracted misery' of the suit (p. 54) – by which he means the misery of its protractedness as well as vice versa – cannot be explained merely as the consequence of gratuitous *additions* to a necessary and proper length, left intact, which they simply inordinately 'pad'. One of the ill effects of the length of the suit has been precisely to render unavailable the reality of a proper measure, of which the suit could be seen as an unwarranted expansion and to which it would be theoretically possible to restore it by some judicious abridgment. The further the length of the suit is elaborated, the more it abandons any responsibility to the telos or finality that originally called it forth, nominally continues to guide it even now, and would ultimately reabsorb it as the pathway leading to its own achievement. And along with the *formality* of an ending – the juridical act of decision – what would constitute the *substance* of one is put in jeopardy: namely, the establishment of the meaning of the original will. So nearly intertwined are ending and meaning that to adjourn the one seems to be to abjure the other: 'This scarecrow of a suit has, in course of time, become so complicated that no man alive knows what it means' (p. 4).

The suit's effective suspension of teleology is, of course, scandalously exemplary of a whole social sphere that seems to run on the principle of a purposiveness without purpose. The principle is enunciated and enforced not only by the bureaucratic officials who, when Jo is sick, 'must have been appointed for their skill in evading their duties, instead of performing them' (p. 432), but even by the various policemen in the novel who enjoin Jo to 'move on' in his perpetually maintained, displaced itinerary to nowhere. Internalised, this lack of purpose emerges as character defects: the long-windedness of Chadband, the aestheticism of Skimpole (who begins sketches 'he never finished'), the flightiness of Richard. Such instances, however, in which the sense of an ending seems entirely given up, are no more symptomatic of the general social suspension of finality than the abstract impatience and hopeful voluntarism with which the sense of an ending is merely imposed on a state of affairs that must thereby be misunderstood. Miss Flite is mad to expect a judgment 'shortly', and Richard is certainly on the way to madness when, choplogically, he argues that 'the longer [the suit] goes on, ... the nearer it must be to a settlement one way or other' (p. 182). In the progress of Hegelian Spirit, 'the length of this path has to be endured because, for one thing, each moment is necessary' to the emergence of the result;[16] whereas, the mere ongoingness of the un-Hegelian suit brings madness to any attempt to make sense of this length as a necessity, or in terms of the end-orientation that it formally retains but from which it has substantially removed itself. Finally, however, the length of the suit is devoid of necessity only in terms of an eventual judgment. Just as the inefficiency of power in Chancery showed up from another standpoint as the power of inefficiency, so too what are in one perspective the superfluous, self-subversive elongations of procedure become in another the necessary developments of a power that – call it the English law – has for its one great principle 'to make business for itself' (p. 548). Accordingly, the delays and remands that amount to an effective suspension of its declared end should not be seen to debilitate Chancery, but rather to allow one to take it seriously as – in Dickens's facetious phrase from *The Old Curiosity Shop* (1841) – 'the long and strong arm of the law'.[17]

In light of the fact that the novel about this long arm itself exercises a considerable reach – that the representation *of* length goes on *at* length too – we are invited to consider the extent to which the novel runs the risk of resembling the Chancery suit that it holds in despite. Certainly, the unfolding of the novel could be thought to parallel the elaboration of the suit insofar as it threatens an analogous failure to bring its ever more abundant materials to a proper or conceivably adequate summation. We already noted how the long novel foregoes 'the immense benefit of *totality*' because it cannot be read at a single sitting; but even if we were to export to the nineteenth century the anachronism of a 'speed-reader', Victorian practices of distributing the novel-product would still render the interruptedness of reading all but inevitable. Serial publication necessarily barred the reader from having full physical possession of the text he was reading until he was almost done with it; and even once the novel was published in volume form as a 'three-decker', the ordinary subscription to the circulating libraries (which provided the majority of readers with their access to it) allowed to a borrower only one volume at a time. These determinations are of course merely external, but they are fully matched by the compositional principles of discontinuity and delay that organise the form from within its own structure: not only in the formal breaks of chapters, instalments, volumes, but also in the substantive shifts from this plot-line to that, or from one point of view or narration to another; and generally in the shrewd administration of suspense that keeps the novel always tending toward a denouement that is continually being withheld. In Dickens, of course, the fissured and diffused character of novel form is far more marked than in the work of any of his contemporaries, extending from the extraordinary multitude of memorably disjunct characters, each psychologically sealed off from understanding any other, to the series of equally disparate and isolated spaces across which they collide. And, like the larger structure of suspense, even individual sentences will frequently derive their effects from the lengths to which they will go in withholding predication.[18] No doubt, both as a system of distribution and as a text, the Victorian novel establishes a little bureaucracy of its own, generating an immense amount of paperwork and sending its readers here, there, backward and forward, like the circumlocutory agencies that Dickens satirises. On this basis, it could be argued that, despite or by means of its superficially hostile attitude toward bureaucracy, a novel like

Bleak House is profoundly concerned to train us – as, at least
since the eighteenth century, play usually trains us for work – in
the sensibility for inhabiting the new bureaucratic, administrative
structures.

To say this, of course, is to neglect what Roland Barthes has
identified as the 'readerly' orientation of the traditional novel: the
tendency of its organisation to knit its discontinuities together by
means of codes such as those ordering our perception of plot and
suspense.[19] Although *Bleak House* baffles us in the first few
hundred pages by featuring a profusion of characters who seem to
have nothing to do with one another, a miscellany of events whose
bearing on a possible plot is undecidable, and even two separate
systems of narration that are unequal and unrelated, it simultaneously encourages us to anticipate the end of bafflement and the
acquisition of various structures of coherence: in the revelation or
development of relationships among characters; in the emergence
of a plot whereby the mysteries of the text will be enlightened and
its meanings fully named; and in the tendency of the two narrations
to converge, as Esther's account comes to include characters and
information that at first appeared exclusively in the anonymous
one. In other words, the novel dramatises the liabilities of fragmen-
tation and postponement within the hopeful prospect that they will
eventually be overcome. We consume the enormous length of a
novel like *Bleak House* in the belief that it is eminently digestible –
capable, that is, of being ultimately rendered in a readerly *digest*: a
final abridgment of plot and character that stands for (and so dispenses with) all that came before it. From the standpoint of this
promised end, the massive bulk of the novel will always have concealed the perfectly manageable and unmonstrous proportions of a
much shorter, tauter form.

Yet however sustained, the mere promise of an ending, far from
being sufficient to differentiate the novel from Chancery, would
positively enlarge on the analogy between the novel's practices and
those of the court, which also entices its subjects by means of
promises, promises. We read the novel under the same assumption
that Richard makes about the suit, that 'the longer it goes on, ...
the nearer it must be to a settlement'; and if the assumption is to be
validated in the one case as it is discredited in the other, the novel is
under obligation to make good its promise by issuing in judgments
and resolutions. For even if we always know about the novel (as we
do not about the suit) that its length is finite, involving only so

many pages or instalments, the vulgar evidence of an endpoint can never amount to the assurance of an *ending*: that is, the presence of a complex of narrative summations that would match or motivate the external termination of discourse with its internal closure. The suit, which attains an endpoint but no ending, embodies the distinction that the novel, to be different, will have to obliterate. Though the suit reaches a point at which it is correctly declared 'over for good' (p. 865), this point is determined extrinsically by the lack of funds that prevents the protracted, complex cause from being pursued to a proper conclusion of its own. 'Thus the suit lapses and melts away' (p. 867), instead of coming to the judgment that would have constituted a proper internal resolution. It is never known, for instance, whether the new will is a genuine document, and the project of finding out has been 'checked – brought up suddenly' upon what Conversation Kenge retains sufficient professional finesse to term the 'threshold' (p. 866).

In a pointed and self-serving contrast, the novel brings its characters to judgment, its mysteries to solution, and its plots to issues that would make further narrative superfluous. Immediately following the end of the suit, as a sort of consequence and reversal of it, Richard's death illustrates the contrast. Insofar as this death is premature, of course, it may look as though Richard will merely re-enact the abrupt check of the suit. Juridical discourse has ceased not because it has said what it wanted to say, but only for lack of funds to say it; and similarly, Richard's utterance is simply 'stopped by his mouth being full of blood' (p. 868). But what is staged on the scene of Richard's deathbed is in fact his full recovery. In the paradoxical logic of nineteenth-century novelistic closure, whereby one sums up by subtracting, Richard is purged of unsteadiness and suspicion and so made whole. Whereas the suit ends as up in the air as ever it was, Richard's end achieves a fundamental clarification: 'the clouds have cleared away, and it is bright now' (p. 869). His tearful recognition that John Jarndyce, whom he mistrusted, is 'a good man' renders him once more a good man himself. And his desire to be removed to the new Bleak House ('I feel as if I should get well there, sooner than anywhere') announces the redemptive turn from public institutional involvements to the domestic haven. As a result, even his death – no longer premature, but occurring only *after* the resolution of his character has been attained – bears witness to the seriousness of his conversion by making it permanent, the last word possible about him.

Unlike Chancery, then, the novel is willing to reward the patience that, like Chancery, it has required. The destiny of the long-suffering Esther is only the most obvious figure for the link the novel everywhere secures between the practice of patience and its payoff. In the reader's case, the link is affirmed each time he gets an answer to one of the questions or riddles he has endured; each time he enjoys the jubilation of recognising a character who has appeared earlier; each time a new instalment comes out to reward his month-long wait for it. It isn't Esther alone in *Bleak House* who is extraordinarily self-deprecating and diffident in the face of authority, be it the heavenly Father in whom 'it was so gracious ... to have made my orphan way so smooth and easy', or simply John Jarndyce, to whom she declares: 'I am quite sure that if there were anything I ought to know, or had any need to know, I should not have to ask you to tell it to me. If my whole reliance and confidence were not placed in you, I must have a hard heart indeed' (pp. 27, 99). The novel puts every reader in an equally subservient position of reliance upon the author, who, if one waits long enough (as, given the nature of the readerly text, one cannot but do), will delight us with the full revelation of his design, offering the supreme example of those happy surprises that Dickens's benevolent father-figures are fond of providing for those they patronise. Still less obviously, the novel develops our trust in the machinery of distribution itself, which can, for instance, be counted upon to provide the next instalment at exactly the interval promised. In short, the novel encourages a series of deferential cathexes – all the more fundamental for being unconscious – onto various instances of authority. What is promoted in the process is a paternalism that, despite the dim view the novel takes of the power structures of the British state, can only be useful in maintaining such structures. To submit to the novel's duration is already to be installed within an upbeat ethic of endurance. If, as we speculated above, the novel trains us to abide in Chancery-like structures – by getting us to wait, as it were, in its very long lines – it does this only insofar as it is organised as a *reformed* Chancery, a Chancery that can moralise its procrastinations in a practice of delayed gratification. Recklessly, the court demanded an attendance so futile that it inspired dangerously anarchistic fantasies of destruction. More prudently, the novel, urging us to wait, also promises (to use the very formula of prudence) that we shall wait *and see.*

VI

Though it goes to great lengths, *Bleak House* also goes to extremities to save these lengths from lapsing into mere unproductive extensions of the Chancery suit. Or rather, it saves them from such a fate *at* the extremities, or end-parts, in the production of a closure. Even so the novel cannot yet be considered to have won free of public, institutional attachments. For the very closure that secures a formal narrative difference between the novel and bureaucracy implicates the novel in a formal narrative resemblance to the institution that has played a sort of rival to the bureaucracy, the police. It is clear that the difference that obtains between Chancery and the novel applies equally in the relationship between Chancery and the police. In determining its own closure as revelation and fixed repose, the novel appears to have rejected the conception of termination proper to bureaucracy only to espouse the one proper to the police. The closural specimen that takes place, for example, at Richard's deathbed, even if it begins as though it will merely reflect the bureaucratic logic of lapse, achieves a permanent clarification of his character that rather subsumes the scene under the police model of closure as a double (cognitive and practical) apprehension. It can be further argued that, insofar as it arouses a desire for expeditious, conclusive solutions but only represents a single agency capable of providing them, the novel subtly identifies the reader's demand for closure with a general social need for the police, thus continuing (with only a considerable increase of cunning) the apologetics for the new forces of order that Dickens began as an essayist in *Household Words*.

The novel, however, is just as little eager to appear an agency of the police as it was to resemble a relay of the Chancery system. The relatively friendly treatment that *Bleak House* accords to the Detective Police is qualified by a number of reservations about the nature and effects of its power. Most of these, like the other aspects of the police, are carried in the characterisation of Inspector Bucket. His black clothes, linking him sartorially with Tulkinghorn and Vholes, darken his character as well with an association to the court; and like the undertaker to whose costume this dress also makes allusion, Bucket induces an ambivalence even in those he works for. Depending on the regularity of corruption, his profession has the doubly offensive aspect of a speculation on human weakness that happens also to be invariably justified. Yet the grief betokened by 'the great mourning ring on his little finger' (p. 310) might as well take Bucket himself for its object as any of his clients. His nature subdued to what it works in, Bucket too may be counted among the victims of crime. 'Pour bien faire de la police', Napoleon is supposed to have said, 'il faut être sans passion.' The moral horror of crime, which Dickens preserves (among other things) in his sensationalistic treatment of it, must be irrelevant – might even be counterproductive – to the professional dispassion required for the task of apprehending the criminal. This task may no doubt be considered itself a moral one. But the game function of detection thoroughly dominates whatever ethical ends it presumably serves; and, as Bucket himself can assure Sir Leicester, his profession has placed him utterly beyond the possibility of being scandalised: 'I know so much about so many characters, high and low, that a piece of information more or less, don't signify a straw. I don't suppose there's a move on the board that would surprise *me*; and as to this or that move having taken place, why my knowing it is no odds at all; any possible move whatever (provided it's in a wrong direction) being a probable move according to my experience' (p. 726). The ethical perspective survives only in the faint melancholy with which Bucket, truly the 'modern prince' in this respect, appears to regret the necessity of his own pessimism; or in the personal ascesis that, when every consequence of desire proves criminal, is perhaps the only humane response remaining. Nonetheless, the melancholy is hardly sufficient to prevent him from eliciting the very weaknesses that are the object of its contemplation. The momentary collabor- ation between Skimpole and Bucket revealed at the end of the novel, an alliance of two species of moral indifference, throws no more discredit on the aesthete who delivers a dangerously ill child over to the police for no better reason than a bribe, than on the officer who extends the bribe for no better reason than to cover his client's prying. Even the ascesis surrenders its moral truth to the extent that it is the very evidence of Bucket's amoral professional- isation. As Tulkinghorn's fate exemplifies, amateur detectives run amok because they are motivated by personal desires for posses- sion. Renunciation is thus for the professional detective a positive qualification, much as what Bucket appears to lament as his barren marriage shows a clear profit as an amicable and highly efficient business partnership.

These reservations are most tellingly inscribed in the novel as a narrative difference, once again centring on the question of ending, between the novel and the detective story that it includes. According to what will later be codified as the 'classical' model, the detective story in *Bleak House* reaches its proper end when Bucket, having provided a complete and provable account of her guilt, arrests Mademoiselle Hortense for Tulkinghorn's murder. In the classical model, one may observe, though the security of its preferred decor, the locked room, is regularly breached, it is also invariably recovered in the detective's unassailable *reconstruction* of the crime. And similarly, in this not yet quite classical example, Bucket's ironclad case against Hortense may be understood as the reparation of Tulkinghorn's tragically vulnerable chambers. Yet if one tradition, the detective story, violates its closed rooms only to produce better defended versions of them in the detective's closed cases, another tradition, let us call it the Novel, violates even these cases. In this latter tradition, to which *Bleak House* ultimately bears allegiance, there is no police case so flawless that a loophole cannot be found through which its claims to closure may be challenged. Here our vision of the loophole is supplied by Mademoiselle Hortense:

> 'Listen then, my angel', says she, after several sarcastic nods. 'You are very spiritual. But can you restore him back to life?'
> Mr Bucket answers, 'Not exactly.'
> 'That is droll. Listen yet one time. You are very spiritual. Can you make an honourable lady of Her?'
> 'Don't be so malicious', says Mr Bucket.
> 'Or a haughty gentleman of *Him?*' cries Mademoiselle, referring to Sir Leicester with ineffable disdain. 'Eh! O then regard him! The poor infant! Ha! ha! ha!'
> 'Come, come, why this is worse Parlaying than the other', says Mr Bucket. 'Come along.'
> 'You cannot do these things? Then you can do as you please with me. It is but the death, it is all the same. Let us go, my angel. Adieu you old man, grey. 'I pity you, and I des-pise you!'

(p. 743)

Hortense enumerates the various existential problems that, outlasting Bucket's solution, make it seem trivial and all but inconsequential. Her purely verbal qualification is soon worked into the actual plot when Bucket sets out in search of Lady Dedlock and finds her dead body instead. However skilfully prosecuted, the work of detection appears capable only of attaining a shell from which the vital principle has departed. Other closural moments in *Bleak*

House similarly end by producing a corpse, as though the novel wanted to attest, not just the finality, but also the failure of a closure that, even as it was achieved, missed the essence of what it aspired to grasp. In its ostentatious awareness of this failure, the novel defines its relationship to the materials of police fiction that it has adopted. On one side of this relationship there would be a detective story whose shallow solution naïvely gratifies our appetite for closure; on the other, there would be a Novel that, insisting at the very moment of solution on the insoluble, abiding mysteriousness of human and literary experience, provides superior nourishment by keeping us hungry.[20] Not to be identified with Chancery, the novel contrasts the aimless suspension of the suit with the achievement of its own ending; but not to be confused with the police either, it counters the tidy conclusion of the case with a conspicuous recognition of all that must elude any such achievement. If in the first instance, the novel must affirm the possibility of closure, in the second it is driven to admit the *inadequacy* of this closure.

In the end, then – precisely there – the novel's attempt to differentiate its own narrative procedures from those of the institutions it portrays falters, and the effort to disentangle itself from one institution only implicates it in another. So the seemingly perverse pattern continues wherein the novel is eager to produce a sheltered space whose integrity it is equally willing to endanger. We have seen how the novel establishes the opposition between the private-domestic and the social-institutional (1) within the representation, as the contrast between Esther's Bleak House and Chancery, and between the former and the police; (2) as a formal practice of consumption, in which the novel-reading subject shuttles to and fro between the home in which the novel is read and the world in which it is verified; and (3) at the intersection of the novel's own representational practice with the represented practice of institutions that it includes in its content. We have also seen how, in every instance, the opposition is accompanied by the possibility that it may be, or have been, nullified. At the same time as the existence of an 'outside' to institutional power is affirmed, that very affirmation is undercut with doubt.

Yet to describe the novel's rhetorical operation in this way, as the work of destructuration and subversion, is to identify it wholly with what is in fact only its negative moment.[21] We need to envision the positivity of this operation too, for what is put in question has also by the same token been put in place, and can be put to use as well. The ideological dividends paid in the difference between the 'inside' and the 'outside' of power are clear. The 'outside' gives the assurance of liberty, that makes tolerable the increasingly total administration of the 'inside' and helps avoid a politicisation of society as a whole. It also provides a critical space from which amendments and reforms useful to this administration can be effectively broached and imposed. As we began by observing, however, *Bleak House* troubles the straightforwardness of this difference, which it transforms into the question of a difference. What, then, are the ideological dividends paid in *bringing the difference in question*? A full answer would have to inquire into a whole range of practices whereby our culture has become increasingly adept in taking benefit of doubt.[22] But we can provide the synecdoche of an answer by turning in conclusion to the specific practice that, though we have seen it continually emerge both as an effect of various institutions and as the term of sundry oppositions, we have stopped short of considering in itself. Yet it is the practice that *Bleak House* is most concerned to promote: the practice of the family.

VII

Even in what otherwise would be her triumph, when the recognition of her merit has assumed public proportions, Esther Summerson retains her modest blindfold: 'The people even praise Me as the doctor's wife. The people even like Me as I go about, and make so much of me that I am quite abashed. I owe it all to him, my love, my pride! They like me for his sake, as I do everything I do in life for his sake' (p. 880). And to Allan's affirmation that she is prettier than ever she was, she can only respond: 'I did not know that; I am not certain that I know it now. But I know that my dearest little pets are very pretty, and that my darling is very beautiful, and that my husband is very handsome, and that my guardian has the brightest and most benevolent face that ever was seen; and that they can very well do without much beauty in me – even supposing –' (p. 880). Just as earlier Esther could barely speak of Allan, or her desire for him, so now, at the moment this desire is returned, she can only stammer. With her unfinished sentence, *Bleak House* 'ends'. Though one easily supplies what Esther keeps from saying ('even supposing I have my beauty back'), the modesty that consigns this assertion to silence is, to the last, radically inconclusive.

Like woman's work, which is the external means to Esther's social recognition, the labours of modesty, its inner correlative, are never done.

What might be a matter for grief or grievance, however, as Esther's 'neurotic' inability to relinquish her self-doubt in the hour of success, also means that the energy that has gone into consolidating and sustaining one Bleak House after another will not be dissipated in the complacency of enjoyment or relaxation. The text has posed the origin of Esther's self-doubt in the question of her proper place in a family structure (her illegitimacy), and this origin has shaped her tacit ambition to instal herself securely within such a structure. Given a twist, however, by the psychology of modesty through which it is obliged to pass, the ambition attains a frustration that is exactly proportionate to its achievements. Esther never ceases to earn her place, as though, were she to do so, she might even at the end be displaced from it. Yet there is a twist to the frustration too, as Esther's endless modesty finds its non-neurotic social validation in the family that, no less precarious than her own sense of identity, requires precisely such anxious and unremitting devotion for its survival. Or, as these relations might be generally summarised: the insecurity of the family subject is indispensable to counter the instability of the family structure, of which it is an effect.

The instability of the family, therefore, is constitutive of its very maintenance. As Jacques Donzelot has shown, the nineteenth-century family develops within two registers, which he calls *contract* and *tutelage*. Contract indicates the free and easy family autonomy ensured through 'the observance of norms that guarantee the social usefulness of [its] members'; whereas tutelage designates the system of 'external penetration' of the family, transformed into an object of surveillance and discipline. The two registers are positive and negative dimensions of a single policy of incentive: if the family satisfactorily performs its social tasks, then it is granted the liberty and autonomy of contract; but should it fail to pay back the privileges thereby conferred upon it in the proper accomplishment of responsibilities, then it must fall back into the register of tutelage.[23]

With these two registers, one can correlate the two causes that Dickens's novels regularly ascribe to the faultiness of the family: on one hand, the external interference of institutions that (like the workhouse in *Oliver Twist*) dislocate and disjoin the family; and on the other, the internal dynamic that (as exemplified in *Oliver Twist* by Monks's oedipal and sibling rivalry) determines its own divisions and displacements. The first cause amounts to a demand for contract; the second is a concession to the necessity of tutelage. The theme of outside interference bears a message to society at large to reform its institutions in the interest of preserving the only natural and naturally free space within it. (The argument is never free from the utilitarianism that Dickens's sentimentality about the family rationalises rather than resists. The novels continually imply the family's advantages over other agencies in producing acceptable citizens of the liberal state both in quantitative terms – as its greater economy – and in qualitative ones – as the superiority of the bonds between its members.) The theme of internal disruption, on the other hand, addresses its message to the family itself, which had better do its utmost to stay together or else face the misery of being dispersed or colonised by remedial institutions. In the first instance, Dickens advises society to police for the family, which would thereby be safeguarded as the home of freedom; in the second, he counsels the family to police itself, that it might remain free by becoming its own house of correction. The two apparently incompatible themes, informing the representation of the family throughout Dickens's work, are in fact complementary. Likewise, the 'practical' recommendations attached to each find their mutual coherence precisely in the way that they cancel one another out. For if society reformed itself so that state institutions would, if not wither away, become minimal and humane, then there would no longer exist an outside threat to consolidate the family in the face of its internal dangers; and to the extent that the family could successfully repress these dangers itself, it would only reproduce such institutions in their worst aspects. With the disappearance of social discipline, the emancipated family would prove in greater need of it than ever; and in the enjoyment of its unobstructed independence, it would restore the discipline from which it was meant as an asylum, either in its own practice or in that of the institutions that would inevitably make their reappearance upon its breakdown.

Neither the social nor the familial 'policing of the family', therefore, can be carried very far without giving rise to the very regimentation it was supposed to curtail. In this respect at least, Dickens's vigorous reformism makes better sense as an undeclared defence of the status quo: the social recommendations would merely be the weights (like most weights, not meant to be carried very far) to preserve the family in its present delicate balance. For the family's freedom is founded in the possibility of its discipline, and thus to enjoy the former means to have consented to the latter. Esther's insecurity, we said, works to oppose the instability of the family structure from which it results. It supplies the constant vigilance wanted to keep the contractual family from lapsing into the subjection of tutelage. It is equally true, however, that Esther's insecurity *confirms* the family in its faultiness. In the same degree that it propagates the worry and anxiety needed to maintain the family, it keeps alive the ever-present danger of its fall. The novel everywhere publishes the same fear of falling and implies the same urgency about holding one's place. The 'outside' of power regularly incurs the risk that it may be annexed – or worse, may already have been annexed – by the 'inside'. So, for instance, the family will sometimes be shown as only a slight modulation of Chancery bureaucracy (comfortably domesticated with the Jellybys), or of the police (one of whose different voices can be heard in Mrs Pardiggle, the 'moral Policeman' who regiments her own family in the same spirit she takes others 'into custody' [p. 107]. And the risk touches us more nearly than do these unadmirable characters, for even the excellent Bagnets rely on an explicitly military order, and Esther herself may be only better directed than Mrs Jellyby when she sits at her desk 'full of business, examining tradesmen's books, adding up columns, paying money, filing receipts, and ... making a great bustle about it' (p. 122). Envisioning the family now as a firm counterweight to social institutions, now as a docile function of them, here as the insuperable refuge from the carceral, there as the insufferable replica of it, the novel poses the question of the family, which it thereby designates as the object of struggle. Rather as Esther takes up this question as the necessity of founding and keeping Bleak House, so the novel extends the question to its readers, both as a principle of hope and an exhortation, as it were, to work at home. Mr Bagnet's famous catchword formulates what is no less the objective than the condition of the family in Dickens's representation of it: 'Discipline' – within the domestic circle as well as outside it – 'must be maintained.'

VIII

Queen Victoria confided to her diaries: 'I never feel quite at ease or at home when reading a Novel.'[24] *Bleak House* makes itself as anxiogenic and incomplete as the home with which it identifies. For in an age in which productivity is valued at least as much as the product, the novel must claim no less the inadequacy than the necessity of closure. This inadequacy can now be understood – not in the old-fashioned way, as a failure of organic form, nor even in the new-fashioned way, as the success of a failure of organic form – but, in the broader context of institutional requirements and cultural needs, as the novel's own 'work ethic', its imposing refusal of rest and enjoyment. Certainly, when reading this novel, though in the reasons of the hearth it finds its own reason for being, one never feels quite at home; perhaps, having finished it, one knows why one never *can* feel at home. For what now is home – not securely possessed in perpetuity, but only leased from day to day on payment of continual exertions – but a House? And what is this House – neither wholly blackened by the institutions that make use of its cover, nor wholly bleached of their stain – but (in the full etymological ambiguity of the word) irresolvably Bleak? 'Bleak House has an exposed sound' (p. 68).

From D. A. Miller, *The Novel and the Police* (Berkeley, CA, 1988), pp. 58–106.

NOTES

[First published in *Representations*, 1 (1983), and then in *The Novel and the Police*, the title of D. A. Miller's original essay derives from *Our Mutual Friend* (I. XVI) where a character, Sloppy, who gives public readings from the newspapers is said to 'do the police in different voices'. The topic of Miller's essay is how the police surface so polyvalently in the text – and in different voices – even in the form of the novel itself. I have commented on the Foucault derivations of this essay in the Introduction, and on its distance from Hillis Miller. Whereas the latter sees Chancery as an aspect of the system of language that holds everyone, in D. A. Miller's essay Chancery is described as 'an organisation of power'. (Yet the text – and this is its part of its danger as a form of ideology – contradicts this sense of the totality of power by suggesting that some people may remain unspoiled outside it.) Hillis Miller's argument that the text suggests the impossibility of interpretation is countered by another that says that Chancery is never willing to become the agency or subject of interpretation – to interpret would be, in fact, a liberating gesture. Interpretation is, rather, deflected into the detective story, whose ideological components (e.g. the notion of individual responsibility), and inspiration come from the ruling party itself – the agents of law. The desire for a narrative with its own coherence produces the real agent of interpretation: the police. They may be seen as the ideological representation of the way the system of Chancery would like to see itself: Bucket takes over from Tulkinghorn. Power, then, newly legitimates itself (the detective police came into being in 1840: the word 'detective', according to the OED, appears in 1856). The novel form, in its length and its serial character, might lend itself to deconstruction's arguments about deferral of meaning and the inevitable *différance* in the text that breaks with the possibility of finding a single and totalisable statement within it, but it is taken by Miller to be another form of policing, disciplining the reader. It operates by the codes that Roland Barthes (in *S/Z*, his 1970 study of the realist text) says sustain the realist text and give it the illusion of continuity, and it gives to the reader the sense that he/she is reading something that unites and links up its various details. The novel in fact disposes of its characters and their destinies with the assurance of a policeman. The desire for 'closure', for an ending to the 'discontents' that narrative breeds is the wish for the resolution the police can provide.

Miller sees Dickens or the novelist as the policeman but with feelings of outrage (e.g. at the end of chapter 47) which conflict with the professionalisation of the police: Bucket may have a 'faint melancholy' but he is also unshockable. Bucket has absorbed shock: he fits the bureaucratic world which is beyond such personal reactions. Hence the importance of the word 'bureaucracy' in Miller's title. Bucket represents the 'administered' society that Max Weber discusses, just as Miller traces the administered, disciplined society through the institution of the family.

Quotations come from the 1948 Oxford edition. Ed.]

1. Charles Dickens, *Oliver Twist* (Oxford, 1949), pp. 95, 94.

2. Charles Dickens, *Bleak House* (Oxford, 1948), p. 7. For all future citations from the novel, page references to this edition will be given parenthetically in the text.

3. John Forster, in an unsigned review for the *Examiner* (8 October 1853), 643–5; reprinted in Philip Collins (ed.), *Dickens: The Critical Heritage* (New York, 1971), p. 291.

4. George Brimley, in an unsigned review, *Spectator*, 36 (24 September 1853), 923–5; reprinted in Collins, *Dickens: The Critical Heritage*, p. 283.

5. A euphoric account of the destiny of Victorian bureaucracy may be found in David Roberts, *The Victorian Origins of the Welfare State* (New Haven, CT, 1961). For a detailed treatment of Dickens's attitude toward the Detective Police, see the pertinent chapter in Philip Collins's invaluable study, *Dickens and Crime*, 2nd edn (London, 1964).

6. I have in mind the tradition founded in Louis Althusser, 'A Letter on Art', in his *Lenin and Philosophy*, trans. Ben Brewster (New York and London, 1971), pp. 221–7, and elaborated in Pierre Macherey, *A Theory of Literary Production*, trans. Geoffrey Wall (London, 1978). Althusser's claim that art performs an 'internal distanciation' on ideology in the course of representing it ('Letter', p. 222) receives its working-through in the theory and practical criticism of Macherey, for whom 'the finished literary work ... *reveals* the gaps in ideology' by 'specifically literary means' (*Literary Production*, pp. 60, 238). The best example of this tradition in English (and also the most relevant to the work in progress here) is Terry Eagleton, *Criticism and Ideology* (London, 1976). In the chapter called 'Ideology and Literary Form', which includes a discussion of Dickens and other nineteenth-century English novelists, 'ideology' (qua 'organicism') once again provides the principle of coherence that 'literary form' once again brings into disarray: 'In English literary culture of the past century, the ideological basis of organic form is peculiarly visible, as a progressively impoverished bourgeois liberalism attempts to integrate more ambitious and affective ideological modes. In doing so, that ideology enters into grievous conflicts which its aesthetic forms betray in the very act of attempted resolution' (p. 161). In all cases, the category of artistic form remains where bourgeois aesthetics used to situate it: beyond social tensions or, what comes to the same, invariably on the right side of the struggle.

7. A first, but decisive expression of this view is given in J. Hillis Miller's introduction to *Bleak House*, by Charles Dickens (Baltimore, MD, 1971), pp. 11–34.

8. Charles Dickens, *Little Dorrit* (Oxford, 1953), p. 104.

9. Trollope, the only other major Victorian novelist to take up the subject of bureaucracy, offers us a similar perception in *The Three Clerks* (1858), where the new system of competitive examinations introduced by the Civil Service Reform inspires one of the examiners with the definitive dream of bureaucracy: to turn the end it serves into the means of its own expansion. 'Every man should, he thought, be made to pass through some "go". The greengrocer's boy should not carry out cabbages unless his fitness for cabbage-carrying had been ascertained, and till it had also been ascertained that no other boy, ambitious of the preferment, would carry them better' (Anthony Trollope, *The Three Clerks* [Oxford, 1943], p. 128).

10. Frequently drawn from the end of the eighteenth century to our own day, the contrast between the law's delay and the dispatch of the police typically emerges (as here in Dickens) on the side of the police. A locus classicus: 'Entourée de formes qu'elle ne trouve jamais assez multipliées, la justice n'a jamais pardonné à la police sa rapidité. La police, affranchie de presque toutes les entraves, n'a jamais excusé

dans la justice, ses lenteurs; les reproches qu'elles se font mutuelle-ment, la Société les fait souvent à l'une ou à l'autre. On reproche à la police d'inquiéter l'innocence, à la justice de ne savoir ni prévenir, ni saisir le crime' (Surrounded by forms that it never finds elaborate enough, the judical system has never pardoned the police its speed. The police, freed from nearly all such shackles, has never forgiven the judical system its sluggishness. The reproaches that each makes to the other are made to both by Society, which upbraids the police for dis-turbing the innocent and the judicial system for being unable to deter or apprehend the criminal.) (Joseph Fouché, Minister of Police, in a circular addressed to the prefects of France, 30 Brumaire, Year VIII; quoted in Henry Buisson, *La police, son histoire* [Vichy, 1949], p. 167).

11. See Michel Foucault, *Discipline and Punish*, trans. Alan Sheridan (New York, 1977), esp. pp. 222–3.

12. In installing criminals and police in the same seat – the conspicuous and closed world of delinquency – Dickens follows what was routine practice throughout the popular literature of the nineteenth century. To quote from a single, but highly influential example: 'Le quartier du Palais de Justice, trés circonscrit, trés surveillé, sert pourtant d'asile ou de rendezvous aux malfaiteurs de Paris. N'est-il pas étrange, ou plutôt fatal, qu'une irrésistible attraction fasse toujours graviter ces criminels autour du formidable tribunal qui les condamne à la prison, au bagne, à l'échafaud!' (The neighbourhood of the Palace of Justice, though very circumscribed and under close surveillance, serves nonetheless as a refuge or a rendezvous for the wrong-doers of Paris. Is it not strange, or rather fated, that an irresistible attraction always draws criminals to the vicinity of the fearful tribunal that condemns them to prison, the hulks, the scaffold!) (Eugène Sue, *Les Mystères de Paris* [1843], 4 vols [Paris, 1977], 1:15).

13. See the editor's summary of the Victorian reception of *Bleak House* in Philip Collins, *Dickens: The Critical Heritage* (New York, 1971), p. 273.

14. Edgar Allan Poe, 'Tale-Writing – Nathaniel Hawthorne', in *The Complete Works of Edgar Allan Poe*, ed. James A. Harrison, 17 vols (New York, 1902), 13:153.

15. Even critics who propose an immediate identification of form and content in *Bleak House* are in practice compelled to acknowledge that the novel resists their enterprise. J. Hillis Miller's claim that '*Bleak House* has exactly the same structure as the society it exposes' has fre-quent recourse to concessive clauses that make allowance for 'Dickens's generous rage against injustice, selfishness and procrastina-tion' or his 'sympathy for Gridley's indignant outrage' against the Chancery system [see above, pp. 46, 39, 44 – Ed.]. And Terry Eagleton,

for whom the novel is 'obliged to use as aesthetically unifying images the very social contradictions ... which are the object of [Dickens's] criticism', is quite happy to register the 'contradictory' nature of the unity thus established (*Criticism and Ideology* [London, 1976], p. 129). Yet since both critics only recognise the difference between the novel and its world in the process of annulling it, they never permit themselves to consider seriously the *question* of the difference, and each is finally willing to pass off as a weakness of the text what is only a weakness in his account of it. In Miller's argument, in the absence of further treatment, evidence of the difference goes only to show that Dickens was curiously inconsistent. And in Eagleton's, such evidence would merely point to a text that is, to use his own expressive phrase about *Dombey and Son* (1846–8), 'self-divided and twisted by the very contradictions it vulnerably reproduces' (*Criticism and Ideology*, p. 127). Yet when, as it begins to appear, the difference between novel and world belongs to a series of analogous difference as an inconsequence or laying it to rest as a contradiction, we neglect a crucial aspect of the novel's own programme, a central feature of its self-definition.

16. G. W. F. Hegel, *Phenomenology of Spirit*, trans. A. V. Miller (Oxford, 1977), p. 17.

17. Charles Dickens, *The Old Curiosity Shop* (Oxford, 1951), p. 553.

18. For example: 'Jostling against clerks going to post the day's letters, and against counsel and attorneys going home to dinner, and against plaintiffs and defendants, and suitors of all sorts, and against the general crowd, in whose way the forensic wisdom of ages has interposed a million of obstacles to the transaction of the commonest business of life – diving through law and equity, and through that kindred mystery, the street mud, which is made of nobody knows what, and collects about us nobody knows whence or how: we only knowing in general that when there is too much of it, we find it necessary to shovel it away – the lawyer and the law-stationer come to a Rag and Bottle shop' (p. 135).

19. 'To end, to fill, to join, to unify – one might say that this is the basic requirement of the *readerly*, as though it were prey to some obsessive fear: that of omitting a connection. Fear of forgetting engenders the appearance of a logic of actions; terms and the links between them are posited (invented) in such a way that they unite, duplicate each other, create an illusion of continuity. The plenum generates the drawing intended to "express" it, and the drawing evokes the complement, colouring: as if the *readerly* abhors a vacuum. What would be the narrative of a journey in which it was said that one stays somewhere without having arrived, that one travels without having departed – in which it was never said that, having departed, one arrives or fails to arrive? Such a narrative would be a scandal, the extenuation, by haem-

orrhage, of readerliness' (Roland Barthes, S/Z, trans. Richard Miller [New York, 1974], p. 105).

20. *Bleak House* is thus one of the first texts to adumbrate a position that with modernism becomes commonplace: namely, that a literature worthy of the name will respect mystery by keeping it inviolate. For a canonical allusion to the position, see Kafka's remarks on the detective story in Gustav Janouch, *Conversation with Kafka*, trans. Goronwy Rees, 2d edn rev. (New York, 1971), p. 133; and among recent rehearsals, see David I. Crossvogel *Mystery and its Fiction: From Oedipus to Agatha Christie* (Baltimore, MD, 1979). Yet insofar as the modernist cult of the irresolvable is perfectly consistent with the efficient workings of the Court of Chancery, *Bleak House* is also one of the first texts to indicate the difficulties with this position, which advancing beyond cheap consolations, may only bind us more profoundly to a society that thrives on delayed and ever-incomplete satisfactions.

21. The moment exclusively occupies those two modes of literary criticism to which this essay may be thought to address itself: Marxism and deconstructionism. Contemporary Marxist criticism would construe the ambiguities we have noticed as the contradictions that inscribe the text's inevitable failure to make its domestic ideology cohere. By virtue of 'internal distanciation', the literary text finds itself compelled to betray this ideology, if only in its hesitations, silences, discrepancies. Not altogether dissimilarly, deconstruction would take such ambiguities for the aporias in an allegory of the process and problems of signification itself. Intended meaning is always exceeded in the signifiers to which it commits its expression, since by their nature those signifiers defer meaning even as they differentiate it. The trace of such differentiation, furthermore, carrying over as a kind of residue from one signifier to another, undermines the integrity of each: so that, in the case of an opposition, one term will invariably prove to be contaminated with the term it is meant to oppose. Without insisting on the comparison, one might say that Marxist criticism, urgently putting under scrutiny the evidence of a text that thereby never fails to convict itself, proceeds rather like the Detective Police; whereas a deconstructive criticism, patiently willing to remain on the threshold of interpretation in the wisdom that every reading it might offer would be a misreading, behaves somewhat like the Court of Chancery. If only from *Bleak House*, however, we know that a practice claiming to resemble neither the bureaucracy nor the police merely uses this pretension to camouflage its alliances with both. For us, therefore, it cannot exactly be a matter of repudiating these critical modes, but rather of writing against them, as against a background. 'Against' Marxism, then, we stress the positivity of contradiction, which, far from always marking the fissure of a social formation, may rather be one of the joints whereby such a formation is articulated.

Contradiction may function not to expose, but to construct the ideology that has foreseen and contained it. And 'against' deconstruction, we should urge (rather as did Hegel in confronting the nothingness of scepticism) that undecidability must always be the undecidability of *something in particular*. The trouble with the deconstructionist allegory of signification is not that it is untrue, but that, despite the deceptive 'closeness' of the readings, it is abstract. Two things, I think, ought to remove the effects of undecidability and contradiction from the void in which deconstruction places them. For one, they have a history or genealogy that determines them and whose traces must be registered. It may be ultimately true, for instance, as J. Hillis Miller has said, that '*Bleak House* is a document about the interpretation of documents' [see above, p. 29 – Ed.], but the formulation elides the rivalrous differentiations among institutional practices through which the concern with interpretation comes to emerge (and then, not as a theme so much as the stakes in a contest). As a result, one misses seeing the extent of the novel's assumption that it is *not* a document like those it is about. For a second, these effects, once formed, are never left at large and on the loose to wreak havoc on discursive and institutional operations. On the contrary, the latter have always already drafted them into a service that takes its toll and whose toll, accordingly, needs to be assessed in turn. Thus, Miller's account keeps characteristic silence about what even *Bleak House* (for highly partisan reasons of its own, of course) is quite willing to publicise: that the hermeneutic problematic itself is an instrument in the legal establishment's will to power.

22. At the level of subjective practices, a central and quite literal example would be the continuity noted by Max Weber between the religious ethos of Protestantism and the mental disposition of capitalism. The Calvinist subject's doubt as to his salvation engages him in intense worldly activity as a means to attain self-confidence. Such self-confidence is thus made to ride on restless, continuous work in a calling – a process that may surpass the moment of possession or remain on this side of it, but in any case never coincides with it. The task of proving one's election becomes as endless as the increase of capital that is the sign of its being successfully accomplished. Dickens is far enough from – or close enough to – this psychological structure to make it a prime target of his criticism, either in the spiritual bookkeeping of a Mrs Clennam or the entrepreneurial pieties of a Bounderby. Yet the end of such criticism is not to repudiate the nexus between personal doubt and worldly duty, but rather to free its terms from their limiting specifications. This means, in effect, re-encoding it within the organisation of the family. Weber's Protestant ethic is replaced by Freud's family romance, as a structure linking self-doubt with worldly ambition. When the specific doctrinal source of doubt (predestination) has been familialised as a problematic of the 'orphan',

uncertain both of his parents' identity and hence of his place in the world; when even the 'calling' has been transferred from the primary capitalist sphere (where with the advent of industrialism its integrity had been seriously compromised) to the still-undisparaged domain of domestic economy, then Robinson Crusoe returns as Esther Summerson: both the doubt-ridden, self-effacing orphan, always on the verge of being overwhelmed by the question of her origin and the consequent problem of her destiny, and the 'methodical' housekeeper (p. 92) 'with a fine administrative capacity' (p. 597), who, admonishing herself 'Duty, my dear!' shakes the keys of her kingdom to ring herself 'hopefully' in bed (p. 80).

23. Jacques Donzelot, *The Policing of Families*, trans. Robert Hurley (New York, 1979). The discussion of contract and tutelage that is paraphrased and cited here appears on pp. 82–95.

24. Viscount Esher (ed.), *The Girlhood of Queen Victoria: A Selection from her Diaries, 1832–40*, 2 vols (London, 1912), 2: 83, reprinted in Collins, *Dickens: The Critical Heritage*, p. 44. The citation comes from an entry for 23 December 1838.

5

Ideology and Critique in Dickens's *Bleak House*

DOMINICK LaCAPRA

D. A. Miller's recent essay[1] is an admirably ambitious attempt to work out a political reading of a literary text. Its series of local insights into *Bleak House* would alone qualify it as a high point in recent criticism. Miller traces with care the complex and often paradoxical relations between carceral and liberal 'topics' or 'spaces' in the novel, and he explores the way Chancery Court seems to blur the oppositions only to give rise to conflict-ridden attempts to contain its own perplexities through the Detective Police and the family. On first appearance, Dickens's novel seems caught up in the contradictions of its social context – in the 'binary opposition' between prison-like, disciplinary 'closures' and contractual sanctuaries of freedom as well as in bureaucratic processes (epitomised in Chancery) that do not resolve contradictions or synthesise oppositions but further confuse and exacerbate them. The movement in the novel to the format of the detective story is genially interpreted by Miller as a formal attempt to reduce Chancery's endless convolutions to a solvable puzzle. He perceptively notes that, in contrast to Chancery's anonymous processes and tentacular permeation into society, the Detective Police is given a 'human face' in that it is represented by one dominant figure, Bucket. The family – notably the family gathered around Esther in the domestic establishment of Bleak House – seems to provide the only place safe from the incursions of both bureaucracy and police. Indeed the anxiety of the family member concerning the domestic group's tenuous position in a complex and invasive society furnishes precisely the motivation needed to shore up or reaffirm its threatened structure. But the Detective Police that polices its own limits as well as those of society at large can at times transgress those limits, as when Bucket serves as both agent of official power and private detective or when he uses his introduction into the family setting to facilitate an arrest. The family itself seems to occupy a position in the novel as a beleaguered fortress whose position finds a curious analogue in the structure of Miller's own argument about it.

I offer the foregoing synopsis not to supersede Miller's account or to render its sinuous complexity but to recall certain of its lineaments to the reader. More generally, Miller attempts to elicit the relation between the literary text and its sociopolitical contexts (or subtexts) while avoiding the twin dangers of sociological reduction and literary formalism. In his own terms, he tries to 'write against' Marxism and deconstruction 'as against a background' [p. 125]. I would like to argue that Miller's formulations in elaborating his mode of antithetical criticism are at times problematic in that they may have ideological implications from which Miller would probably want to distance himself. The general issue, as I see it, is how symptomatic, critical, and possibly transformative forces interact in relating a text to its various contexts (or subtexts). I think Miller's formulations often rearticulate the symptomatic or legitimating functions of a text but do not allow for the complications arising through significant critical effects. At best they revalorise legitimation as necessary for the production of a text.

Miller asserts that *Bleak House* is a 'contradictory text' but that 'we should be wary of prejudging it, in a certain Marxist manner, as the "symptom" of an ideological bind, obligingly betrayed to our notice in the text's taken-for-granted "distanciation" from its own programme'. Certain Marxists in whom Miller finds this objectionable manner are Louis Althusser, Pierre Macherey, and Terry Eagleton [pp. 92, 122]. Miller insists that 'we need rather to be prepared to find in the source of "incoherence", the very resource on which the text draws for its consistency; in the ideological "conflict", a precise means of addressing and solving it; in the "failure" of intention on the part of the text, a positively advantageous *strategy*' [p. 92].

Miller may be justified in insisting that the concepts of a symptomatic relation to ideology (or ideologies) and an 'internal distanciation' from it (or them) are too simple to account for the interinvolvement of a text and its contexts. But his own wavering and at times unexplicated formulations do not go very far in elucidating this problem. The notion that the 'source of "incoherence"' is 'the very resource on which the text draws for its consistency' seems to limit a text to the uncritical harmonisation of inconsistencies – and to do so through the kind of verbal conceit characteristic of the most dubious form of deconstructive criticism against which Miller inveighs. The idea that a text finds in 'the ideological "conflict", a precise means of addressing and solving it' would seem (for the formulation is rather imprecise) to attribute to a text, both in its internal performance and in its bearing on larger sociopolitical processes, an ability to transcend social problems in a manner Miller elsewhere sees as mystified. And the assertion that the '"failure" of intention' may conceal 'a positively advantageous strategy' does not find its necessary explication in Miller's later discussion, for the strategy of a text seems to be little more than an anonymous process of employing existing ideologies to generate further ideological variations or legitimating reinforcements of them. Thus Miller writes a few pages later:

> We cannot too strongly insist that these 'paradoxes' are not merely confusions or historical contradictions that tug and pull at a text helpless to regulate them, but rather productive ambiguities that facilitate the disposition, functioning, and promotion of certain ideological effects, some of which we have already suggested. Neither, however, should '*Bleak House*, by Charles Dickens' be denounced – or congratulated – as the ultimate strategist of these effects, as though one could allow such effects their broad cultural resonance without also recognising their broad cultural production and distribution. Yet if the novel no more 'manipulates' the equivocations we have traced than 'succumbs' to them, perhaps the most pertinent reason is that it lacks the distance from them required to do either.
>
> [p. 103]

It is difficult to infer more 'positive' statements from the neither/nor formulations Miller puts forth (another deconstructive residue?), but the resulting image of the text seems to make it more passively 'symptomatic' than it is in the writings of the Marxists Miller criticises. Participating fully in sociocultural equivocations, the text merely recycles ideological effects to produce more ideological effects through a mysterious strategy devoid of a strategist (the death of the author?). At least the Althusserian notion of 'internal distanciation' provided the possibility of a space in which a text reworks its social contexts and thus 'produces' critical effects to complicate its inscription of ideology. And it allowed for the possible relation of these effects to the difference and the distance between author and narrator as roles of the complex social individual – a problem Miller tends to ignore despite his (largely empty) concern for the specificity of the novel form. One might hypothesise that one reason why the nineteenth-century novel at times allowed for certain critical effects in its relation to ideology was because of the problematic relation between author and narrator characteristic of its 'form'. This distinguished it from historiography, for example, where the convention was (and is) for the author to speak in his own undivided and clearly defined voice – a voice that is essentially objective but that may on occasion wax subjective, as in a preface or conclusion. (Tocqueville – right balance, serious historian: we may not agree with all of his theses, but we share his over-all frame of reference. Michelet – too subjective, hence 'romantic': we may applaud some of his genial insights, but we take our distance from him.) In historiography, voice might in fact be at times split or internally divided (as in Michelet's equivocal relation to 'the people' or even in Tocqueville's doubts about the compatibility of democracy and liberty in modern society), but the divisions were often repressed and hence less subject to responsible modulations, including an element of critical control (which need not be purely 'carceral'). In any case, the convention concerning unity of voice made it more difficult for the historian to question his own beliefs or hopes without resorting to certain devices ('The reader may object ...') that seemed to jar with the quest for an objective representation of reality expressed in a firm and coherent narrative style.

Here one might note that Miller, despite his theoretical emphasis upon the problematic relation of form and content, often relies on rather orthodox thematic and character analysis. His discussion centres on the nature of the representation of certain 'objects' in the novel (bureaucracy, police, family; Esther, Bucket, etc.). He does nothing with the fascinating problem of dual narration in *Bleak House* (the anonymous ironic narrative and Esther's seemingly naïve and innocent narrative) and the way it might bear on the 'internal dialogisation' of the voice of the Dickens-narrator, thereby problematising the inscription of ideological effects. And his excursus on the reading process as one of withdrawal into privacy followed by a return to society [pp. 104–5] is not specific to the novel form; it would apply to any long written text. One might argue that the novel tends, if anything, to be more critical than other forms in coming to terms with this problem. Yet even in his stimulating discussion of the novel's attempt to distinguish itself from Chancery Court and the Detective Police, Miller does not inquire into the importance of critical effects in the novel's relation to ideology and sociopolitical processes. Instead he relies overmuch on Barthes's notion of the delights of the *lisible* and the issue of closure.

The one crucial institution in reference to which Miller sees Dickens as a writer who recycles and legitimates dominant ideological stereotypes is the family. Here Dickens presumably presents the family as a haven in a heartless world (to coin a phrase), and he tacitly reiterates in his image of it the dual bases of its real instability: its 'registers' of (liberal) contract and (carceral) tutelage. The one complication in this interpretation that Miller fails to observe is that if Dickens idealises any type of family, it is the *pre-capitalistic* family in which a 'moral economy' (in the phrase of E. P. Thompson) counteracts through its modes of solidarity and mutual aid the effects of both contract and tutelage. This nostalgic utopia is directly evoked in the explicitly artificial family assembled by John Jarndyce. It may of course serve conservative or legitimating functions, thereby providing in a different way what Miller argues is Dickens's 'undeclared defence of the status quo' [p. 118]. But it may also have contestatory functions as it did at least in part for workers' movements in the nineteenth century. These functions would support Raymond Williams (a Marxist not mentioned by Miller) in his excessively general but still noteworthy argument in defence of the critical role of Dickens's texts.[2]

Miller suggests that 'contemporary' Marxism is allied with the Detective Police in its predilection for closure and manageable solutions, and he further suggests that deconstruction forges an unholy alliance with Chancery Court in its spinning out of endless, inconclusive commentaries. In what is by now a familiar (and rather uncritical) gesture, he identifies J. Hillis Miller as the authoritative voice of deconstruction. And there is at least a hint of paranoia in the vehemence with which D. A. distances himself from the possibility that J. H. is a hermeneutic *frère ennemi*.

D. A. argues that J. H. misleadingly provides an interpretation of Chancery Court as a direct allegory of the problem of interpretation in general. 'No response would serve Chancery or the logic of its law better than to see this manufacture as inhering in the nature of "textuality" rather than belonging to an institutional practice that seeks to implant and sanction its own technical procedures' [p. 93]. D. A.'s indictment becomes more inclusive when he charges deconstruction with furnishing deceptively close readings that are really abstract and with what Hegel saw as 'the nothingness of scepticism' [p. 126].

Despite its shrillness and its tendency to scapegoat the other who is in certain respects too close for comfort, D. A. Miller's critique of certain tendencies in deconstruction (or of the tendencies of a certain deconstruction) is, I think, one of the strongest moments of his text. Even if one accepts the value of the textual analogy for the interpretation of society and culture, one must actively acknowledge and explore the differential relations within and between written and lived 'texts'. One cannot read all texts in the same way. It *is* misleading and politically suspect to identify undecidability or aporia on a 'foundational' level with the sort of muddling confusion and equivocation in a bureaucracy that serves certain social and political interests more than others. As Dickens himself puts it early in *Bleak House*, the Chancery 'gives to monied might the means absolutely of wearing out the right'.

Thus I would agree with Miller's objection to the overly direct and indiscriminate allegorisation of institutional and sociopolitical questions in philosophical terms – to reading bureaucracy as an allegory of aporia or *mise en abyme*. But I don't think Miller does enough to articulate better the relations of the institutional and the philosophical. At times his own account even threatens to replicate the 'deconstructive' manoeuvres he deplores. Derrida himself has warned against drawing overly direct political inferences from deconstructive strategies, and he has stressed the difficulties of joining deconstruction as a mode of reading complex and fruitfully divided texts with political practice.[3] (The text being deconstructed must be strong enough to have the inner resources that one brings to bear against it.) I would suggest that the problem is how to relate a critique of foundational philosophy that is itself acritical in its attempt to undo pure binary oppositions, on the one hand, and a critique of institutions that is indeed critical in its attempt to change society, on the other. These critiques are not dissociated, but neither are they related by direct derivation or unproblematic inference.

Despite the hazardous nature of the undertaking, I would nonetheless like to be more 'affirmative' in attempting to relate deconstruction to the issues with which Miller is justifiably concerned. What implications might deconstruction be argued to have for the critique of certain institutions and for the development of alternative institutions? Institutions (including bureaucratic institutions) may seek legitimation by an appeal to a 'logocentric' myth of origins in either religious or secular form. A deconstructive strategy places in radical question this mode of legitimation and all associated types of absolute sovereignty, including the sovereignty of 'the people'. It forces one to look for other modes of legitimation that are more open to contestation. In addition, its critique of pure binary opposites and attendant hierarchies places in jeopardy rigid social structures that rely on them to constitute collective life. Especially significant in this respect is its attempt to undo the scapegoat mechanism which is essential for the generation and maintenance of pure binary opposites in society. Scapegoating is a short-cut to solidarity that projects all undesirable 'alterity' or otherness onto the clear and distinct, separate 'other' thereby providing a sense of purity or innocence for the in-group. (Scapegoating via extreme analytic purification is also necessary for speculative dialectics – including the speculative dialectic of history – that attempt to regain identity or wholeness 'on a higher level' by overcoming analytic oppositions.) In its exploration of internal alterity or differences *within* that are occulted or denied by extreme analytic or binary oppositions and related dialectical ventures, deconstruction not only helps to unsettle the scapegoat mechanism. It poses the problem of how to relate to the 'other' that is always to some extent within. This aspect of deconstruction is quite significant institutionally, not only in obvious but still crucial respects (e.g., anti-Semitism) but in the institutional organisation and self-understanding of genres and disciplines. It forces the issue of how to come to terms with what is conventionally taken as 'other', e.g., the literary in philosophy, the sub-or contextual in literary criticism, or the critical reading of texts in historiography. It may enable one to perceive subtle methodological displacements of scapegoating in the way certain experimental or 'transgressive' approaches are castigated or dismissed by defenders of conventional disciplinary lines. Deconstruction more than suggests that any form of identity is never pure other than through questionable processes of inclusion and exclusion, and it simultaneously raises the issue of how to articulate modes of relative specificity that remain subject to questioning and contestation.

Vital in the latter respect is the rethinking of the role of margins, thresholds, and the problem of liminality. Deconstruction indicates ways in which the marginal is not merely the realm of borderline or parasitic cases that may be bracketed or set aside in the definition of problems or institutions. It insists on the crucial role of the marginal in the constitution of the central, the dominant, or the mainstream. More significantly, it activates the marginal and enters it into a more even-handed contest or *agon* with the central or dominant. Hence it not only emphasises the importance of seemingly mixed modes and the manner in which pure types or 'essences' are idealisations that achieve dominance through other than purely ideal – that is, through rhetorical and institutional – gestures, including the workings of force and hegemony. It also insistently brings about the need to reformulate and even to reconstitute the general way one relates to the marginal or threshold in thought and in life.

Here I would suggest a link between deconstruction and the carnivalesque – not as a free-standing or autonomous possibility but as a necessary supplement to work *and* as an alternative to scapegoating in offering a way of relating to the marginal or the 'other' that is always to some extent within. The carnivalesque may be seen as a 'double inscription' of the serious, the productive, the workaday. And Derrida's own texts, which bring about a carnivalisation – prominently including a carnivalesque uncrowning – of traditional assumptions, may be taken to imply the need for a larger inquiry into actual and desirable relations between the carnivalesque and its 'others' or 'doubles' in society and culture. Indeed the hyperbolic exuberance in Derrida is not altogether alien to the qualities of Dickens that made him so attractive to a writer like Dostoevsky or, for that matter, to readers even today.

The above comments do little more than broach a complex set of problems, and, given the format in which they are made, they do so in a tediously cathechismal form. But they might suggest paths around the overly devout replication of the polemic between Derrida and Foucault by indicating junctures at which their initiatives intersect. The difficulty I see in Miller's analysis is a rather precipitous turn toward the most indiscriminate recent Foucauldian discourse on power in order to compensate for the presumed defects of deconstruction. In the process, the notion of power becomes a surrogate for the kind of *passe-partout* or misleading smear word Miller thinks 'aporia' or *'mise en abyme'* readily becomes in deconstructive criticism that reprocesses all texts into its own terms. In fact, Miller himself shifts a bit too quickly from the treatment of bureaucracy (Chancery Court) in the novel to what can only be called the aporetics of its displacement onto the police and the family. One tends to lose sight of the potent critique, indeed the grotesque carnivalisation, of bureaucracy in *Bleak House*. The world represented in the novel is a *monde à l'envers*, and Dickens must use fire to fight fire – not fire in the stereotypical image of anarcho-apocalyptic conflagration (an image, that is, by the way, unjust to the complexities of anarchism) but the fire of powerfully carnivalised criticism – irony, parody, outrageous caricature, self-consuming characters, and so forth. One may even raise the question of whether the text is contradictory in its representation of bureaucracy as both carceral and diffuse (as Miller maintains) or whether it critically inscribes the contradictions of a state agency that is indeed both centralised and in touch with multiple facets of daily life – and whether it does so more pointedly than does Miller with his reliance on 'power' as a universal solvent.

Miller's concluding conception of what is the *telos* of his entire account – the family (and, by further extension, the novel form itself) as involving necessary and inadequate 'closure' – itself involves a telling instance of an unannounced return to one of the most questionable deconstructive gestures denounced by Miller himself: the direct allegorisation of a social institution.

> Certainly, reading this novel, though in the reasons of the hearth it finds its own reason for being, one never feels quite at home; perhaps, having finished it, one knows why one never *can* feel at home. For what now is home – not securely possessed in perpetuity, but only leased from day to day on payment of continual exertions – but a House? And what is this House – neither wholly blackened by the institutions that make use of its cover, nor wholly bleached of their stain – but (in the full etymological ambiguity of the word) irresolvably Bleak? 'Bleak House has an exposed sound'.
>
> [p. 120]

By signing off with grandiloquent rhetorical questions abruptly followed by a tell-tale quotation, Miller even pays emulative homage to the pun-filled, etymological 'surprise' ending that has become *de rigueur* in a certain form of deconstruction. For what now is home, indeed? Miller's waning voice seems to merge with his 'image' of Dickens's, as the family is magnified into an undifferentiated allegorical figure facing a perennial, intractable problem. This view of the family overshadows the specificity of the treatment of *families* in Dickens, and it threatens to become an ideological abstraction serving the legitimating functions Miller ostensibly deplores. The Family as Bleak Allegory of closure-in-general ends Miller's account at a point where a critical analysis would rather begin. His 'sense of an ending' reopens the question of the extent to which Miller, rather than 'writing against' Marxism and deconstruction, at times settles for an unwieldy pastiche of Foucault on Power and some of the weaker ploys of deconstruction itself. Lost in the pastiche are a number of the strengths of both Marxian and deconstructive criticism.

From *Representations*, 6 (1984), 116–23.

NOTES

[My summary of D. A. Miller's argument (p. 120–1) may be compared with Dominick LaCapra's first paragraph which starts his counter to Miller's argument. LaCapra finds Miller's essay too Foucauldian in resisting both Marxist readings of the text and deconstruction. To deal with the second of these first, he disengages himself from Hillis Miller, but then argues that D. A. Miller underestimates the potentialities of deconstruction, and refers to its affiliations with Bakhtin and carnival. (Bakhtin on carnival is best approached through his study *Rabelais and his World*, written by 1940 but not published until 1965, and not translated into English until 1968.) And Dickens is carnivalesque – in his use of grotesque, in his presentation of Chancery as the world turned upside down, in his attention to the body as monstrous – e.g. with the Smallweeds, or in the case of spontaneous combustion, where the text seems to revert to an older, Rabelaisian or Shakespeare-like model of the body current in the early modern period, referring to the 'corrupted humours of the vicious body itself' (ch. 32, p. 512). Seeing the text as thus unstable, destabilising, draws attention to the affinities between Dickens and Bakhtin's concept of the novel as impure, a mixture of genres, riddled with the voice of the other in its dialogism. It contrasts with Miller's sense of the realist novel form colluding with the discourse of the police.

LaCapra also considers how Miller deals with contradictions in Dickens's text. Contradictions would be seen by a Marxist criticism such as that of Macherey, Louis Althusser, or Terry Eagleton (in his 1976 study *Criticism and Ideology*) as evidence of the split of discourses in Dickens: evidence of the non-total aspect of the power that Miller considers so dominant, so total. A Marxist reading of novels, using the work of Althusser (Fredric Jameson in *The Political Unconscious* [1981] is the obvious example) would take such gaps and splits in a text as symptoms of ideological rifts within the text. For Althusser, at such moments the text shows its 'inner distantiation' from the ideology that subtends it. Such splits are also the material that deconstruction works on: indeed, they provide LaCapra with the motivation for his article, which is to bring Marxism and deconstruction together. LaCapra says Miller ignores the existence of both: contradictions merely serve the workings of power: they can be assimilated into the pattern of the novelist as the police. It seems that LaCapra scores an important point when he notes that the total thesis of the novel as vehicle for the police ignores the dual narrative. Taking Virginia Blain's point about the gendered nature of the two narratives, this would imply that the gender-issue might complicate or split open arguments about realism and the convergence of the two narratives that Miller refers to.

D. A. Miller returned to the attack in 'Under Capricorn' in the same issue of *Representations*. His argument is sceptical about carnival in its suspicion that carnival is as much a strategy of the ruling class as a subversion of it. It repeats the terms of Foucault in finding deconstruction (plus its affiliations with carnival) as professional pedagogy (see Introduction, p. 10). Ed.]

1. D. A. Miller, 'Discipline in Different Voices: Bureaucracy, Police, Family, and *Bleak House*', *Representations*, 1:1 (1983), 50–89. [Further page references included in the text are to the page numbers of essay 4 in this volume – Ed.]

2. Raymond Williams, 'Social Criticism in Dickens: Some Problems of Method and Approach', *Critical Quarterly*, VI (1964), 214–27. Reprinted in *Bleak House*, ed. Duane De Vries (New York, 1971), pp. 949–65.

3. Jacques Derrida, 'Entre crochets', *Digraphe*, 8 (1976), 97–114.

6

Telescopic Philanthropy: Professionalism and Responsibility in *Bleak House*

BRUCE ROBBINS

In the decade of the 1840s, 'there occurred a cataclysmic event, far more dramatic than anything that happened in England, a very short geographical distance away. ... That was, of course, the famine in Ireland – a disaster without comparison in Europe. Yet if we consult the two maps of either the official ideology of the period or the recorded subjective experience of its novels, neither of them extended to include this catastrophe right on their doorstep, causally connected to socio-political processes in England.' According to the editors of *New Left Review*, who offer this statement for Raymond Williams' consideration in *Politics and Letters* (1979), English fiction of the nineteenth century and the English criticism concerned with it have both privileged 'national experience', and thus have omitted what by many accounts would be the most significant aspects of the period. Because the French Revolution of 1848, for example, is 'not a national experience in the direct sense', neither it nor other 'foreign or overseas developments' can turn up in Williams' account of the English literature of the 1840s. For Williams' interlocutors, the conclusion extends to literary criticism as a whole: 'It is not possible to work back from texts to structures of feeling to experiences to social structures.'

Since literary texts are tied to 'experience' and since 'experience' seems to neglect whatever is distant or international, the study of literature cannot be asked to furnish knowledge of 'the total historical process' or of how human beings might act in and upon 'an integrated world economy'.[1]

In response to this challenge, Williams offers the counter-example of Dickens. Dickens' novels, he says, attempt 'to find fictional forms for seeing what is not seeable' (p. 171). If it is generally true that the novel produces knowable communities only at the cost of blindness to international effects, determinants, and analogues, it is no less true that Dickens managed to represent a world 'increasingly dominated by processes that could only be grasped statistically or analytically – a community unknowable in terms of manifest experience' (p. 247). In effect, Williams suggests, Dickens has made experience out of what seemed beyond experience – and in so doing has proved the possibility of continuing to write novels adequate to 'an integrated world economy'.

Whether or not a political defence of literary study rests upon it, this argument seems a valuable one to interrogate further. The current dialogue between Marxist humanism and poststructuralism, like the dialogue between Williams and *New Left Review*, hangs precisely on rival views of the achievement Williams ascribes to Dickens: occupation of the politically dangerous territory outside humanist 'experience', involving both the risks of wandering away from ethical home truths and the potential advantages of learning to understand and act in a dispersed global system which now exceeds experiential categories. This essay will try to follow Williams' lead into this 'post-humanist' domain. Taking the example of professionalism – a hinge joining these risks and advantages, a context for Dickens' social analysis, a site of his personal ambivalence – it will examine the way Dickens' political position is both jeopardised and enlarged by his willingness to imagine professional 'dehumanisation' as a new (international, post-humanist) condition of 'action at a distance'.

Williams himself writes that imperialism still seemed 'distant or marginal' to Dickens (p. 262). Nothing could be more distant than the allusion to Africa in *Bleak House*. The fourth chapter, entitled 'Telescopic philanthropy', introduces the heroine and the reader to Mrs Jellyby, who is described as 'a lady of very remarkable strength of character, who ... is at present (until something else attracts her) devoted to the subject of Africa; with a view to the general cultivation of the coffee berry – *and* the natives – and the settlement, on the banks of the African rivers, of our superabundant home population'.[2] Mrs Jellyby is 'too much occupied with her African duties' to brush her hair or take care of her children; her eyes have 'a curious habit of seeming to look a long way off. As if ... they could see nothing nearer than Africa!' The moral is quickly drawn, and it pushes Africa farther into the distance. Esther Summerson, who narrates the episode, expresses the opposite philosophy of social action. Rather than neglect the near in favour of the far, she concentrates her efforts on what is close at hand. 'I thought it best to be as useful as I could ... to those immediately about me; and to try to let that circle of duty gradually and naturally expand itself' (ch. 8). The satire of Mrs Jellyby – 'just the style in which vulgar men used to ridicule "learned ladies" as neglecting their children and household', John Stuart Mill wrote to his wife[3] – makes Africa a distraction, an ineligible elsewhere. Instead of founding piano-leg factories on the left bank of the Niger, enlightened English women and men should see to it that their offspring don't fall down the stairs at home or go without their dinner. Jo, the slum-child of Tom-All-Alone's, is representative: 'he is not one of Mrs Jellyby's lambs, being wholly unconnected with Borrioboola-Gha; he is not softened by distance and unfamiliarity' (ch. 47). It is not Mrs Jellyby but Esther, fully present to those immediately around her and refusing to be distracted into anything but personal, face-to-face contact, who takes care of him.

However naïve Esther has seemed to later readers, there is no doubt that Dickens endorsed her amateurish, slowly dilating 'circle of duty' as a paradigmatic alternative to Chancery's expansive 'circle of evil'. In his article on the Niger expedition – the original of Mrs Jellyby's project – in 1848, he had written:

> The stone that is dropped into the ocean of ignorance at Exeter Hall, must make its widening circles, one beyond another, until they reach the negro's country in their natural expansion. There is a broad, dark sea between the Strand in London, and the Niger, where those rings are not yet shining; and through all that space they must appear, before the last one breaks upon the shore of Africa. Gently and imperceptibly the widening circle of enlightenment must stretch and stretch, from man to man, from people on to people, until there is a girdle round the earth; but no convulsive effort, or far-off aim, can make the last great outer circle first, and then come home at leisure to trace out the inner one. Believe it, African Civilisation, Church of England

Missionary, and all other Missionary Societies! The work at home must be completed thoroughly, or there is no hope abroad. To your tents, O Israel! but see they are your own tents![4]

These expanding circles are the perfect contrary of what we mean by the verb 'to telescope': a forcible, sometimes violent compression in which circles collapse into one another and the result is closure and perhaps loss. Yet Esther's concentric gradualism, 'responsible' in that all action remains continuous with and answerable to its originary centre, sounds more troubling when transposed into international terms. Like his older contemporary Michael Faraday, Dickens here refuses the concept of 'action at a distance', or rather sees it as inherently destructive. Mrs Pardiggle's charity, 'overturning, as if by invisible agency, a little round table at a considerable distance' (ch. 8), is a figure of telescopic destruction. Dickens' circles on the water, like Faraday's ether or the 'webs' of George Eliot, presume a full, dense medium which impedes 'convulsive' action and judges 'far-off aims' by their first impact at home. Like *The Little Drummer Girl*, which respects the authentic commitment of 'natives', whether Palestinian or Israeli, while scorning the consciously chosen, 'telescopic' commitment of a non-native to a distant struggle, these passages articulate a politics of presence whose appeal must by the same token exclude or discourage a good many of the connections, national and international, which today compose political reality. And yet if, as Le Carré's novel suggests, we continue to respond to this privileging of proximity, we should not be surprised that it has continued to inform the most frequent ethical and political readings of *Bleak House*, which agree in setting local responsibility, as exemplified by Esther, against the novel's many versions of irresponsibly telescopic philanthropy, of which Chancery's is the most evident.

Critics have remarked that in *Bleak House* Dickens moves away from the individual villains of his earlier novels toward an understanding of social evil as, in Terry Eagleton's term, 'systemic'.[5] 'The Law is administered by people who are at best, like Conversation Kenge and Guppy, absurdly, at worst, like Tulkinghorn and Vholes, wickedly inhuman', Arnold Kettle writes.

Mr Tulkinghorn may not have a very coherent personal motive for his vendetta against Lady Dedlock, but the point is that he is the agent of an impersonal system more potent and more sinister than any expression of personal spite or hatred. ... It is this very impersonality that

makes Mr Tulkinghorn so formidable. It is not his personal wicked-
ness that Lady Dedlock is up against any more than it is the personal
kindliness of the Lord Chancellor that determines the workings of the
Court of Chancery. The sense of the Law as a force in itself, an independent business, self-perpetuating within its own closed circles of
privilege and procedure, is basic to the meaning of *Bleak House*.[6]

But if personal motive and character have indeed become irrelevant,
if agency has become transpersonal – as Kettle recognises, in an
Althusserian moment, when he observes that this is a revolutionary
novel without revolutionaries – and if we are thus dealing with a
new 'impersonality', then the 'responsibility' reading and the comfortable conflation of the ethical with the political which supports it
would seem to require some rethinking.

The point made in *Politics and Letters* holds here as well: to
clutch the ethical and experiential, while letting go of the global
and the systematic, is to give up on teaching people how they can
act in, on, and against System. Critics have largely done just this,
escaping the strain between the ethical level of 'responsibility' and
the analytic level of 'system', between the impersonal institution
and the accountable individual, by accusing that institutional category to which they themselves largely belong, namely the professions. For many critics, the professions are the true villains of *Bleak
House*. In a representative opinion, Robert Alan Donovan writes:

> the lawyer cares nothing for justice; he cares only for the law. Of the
> justice, that is to say, of the social utility, of his professional activity he
> is presumably convinced antecedently to his engaging in it, but he goes
> about his business secure in the knowledge that justice will best be
> served by his shrewdness in outwitting his adversary ... the evil they
> give rise to is not a consequence of their abusing their functions but of
> them performing them as well as they do.[7]

In addition to all the incidental professional satire, there is of course
a substantial case against the professions, and especially against the
legal profession. It is by means of their profession that the Chancery
lawyers evade the responsibility for their actions, that they shoot
their daily arrows in the air without being obliged to consider on
whom the arrows are falling. The Court of Chancery that sits at the
centre of the London fog in the first chapter and is the central
symbol of English society throughout the novel is the court that is
supposed to take care of the helpless, the widows and orphans who
make up a large percentage of this novel's cast of characters. But

instead of taking care of them, it takes care of itself. Dickens shows lawyers and judges getting rich off the notorious cases that go on for years, caught up in legal red tape and gobbledy-gook that it is of course in their interest to maintain, while Chancery suitors go mad, commit suicide or murder, and live in run-down Chancery-held properties like the slum Tom-All-Alone's. The profession could be defined as a sort of organised, legitimated irresponsibility.

Yet in several ways this indictment is both inaccurate and inadequate. To begin with, it ignores Dickens' own ambivalence about the increasingly dominant mode of institutional impersonality. The contradictory feelings that he entertained with regard to professionalism make themselves apparent before *Bleak House* even begins. In the preface to the first edition, dated August 1853, Dickens responds to 'a Chancery Judge' who has informed him that the 'Court of Chancery, though the shining subject of much popular prejudice ... was almost immaculate'. Dickens writes:

> This seemed to me too profound a joke to be inserted in the body of this book, or I should have restored it to Conversation Kenge or to Mr Vholes, with one or other of whom I think it must have originated. In such mouths I might have coupled it with an apt quotation from one of Shakespeare's sonnets:
>
> > My nature is subdued
> > To what it works in, like a dyer's hand:
> > Pity me, and wish I were renewed!

This is a familiar view: it is in the nature of work to subdue the worker to its habits, tendencies, and interests. Professions distort, and judges are as subject to this professional deformation as dyers. One sentence later, however, Dickens marshals evidence that 'everything set forth in these pages concerning the Court of Chancery is substantially true, and within the truth' by appealing to no other authority than professional disinterestedness: 'The case of Gridley is in no essential altered from one of actual occurrence, made public by a disinterested person who was professionally acquainted with the whole of the monstrous wrong from beginning to end.' Is professionalism a proof of self-interest and distortion, or on the contrary of disinterestedness and impersonal clarity?

Much the same ambivalence animates the novel's plot. Esther herself is a firm believer in professions, as we discover when she pushes Richard Carstone into one and then worries that he 'has not that positive interest in it which makes it his vocation'. Devoting oneself to a profession, Richard remarks, is 'like making a great disturbance about nothing particular' (ch. 17). But Esther shares Mrs Bayham Badger's opinion that to feel 'languid about the profession' is to disregard a moral imperative:

> 'It was a maxim of Captain Swosser's,' said Mrs Badger, 'speaking in his figurative naval manner, that when you make pitch hot, you cannot make it too hot; and that if you only have to swab a plank, you should swab it as if Davy Jones were after you. It appears to me that this maxim is applicable to the medical, as well as to the nautical profession.' 'To all professions,' observed Mr Badger.
>
> (ch. 17)

Reference has just been made to Captain Swosser's ship as 'the dear old Crippler'. And what immediately follows is an example of the professional deformation of Mrs Badger's second husband, the archaeologist Professor Dingo: 'The Professor made the same remark, Miss Summerson, in his last illness; when (his mind wandering) he insisted on keeping his little hammer under the pillow, and chipping at the countenances of the attendants. The ruling passion!' Within the comic mode, Dickens takes pains to associate professional passion with violent inhumanity. What is remarkable is not that Richard could feel 'languid' about such professionalism, but that Esther, hearing all this, continues to urge him on. And yet, despite all the comedy, Dickens puts the plot solidly behind her. If lawyers, ministers, and politicians are devastating England by faithfully pursuing their callings without asking larger questions about what they ultimately achieve or destroy, the plot also suggests that not having a calling is likely to be fatal, as it is for Richard, and precisely because the individual is then forced to confront the question of ultimate consequences. Richard Carstone's tragedy is that in hoping for justice – that is, the speedy termination of the Chancery suit – he cannot devote himself to a profession, which would suspend issues of justice. Could he have done so, the novel suggests, could he have chosen Allan Woodcourt's limited but systematic professional action instead of a heroic but foolhardy confrontation with Chancery, he could have done more good to others as well as saved his own life; as Esther in a sense saves hers by marrying Woodcourt, a character so thin that in effect she is not so much marrying a man as his work. Work is salvation, in *Bleak House*, not despite but because of its evasion of ultimate questions about the system.

The Victorian gospel of work flirted with nihilism: the fear that local professional activity, though possibly meaningless in itself, must be pursued as a blind therapy, since despair and self-destruction waited upon anyone who dared interrogate its distant meaning or end. To the extent that it resigns itself to this nihilism, *Bleak House* would seem to advocate not responsibility but irresponsibility. And in the context of the 1840s, there are other reasons why this should not surprise us. Among those reforms with which Dickens sympathised were several that loosened rather than tightened the legal rigour of responsibility. The most obvious is the end of imprisonment for debt, which he had of course suffered with his family as a child and which he attacks head-on in *The Pickwick Papers*. In the year when imprisonment for debts of less than £20 was abolished, 1844 (the year after the Borrioboolan expedition), the Companies Act was passed, taking the first step toward limited liability. The same concept of responsibility that incarcerated a body in exchange for a business debt also of course precluded the modern corporation. For 'it was still widely felt to be immoral for an ordinary commercial business to be carried on under conditions which might allow the "partners" to escape paying its debts'.[8] The whole point of joint stock companies, as N. N. Feltes writes, was to produce 'a new form of business association in which the members might not know each other personally, need not necessarily work together, and could not "be called upon to contribute to the debts and liabilities of the company"' beyond what they had invested in it.[9] With some indirection, the joint stock company takes us back to Africa. For it was only by means of limited liability, the outstanding modern form of economic irresponsibility, that what Eric Hobsbawm calls 'the emigration of capital' could take place:

> businessmen and promoters (contemporaries would have said 'unsound businessmen and shady promoters') were now better able to raise capital not only from potential partners or other informed investors, but from a mass of quite uninformed ones looking for a return on their capital anywhere in the golden world economy.[10]

To say this, however, is not simply to identify the overcoming of ethical responsibility with capitalism and imperialism. Today, when millions of lives depend on decisions about such distant, all-but-invisible matters as the Third World debt, one of the tasks of the global imagination is surely to teach us to see beyond the personal ethical simplicities of an earlier system (you pay back what you borrow) and to prepare the way for such 'unethical' options as repudiation or restructuring. Such shifts were already characteristic of Dickens' time. The word 'responsibility' itself was in fact undergoing a notable transformation. In the eighteenth century, to be 'responsible' was not to possess a trait of character but to occupy a position, within a system of social relations, where one could be made to answer for oneself. A servant, to take Edmund Burke's example, could not be made responsible. According to the *OED*, the first use of the word in the sense of 'morally accountable for one's actions', that is, as an inherent moral quality, comes as late as 1836. In short, it was in Dickens' lifetime (the *OED* in fact cites *Bleak House*) that the meaning of the word came to inhere not in relations of accountability but in the individual character. There was of course self-consciousness about this ethical shift in the nineteenth century; the rebellion against it is generally associated with Nietzsche, whose *Genealogy of Morals* tells 'the long story of the origin or genesis of responsibility'.[11] In our own time, this history has been filled in by Michel Foucault's revisionary reading of the institutions which produce the modern individual. The liberal recorders of the nineteenth century, Foucault writes in *Madness and Civilization*, 'substituted for the free terror of madness the stifling anguish of responsibility':

> the madman, as a madman, and in the interior of a disease of which he is no longer guilty, must feel morally responsible for everything within him that may disturb morality and society, and must hold no one but himself responsible for the punishment he receives.[12]

For Foucault, what is wrong with modern society is not, as criticism of *Bleak House* tends to assume, that it permits so much irresponsibility, but rather that it produces so much responsibility.

Dickens was of course one of these liberal reformers, cheering when imprisonment for debt was eliminated and sneering at those who resisted the extension of the state's social welfare efforts; fear of 'centralisation', he wrote, was a mere mask for 'irresponsibility'.[13] In turning to Chancery after the prison as his central image of society, Dickens' career followed the path of enlightenment as Foucault has described it: people are released from behind bars only in order to submit to a new, less visible mode of power. This power permeates rather than encloses its objects; the state can now afford to reform its prisons, for people carry their walls and surveillance around inside them. They have become responsible. And yet

Dickens' social vision is not simply reversed by Foucault. To an extraordinary extent, *Bleak House* anticipates Foucault's own complex and difficult position. Dickens' critique of institutional modernity, like Foucault's, is wary of such humanist values as responsibility, which it shows to be produced by the system. And Dickens, again like Foucault, courts paradox by looking for new sorts of resistance in post-humanist forms which the system has also generated.

We know that Dickens planned to call *Little Dorrit* 'Nobody's Fault'. Samuel Smiles later used the same figure: 'When typhus or cholera breaks out, they tell us that Nobody is to blame. That terrible Nobody! How much he has to answer for. More mischief is done by Nobody than by all the world besides. Nobody adulterates our food. Nobody poisons us with bad drink ...'[14] Smiles was speaking in favour of self-help, whose other side is the need to pin responsibility to a definite individual target. But Dickens would seem to have access to a more nuanced attitude toward responsibility. Not only does he devote a great deal of attention to the psychological damage done by an *over-acute* sense of responsibility, as in Esther's case, but he also directs much of *Bleak House's* humour precisely at the misattribution of responsibility to individuals for phenomena that are clearly collective. One instance among many is Boythorn reducing the system of public transport to a matter of individual character and thus proposing that late coachmen should be shot:

> It is the most flagrant example of an abominable public vehicle that ever encumbered the face of the earth. It is twenty-five minutes after its time, this afternoon. The coachman ought to be put to death! ... With two ladies in the coach, this scoundrel has deliberately delayed his arrival six and twenty minutes. Deliberately! It is impossible that it can be accidental!
>
> (ch. 18)

In the same line, there is the principle of treating collectivities as if they were responsible individuals. One of the first examples is the rebellious outburst of Mrs Jellyby's daughter, Caddy, who serves as her reluctant amanuensis: 'I wish Africa was dead! ... I hate it and detest it. It's a beast!' Alternatively, there is a series of jokes on the habit of attributing agency to processes, like spontaneous combustion, which *have* no agents. 'You don't suppose I would go spontaneously combusting any person, my dear?' Snagsby asks his wife. 'I can't say', returns Mrs Snagsby (ch. 33). In associating the novel's revolutionary hopes with Krook's spontaneous combustion, Dickens, like Althusser, proposed a vision of history as a process without a subject.

Althusser's anti-humanism is a curiously valuable touchstone at other points as well. Dickens offers a textbook illustration of ideology as interpellation, for example, in describing Chadband's

> pulpit habit of fixing some member of his congregation with his eye, and fatly arguing his points with that particular person; who is understood to be expected to be moved to an occasional grunt, groan, gasp, or other audible expression of inward working; which expression of inward working, being echoed by some elderly lady in the next pew, and so communicated, like a game of forfeits, through a circle of the more fermentable sinners present, serves the purpose of parliamentary cheering.
>
> (ch. 25)

As the word 'circle' suggests, this resembles Esther's version of 'responsibility': the 'answering' by a particular individual of a general 'hailing'. The mistake and the joke lie in the incongruity between the utter arbitrariness of the particular 'subject' thus brought into existence and the discursive system which generates these effects. 'From mere force of habit, Mr Chadband in saying "My friends!" has rested his eye on Mr Snagsby; and proceeds to make that ill-starred stationer, already sufficiently confused, the immediate recipient of his discourse.' Chadband asks one of his usual rhetorical questions: why is Jo poor? Snagsby 'is tempted into modestly remarking, "I don't know, I'm sure, sir." On which interruption, Mrs Chadband glares, and Mrs Snagsby says, "For shame!"' In being 'lured on to his destruction', Snagsby parodies and, one might say, refutes Esther's personalised philosophy of responsible action: thinking that the call is truly for him, he offers a personal 'response' that is 'battered' and 'smashed' by a systematic 'Terewth'.

Scapegoating, the misguided ascription to available local objects of responsibility for circumstances that are systematic or otherwise ungraspable, is explained succinctly by a debilitated member of the Dedlock family: 'better hang wrong fler than no fler'. Responsibility must be attributed to *someone*, if only to relieve feelings that have no other outlet. It is this principle that underlies the extraordinary violence of everyday life in *Bleak House*. According to Nietzsche, violence is in fact the source of responsibility: it is violence from the outside, he explains, which creates the reflexive relation to oneself which is the foundation of moral consciousness, of the right to make promises, and hence the guarantee of future action. In *Bleak House*, too, responsibility results from Chancery's release of surplus violence into society, which cannot be directed at the System itself and must find particular, inappropriate targets, often oneself. After saying that she hates Africa, Caddy Jellyby says 'I wish I was dead! ... I wish we were all dead' (ch. 4). When Guppy says 'How do you do, sir?' to Krook, the old man, 'aiming a purposeless blow at Guppy, or at nothing, feebly swings himself round' (ch. 20). Guppy, in the same chapter, is shown stabbing his desk with a knife: 'Not that he bears the desk any ill will, but he must do something.' Richard blames Jarndyce for Chancery, unemployed brickmakers beat their wives, and at Mr George's Shooting Gallery, where people come to displace Chancery-generated violence, Phil Squod 'makes a butt' at his master 'intended to express devotion to his service' (ch. 26). In the 'Telescopic philanthropy' chapter Esther and her friends come upon a child with his neck stuck between railings 'while a milkman and a beadle, with the kindest intentions possible, were endeavouring to drag him back by the legs, under a general impression that his skull was compressible by those means'. Released into Mr Guppy's arms, the child 'began to beat Mr Guppy with a hoopstick in quite a frantic manner'. It is another comic refutation of Esther's philosophy: in the impersonal system dominated by Chancery, 'the kindest intentions' may be received as and rewarded with violence.

Bleak House does however contain an alternative attitude toward violence and responsibility. Skimpole, who declares himself to be irresponsible, also refuses to find others responsible. Skimpole rewrites the scene of Oliver Twist asking for more, for example, by putting responsibility not on the individual criminal but on the social system:

> At our young friend's natural dinner hour, most likely about noon, our young friend says in effect to society, 'I am hungry; will you have the goodness to produce your spoon, and feed me?' Society, which has taken upon itself the general arrangement of the whole system of spoons, does *not* produce that spoon; and our young friend, therefore, says, 'You must really excuse me if I seize it'.
>
> (ch. 31)

If Esther represents Dickens at the level of ethics, it is surely Skimpole who represents him better at the level of analysis. And the contrast may not work entirely in Esther's favour. At some risk to herself, Esther takes the sick Jo into her house; fearful for himself, Skimpole accepts a bribe from Bucket and helps turn Jo out of the house. But Skimpole is in effect placing the burden on the public, where Dickens would agree it ultimately belongs; and Esther, taking the burden upon herself, falls ill, nearly dies, and is scarred for life.

Skimpole imagines Gridley, before his final entanglement in Chancery,

> wandering about in life for something to expend his superfluous combativeness upon ... when the Court of Chancery came in his way, and accommodated him with the exact thing he wanted. There they were, matched, every afterwards! Otherwise he might have been a great general, blowing up all sorts of towns ... but, as it was, he and the Court of Chancery had fallen upon each other in the pleasantest way, and nobody was much the worse.
>
> (ch. 15)

This fanciful computation of the social cost and benefit of an individual tragedy depends, of course, on a detached, impersonal point of view which subordinates individual feelings to the perspective of the system as a whole. But such impersonality seems to have become indispensable. Otherwise, Chancery is reduced to the Lord Chancellor, who is 'affable and polite', as Esther sees him. To Esther, the army, Richard's second choice of profession, is no worse than medicine, his first choice. To Skimpole, on the other hand, society would certainly be 'the worse' for another 'great general, blowing up all sorts of towns'. Which of them would be a better judge of 'the dear old Crippler'?

It is interesting that Bucket, attempting the neat trick of arresting the dying Gridley and cheering him up at the same time, presents Gridley's case to him in exactly Skimpole's terms: 'You want excitement, you know, to keep *you* up; that's what you want. ... What do you say to coming along with me, upon this warrant, and having a good angry argument before the magistrates. It'll do you good' (ch. 24). And in the ending, Dickens' narrator will again apply Skimpole's view of violence, this time in Boythorn's quarrel with Sir Leicester: 'Mr Boythorn found himself under the necessity of committing a flagrant trespass to restore his neighbour to himself' (ch. 66). The same insensibility that makes Skimpole's theories funny also makes them capable of discovering supraethical coherence in English society: here, the poststructuralist insight that ordinary individuality is constituted by a displacement of violence from the system to more or less arbitrary individuals. In fact, his theories sound very much like the statements of early sociology, and the parallel is more than parodic. Through the intermediaries of Comte, Spencer, and Durkheim, a common attention to the disparity between the morality of individual actions and their eventual social value or function provides a historical link between Dickens and Foucault.

Since it is social facts that must be altered, the argument must keep to the level of social desirability, which is not congruent with the domestic virtues. In terms of those virtues, Vholes, for example, who supports three daughters and an aged father in the Vale of Taunton, is an eminently moral, professionally respectable barrier to reform.

> Take a few more steps in this direction, say they, and what is to become of Vholes' father? Is he to perish? And of Vholes' daughters? Are they to be shirt-makers, or governesses? As though, Mr Vholes and his relations being minor cannibal chiefs and it being proposed to abolish cannibalism, indignant champions were to put the case thus: Make man-eating unlawful, and you starve the Vholeses!
>
> (ch. 39)

Face to face with Mrs Jellyby, Esther was not interested in Africa, but in how Mrs Jellyby was treating her family. Here Africa in a sense regains its rights: it is not proximate ethics but distant politics, Dickens' narrator declares, that should be decisive. The social system can neither be comprehended nor acted upon as long as one consults the wellbeing of Mr Vholes' family. Without a humorous, apparently immoral detachment from such questions, one is left with a moral purity that paralyses all supra-individual change.

Dickens' own humanism was of course troubled by this paralysis. Trying to be ethically responsible to everyone, it could not easily accept, for example, retributive violence, as Gridley's crucial speech indicates:

> The system! I am told on all hands, it's the system! I mustn't look to individuals. It's the system. I mustn't go into the court and say, 'My Lord, I beg to know this from you – is this right or wrong? ... *He* is not responsible. It's the system. But, if I do no violence to any of them, here – I may! I don't know what may happen if I am carried beyond myself at last! – I will accuse the individual workers of that system against me, face to face, before the great eternal bar!
>
> (ch. 15)

Like Mr Bumble, Dickens wishes the eye of the law to be opened 'by experience'. But Dickens' politics is not exhausted by 'face-to-face' confrontation, whether in this world or the next. Gridley demands that the judges 'have the face' to answer him directly, but instead he is tracked down by the disguised Bucket, the faceless or two-faced professional. As he dies he too becomes faceless: there is 'no likeness in his colourless face' to its 'former combative look' (ch. 24). Esther performs an act of responsible, face-to-face philanthropy when she opens the door to social forces that not even Bleak House can hold by taking Jo into her home. The result is that she literally loses her face. Self-effacement, it would appear, is both the price of amateurism and the definition of a more efficient professionalism. Abdicating his responsibility as a moral agent, Skimpole speaks of himself 'as if he were not at all his own affair, as if Skimpole were a third person' (ch. 6). Through the usurer Smallweed and his imaginary 'friend in the city' this phenomenon is associated, significantly, with the general irresponsibility of finance capitalism. However, the same detachment characterises the virtuous Jarndyce, who proposes marriage to Esther as passionlessly 'as if he were indeed my responsible guardian, impartially representing the proposal of a friend' (ch. 44). And George Rouncewell, who is told after his indictment for murder, 'you talk of yourself as if you were somebody else!' replies, 'I don't see how an innocent man is to make up his mind to this kind of thing without knocking his head against the walls, unless he takes it in that point of view' (ch. 52). Given a social system which distracts attention from its own irresponsibility by distributing false accusations of responsibility among the innocent, these characters find their only freedom of thought and action in adopting the impersonality of Skimpole, of the lawyers, of professionals.

If the mode of action proper to the world of finance capital is not Gridley's self-assertion but rather, in Esther's words, 'the art of adapting my mind to minds very differently situated, and addressing them from suitable points of view' (ch. 8), then Bucket, whose 'adaptability to all grades' (ch. 53) is the institutional version of Esther's selflessness, presents professionalism as a necessary component of a new, impersonal mode of action. Although the professions stand for an impersonality that may provoke the individual to be 'carried beyond' himself into violence, they also suggest, in the same impersonality, a means of being carried beyond the individual's rage, madness, and impotence. Paradoxically, Bucket's suppression

of any private self – he is childless, and his 'occupations are irre-
concilable with home enjoyment' (ch. 53) – gives him both a professional deformation and exceptional powers of spontaneous,
charming, manipulative action, a combination expressed in the
paradox of a repetitive comic tag based on the non-repetitive variety
of *ad hominem* address, as well as the 'fat forefinger', his powerful
substitute for a full face. If the abandonment of a private household
for a wider field of action makes Mrs Jellyby a telescopic philanthropist, then Bucket is another one, and despite all his reservations
about Bucket's character, Dickens has come almost full circle. Like
the 'unmoved' policeman looking 'casually about for anything
between a lost child and a murder', Bucket's professional callousness
is both morally questionable and socially powerful. 'Angel and devil
by turns, eh?' he replies to Hortense. 'But I am in my regular employment, you must consider' (ch. 54). For *Bleak House*, this alternation
seems to define regular employment. Even in Woodcourt, whose
attachment to the medical profession seems an unqualified ideal,
Dickens hints at a certain inhumanity. Woodcourt is introduced to
the reader, at the deathbed of the man who would have been his
father-in-law, through his 'professional interest in death, noticeable
as being quite apart from his remarks on the deceased as an individual', and speaks 'in his unmoved, professional way' (ch. 11). Yet
only his medical professionalism seems to answer directly the 'class
revenge as disease' figure. Outside Krook's door a policeman 'stands
like a tower, only condescending to see the boys at the base occasionally; but whenever he does see them, they quail and fall back'
(ch. 11). To be subsumed by one's function is to acquire at once the
blindness of comedy and the potency of a telescopic regard.

   To speak of Dickens as endorsing telescopic philanthropy would
be an overstatement. Yet his complicity in the inhumanity he
attacks has been widely attested, if in other than 'post-humanist'
terms. '*Bleak House* itself has the same structure as the society it
exposes', J. Hillis Miller wrote in 1971.[15] Terry Eagleton, Jonathan
Arac, and David Miller have developed the theme, which has
become a critical commonplace.[16] Esther's ethical myopia is of
course brought to the reader's attention by the contrasting version
of the second, impersonal narrator, who like the far sighted
Mrs Jellyby sees telescopically. Robert Garis calls this narrator's
style 'a tyranny over us which is at least as oppressive as the
tyranny of Chancery', while Robert Kincaid finds in this narrative
detachment 'the central sin of remaining untouched'.[17] Indeed, this

narrator often sounds a good deal like the Reverend Chadband; he too makes use of tautologies and answers all his own questions. Like the Law, his self-enclosed and systematic rhetoric mimics the social system it comes out of. We are speaking of course of Dickens' humour – but wasn't humour precisely Dickens' own professional secret as an entertainer? And to the extent that comic villains like Chadband are always slipping out of Dickens' ethical and political control, as generations of readers have observed, isn't humour also the special repository of his own 'irresponsibility'? The principle is familiar: 'a child is destroyed, as in *Dombey and Son*, by the subjection of a human being to a social role'. Raymond Williams notes, 'but then Toodles or Cuttle are similarly subjected, by their author, who defines their whole reality by the jargon of their job.'[18] This is narrative at a distance: the distance, the withdrawal of sympathy, by which the Victorians themselves defined the comic, by which Dickens defined 'telescopic philanthropy', and by which we continue to define professionalism. The Dickens we hear or imagine behind the narrator is very clearly, as Gabriel Pearson has argued, a professional.[19]

To see Dickens' complicity with the social structures he deplored, however, is no longer the point. These complicities are only interesting – that is, they only impinge upon that balance between past contextualisation and present celebration that makes up our usual treatment of cultural monuments – if the standpoint from which we now observe them is also thrown into question. Indeed, not to throw it into question seems both politically incautious and intellectually timid. For there are few topics which so insistently demand reflexivity as the question, addressed to a political interpretation by a professional critic, of the politics of professionalism.

Recent criticism of Dickens has made little headway with such questions, largely it seems because it has been unwilling to acknowledge its own institutional basis. F. R. and Q. D. Leavis, who of course did a great deal to professionalise literary study, make a case for Dickens as an earnest professional, but in so doing plunge headlong into inconsistency. Dickens himself is praised, in the preface to *Dickens the Novelist*, for 'his high standard of conscientious professionalism', while Inspector Bucket is later accused of 'bloodhound professionalism'.[20] We are given no significant way of distinguishing 'bad' from 'good' professionalism, and the latter is extracted from *Bleak House* in pure form only at the cost of an astonishing neglect of the novel's humour. Indeed, Q. D. Leavis

takes the exchange on professions with Mrs Bayham Badger with
full seriousness:

> Mrs Badger notices Richard's lack of the sense of vocation for medi-
> cine because, as her husband points out, 'her mind has had the rare
> advantage of being formed by two such very distinguished public men
> as Captain Swosser and Professor Dingo', her two previous husbands.
> She is therefore able to point to the Captain's maxim, 'that if you have
> only to swab a plank, you should swab it as if Davy Jones were after
> you' (a maxim which, Mr Badger says, applies to all professions) and
> to Professor Dingo's reply when accused of disfiguring buildings with
> his geological hammer, 'that he knew of no building save the Temple
> of Science'. No doubt Dickens felt that literature as he himself prac-
> tised it was like the navy, science and medicine in requiring to
> be pursued in the spirit of these maxims, which he undoubtedly
> personally endorsed.

(p. 140)

Criticism which does not flee self-contradiction by omitting
Dickens' humour has tended to do so by labelling it anarchistic.
V. S. Pritchett: 'All bureaucracies are tyrannies of the individual.
Dickens' ridicule is the soliloquist's protest against institutions.'[21]
The trouble is not only that those who happily agree are themselves
professional critics firmly established in institutions, but also that –
as this comfortable consensus indicates – anti-institutional anarchism on this level is indistinguishable from liberalism, and of no
more use in teaching us how to deal with the institutions we inhabit
than the symmetrical mobilising of Dickens' humour against any
and all political engagement. 'If we strain at accepting Dickens as a
thoroughgoing rebel or outcast', John Gross comments, 'it is, above
all, on account of his humour.'[22] Setting Stuart Tave's *Amiable
Humorist*, which traces the rise of democratically inclusive, sentimental humour through *Pickwick*, next to R. B. Martin's *The
Triumph of Wit*, which shows how in the rest of the century sentimental humour is replaced by unsentimental wit, the effect is to
trace, from Carlyle to Bergson, the blunting of comedy as a progres-
sive political instrument. This same trajectory also results from
Roger Henkle's *Comedy and Culture*, which takes Dickens as paradigmatic. 'The shift from a comedy that exposes the excesses ... of
the members of a society to one that relies largely on the exploration of paradoxes', Henkle writes, is 'perhaps the greatest change
in English comedy in the 19th century.'[23] Substituting *aporia* for
paradox, the same turn separates Hillis Miller's epoch-making

account of Dickens in 1958, where professional automatism and repetition signal 'dehumanisation', from his equally influential preface to the Penguin *Bleak House* in 1971, where it is no longer the professions which 'assimilate the particular into a system' but language, and where the theme of the novel thus becomes the impossibility of interpretation: that is *aporia*.[24]

The replacement of 'comedy as ridicule of the professions' by 'comedy as *aporia*' has less political impact than one might imagine. Both are critiques of all system as such, and are thus unable either to acknowledge that their own critiques emanate from institutions, or to distinguish (*within* the system) between the times and places when institutions must be attacked and the times and places when institutions may be defended. They cannot concede that professions, as in *Bleak House*, might belong both to the problem and to the solution. There is some comfort, finally, even in the commonplace that all the social injustices of *Bleak House* can be traced back to the single centre of Chancery. As the antagonist becomes all-encompassing, it becomes more difficult to imagine overthrowing it. Foucault's critique of current definitions of power makes this point: to think of power as a totality is to think oneself into impotence and passivity. Even so brilliant a Foucaultian reading of *Bleak House* as David Miller's 'Discipline in different voices' succumbs – as does Foucault himself, according to some critics – to this totalising trap. Against 'the feasible politics of reformism', Miller writes, 'the total social reticulation of Chancery finds its corresponding oppositional practice in the equally total social negation of anarchism'[25] – the urge to see the court go up in flames. Anarchism of a subtler sort underlies Miller's own moral:

> it could be argued that, despite or by means of its superficially hostile attitude toward bureaucracy, a novel like *Bleak House* is profoundly concerned to train us – as, at least since the eighteenth century, play usually trains us for work – in the sensibility for inhabiting the new bureaucratic, administrative structures.
>
> (p. 76)

The point is that Miller's essay, like my own, comes out of a bureaucratic, administrative structure. It is easy but disingenuous, therefore, to leave the reader to assume one's unexpressed and unlocated horror before such structures. In pointing out the novel's undecidability, which resembles and resists both the openness of Chancery and the closure of the police, Miller leaves undone the job of instructing those who, when analysis is finished, must decide to act from positions within the system. His analysis discourages action by providing no room for it. As a practice of interpretation that respects the text itself to the exclusion of imperatives to action which may lie outside it, the 'close reading' that discovers *aporia* leaves the reader before an *aporia* – a 'No Way Out' sign.

An argument that would return to ethical responsibilities, therefore, would have to say something on behalf of distance. Today, a responsible criticism cannot run from distant structures into the illusory consolations of presence, but must learn to extend its range, teaching the imagination to deal with the apparent inhumanity of our new distances. 'Many writers have not yet forgiven the English nineteenth century', Jonathan Arac writes, 'for giving us not a workers' revolution but instead the practical basis, both in government and industry, of modern management and bureaucracy.' Professional or telescopic overview, as Dickens fashioned it, 'may be understood as part of a coercive, manipulative stance to the world that coincides with many of the economic and social relations of the nineteenth century most productive of misery for that time and ours', such as the Panopticon and factory organisation.

> To find the techniques of overview evil in themselves is a strong metaphysical temptation, and to condemn all bureaucracy, administration, organisation is an anarchist temptation almost irresistible in our society for the spirit that would be free. The fundamental historical issue, however, remains who is surveying whom and for what purposes.[26]

Instead of confronting 'system' with *aporia*, we need to look farther afield. If we require, say, new links between local constituencies and international actions, then we need 'systems' of our own, and we need to know how such 'artificial' collectivities of postmodern anomie as the professions might yet be harnessed to other ends than at present.

Taking my materials from a considerable distance, I will end by suggesting an ancient 'way out' of *aporia*. As many footnotes have mentioned, *aporia* comes from the Greek *poros*, which means path, passage, or ford; *aporia* is in fact a near synonym of 'no way out'. But *poros* also means – in the definition of Marcel Détienne and Jean-Pierre Vernant – 'a stratagem, the expedient which the cunning of an intelligent being can devise in order to escape from an *aporia*'.[27] As Détienne and Vernant point out, this cunning is strongly associated with the skill or craft of specialised workers. Through its involvement in *metis*, the subject of Détienne and Vernant's *Les Ruses de l'intelligence, poros* belongs to 'the entire collection of technical activities represented in the world of men by a wide range of know-how from metallurgy and pottery to weaving and carpentry and including the skills of the charioteer and the pilot' (p. 280). As part of the pilot's craft, *poros* belongs, by one of our oldest metaphors, to the very essence of politics. Unlike contemplative philosophy – a later invention – it is a practical and professional know-how associated not with universals but with particular local situations of conflict, danger, and rapid change, like those of the navigator, the doctor, the athlete, the politician, and the sophist. If *aporia* continues to judge the professions against a universal standard, *poros* is the 'way out' – one translation of the term – which, by ditching universals, both retains rationality and maintains professional respect.

I don't want to suggest that this local, professional form of rationality solves the political problem of the professions. As in *Bleak House*, the ultimate ends and values beyond its instrumentality remain obscure. The limits of *poros* are indeed part of the term itself, which combines the antithetical meanings of 'indication' – how to do it – with 'bond' and 'limit'. But the suggestion that knowing how to involves knowing limits seems a very useful one for the revaluation of the rational subuniversality of professional work. And as a provisional alternative to *aporia, poros* certainly seems a good working choice.

From *Nation and Narration*, ed. Homi Bhabha (London, 1990), pp. 213–30.

NOTES

[This essay uses the work of two Marxist critics, Terry Eagleton and Raymond Williams. Williams's criticism stresses Dickens's ability to 'find fictional forms for seeing what it not seeable'. This statement about the unrepresentability of nineteenth-century capitalist existence is perhaps explained by Terry Eagleton, who points out that Dickens in his later fiction uses as aesthetically unifying images the social institutions – such as Chancery – that he criticises. A system of division and contradiction provides him with 'a principle of symbolic coherence'. 'It is not that the early Dickens's perception of character as idiosyncratic and non-relational yields to a vision of social unity; it is rather that such non-relationship is now shown to be *systemic* – the function of decentred structures like Chancery ...' (*Criticism and Ideology* [London, 1976], p. 129). This description of a system is like Hillis Miller's account of the world of language in his essay on *Bleak House*, with this difference: that in Eagleton's Marxist reading, which inspires Robbins's no less Marxist essay, the decentred structure is now an image of the deterritorialised space which is opened up by finance capitalism. To interpret that decentred structure, or to find any stance from which to write about it, or assess it, is the issue, and each of Robbins's key terms in his title – 'philanthropy', 'professionalism' and 'responsibility' – belongs both to the problem and to the solution. Philanthropy – a key to *Bleak House* and the obsession of John Jarndyce – leaves the system unaltered; professionalism supports it, and responsibility is what it produces in the individual (Robbins uses Nietzsche and Foucault to focus on this point). Dickens professionalised literature: professionals in universities, for instance, or in the 'media' discuss it, so that even the most passionate writing about 'the system' is already part of that system, on the wrong side (just as Dickens's novel is seen by D. A. Miller to bring about bureaucratic habits of mind in its readership). If to write about this unrepresentable society presents the writer/reader – whether deconstructionist or Foucauldian – with an impossibility, an *aporia*, Robbins finishes by finding some kind of *poros* – a way through – to set against it. He looks for a writing which is aware of limits (of knowing, of competence), and which will work with these. Perhaps the division of the text of *Bleak House* might serve as something of an illustration of what Robbins means, with Esther so different from the impulse in the omniscient narrative to know fully, and to find meaning. Ed.]

1. Raymond Williams, *Politics and Letters: Interviews with New Left Review* (London, 1979), pp. 165–70.

2. Charles Dickens, *Bleak House*, ed. Norman Page with an introduction by J. Hillis Miller (Harmondsworth, 1971), ch. 4. Further chapter references will be given in the text.

3. Quoted in Edgar Johnson, *Charles Dickens: His Tragedy and Triumph* (New York, 1952), p. 761.

4. Quoted in Humphry House, *The Dickens World* (London, 1942), p. 89. It is worth noting that in at least one sense Dickens was wrong. One year after *Bleak House* was published, an expedition up the Niger was successfully accomplished without deaths from malaria, thanks to the use of quinine. There were of course other things to say about such expeditions, but Dickens did not say them. Critics of American intervention in Central America should learn that the 'impracticality' argument is not strong enough. See Howard J. Pedraza, *Borrioboola-Gha: The Story of Lokaja, The First British Settlement in Nigeria* (London and Ibadan, 1960). Dickens in fact supported the emigration

scheme of Caroline Chisholm, on whom Mrs Jellyby is partly modelled. See 'A Bundle of Emigrants' Letters', in Harry Stone (ed.), *Charles Dickens' Uncollected Writings from Household Words 1850–1859* (Bloomington, IN, 1968), vol. 1, pp. 85–96.

5. Terry Eagleton, *Criticism and Ideology* (London, 1976), p. 130.

6. Arnold Kettle, 'Dickens and the popular tradition', in David Craig (ed.), *Marxists on Literature: An Anthology* (Harmondsworth, 1975), pp. 231–2.

7. Robert Alan Donovan, 'Structure and idea in *Bleak House*', in Ian Watt (ed.), *The Victorian Novel: Modern Essays in Criticism* (New York, 1971), p. 87

8. G. D. H. Cole and Raymond Postgate, *The Common People 1746–1938* (London, 1938), p. 288.

9. N. N. Feltes, 'Community and the limits of liability in two mid-Victorian novels', *Victorian Studies*, 17: 4 (June 1974), p. 359.

10. E. J. Hobsbawm, *Industry and Empire* (Harmondsworth, 1968), p. 118.

11. Friedrich Nietzsche, *The Birth of Tragedy and The Genealogy of Morals*, trans. Francis Golffing (New York, 1956), p. 190.

12. Michel Foucault, *Madness and Civilization: A History of Insanity in the Age of Reason*, trans. Richard Howard (New York, 1965), pp. 246–7. See also Peter Dews, 'Power and subjectivity in Foucault', *New Left Review*, 144 (March–April 1984), 72–95.

13. Jonathan Arac, *Commissioned Spirits: The Shaping of Social Motion in Dickens, Carlyle, Melville, and Hawthorne* (New Brunswick, 1979), p. 183.

14. Quoted in Asa Briggs, *Victorian People* (Harmondsworth, 1965 [1954]), p. 134.

15. Miller, in Dickens, *Bleak House*, p. 29.

16. For example, Eagleton, *Criticism and Ideology*: 'Dickens is forced in his later fiction to use as aesthetically unifying images the very social institutions (the Chancery Court of *Bleak House*, the Circumlocution Office of *Little Dorrit*) which are the objects of his criticism', p. 129. For Arac and Miller see notes 13 and 25.

17. Robert Garis, *The Dickens Theatre* (Oxford, 1965), p. 117; R. Kincaid, *Dickens and the Rhetoric of Laughter* (Oxford, 1971), p. 63. For Dickens on work, see also Alexander Welsh, *The City of Dickens* (Oxford, 1971), pp. 82–4.

18. Raymond Williams, *The English Novel from Dickens to Lawrence* (London, 1971), p. 58.

19. Gabriel Pearson, 'Towards a Reading of *Dombey and Son*', in Gabriel Josipovici (ed.), *The Modern English Novel* (London, 1976), pp. 54–76.

20. F. R. and Q. D. Leavis, *Dickens the Novelist* (London, 1973), p. xvi.

21. V. S. Pritchett, 'The Comic World of Dickens' in Watt (ed.), *The Victoria Novel*, p. 38.

22. John Gross, 'Dickens: Some Recent Approaches', in John Gross and Gabriel Pearson (eds), *Dickens and the Twentieth Century* (Toronto, 1962), p. xii.

23. Roger Henkle, *Comedy and Culture* (Princeton, NJ, 1980), p. 183.

24. J. Hillis Miller, *Charles Dickens: The World of his Novels* (Bloomington, IN, 1958), p. 207; Miller, in Dickens, *Bleak House*.

25. D. A. Miller, 'Discipline in Different Voices: Bureaucracy, Police, Family and *Bleak House*', *Representations*, 1 (February 1983), p. 61 [p. 60, above – Ed.]. See also Dominick LaCapra's 'Ideology and Critique in Dickens' *Bleak House*', and Miller's reply, 'Under Capricorn', both in *Representations*, 6 (Spring 1984). [See above, pp. 87–138 – Ed.]

26. Arac, *Commissioned Spirits*, pp. 189–90.

27. Marcel Détienne and Jean-Pierre Vernant, *Cunning Intelligence in Greek Culture and Society*, trans. Janet Lloyd (Sussex, 1978), p. 150. Further page references are in the text.

7

David Copperfield and *Bleak House*: On Dividing the Responsibility of Knowing

AUDREY JAFFE

[Audrey Jaffe begins by discussing the first-person narrative of *David Copperfield*, the novel written immediately before *Bleak House*, showing how 'David returns to his past in order to fix it, and to experience it as fixed, thereby establishing his present distance from it' (Jaffe, p. 123) – suggesting that David the narrator disposes others about him as he wishes, and denies his own complicity in constructing knowledge.]

Whereas *David Copperfield* attempts to collapse the distance and difference between the individual subject and the world, *Bleak House* insists on their separation. In this novel, third-person, omniscient, 'impersonal' narration has one place, and limited, individualised, 'personal' narration another. But what does it mean for omniscience to have a place? The double narrative, constituting as it does a boundary omniscience cannot cross, raises a problem for the very notion of omniscience. Though the contrast with Esther's narrative contributes to the other narrative's omniscient effect, the presence of her narrative also suggests its limitations. Omniscience in *Bleak House* is paradoxically proscribed, limited to one half of the novel.[1] The idea of omniscience as all-knowing is thus undermined by Esther's narrative, which, as supplement, to use Derrida's term, reveals a lack in what is supposed to be complete.[2] And the existence of Esther's narrative immediately suggests the possibility of other narratives: Richard's, Ada's, Jarndyce's, Guppy's. Thus although omniscience need not signify only distance – indeed, the term implies the ability to move inside and outside character – in *Bleak House*, it seems, omniscience cannot 'do' the personal.

The kind of supplementary relationship the split narration of *Bleak House* suggests, in which one part supplies knowledge the other doesn't possess, or in which two halves appear to make up a whole, appears in other forms throughout the novel. The Bagnets, the Badgers, the Smallweeds, the Jellybys – even Boythorn and his bird, Bucket and his finger – are similarly divided entities, in which one member of the couple either speaks for the other (the Bagnets), or represents a kind of complement to the other (as Mr Jellyby's silence does to Mrs Jellyby's busyness), or metonymically expresses what is hidden within the other (the way Bucket's finger represents his seemingly magical powers, or Boythorn's bird reveals his gentleness). In form, as split subjects whose parts do not acknowledge or fail to know one another, these characters reproduce the novel's divided structure.[3]

Given one narrative that, we are explicitly told, someone has written, we are also offered one that it seems no one has – at least no human agent who will acknowledge it. This general premise is so compelling that readers tend not to care about those ways in which the fiction sustaining each narrative cannot be upheld: about the fact that the third-person narrator speaks, for a moment, in the first person (p. 620), or about the numerous times when Esther's 'little body' does 'fall into the background', as she says (p. 74) – times when she records conversations in such detail that, if the narrative's premise is to make sense, we must imagine either that she writes constantly or possesses an uncanny capacity for memorisation. For much of her narrative, that is, Esther might as well be omniscient.

At times, the tension between Esther's role as character and her role as narrator places her in an awkward position, as, for instance, when she sits with Richard and Ada:

> I had never seen any young people falling in love before, but I found them out quite soon. I could not say so, of course, or show that I knew anything about it. On the contrary, I was so demure, and used to seem

so unconscious, that sometimes I considered within myself while I was
sitting at work, whether I was not growing quite deceitful.

(p. 163)

What are we to make of the relationship between character and
narrator in this passage, in which the former's meekness or 'unconsciousness' is subverted by the latter's active mind and eye? Telling
what she knows, making it clear that she knows, Esther speaks at
the same time of her need to remain 'in character'. But her qualms
about deceitfulness, like Florence Dombey's when she catches a
glimpse of Carker leaving Dombey's house, register the tension produced in these figures by their double role as observers – narrators
or narratorial surrogates – and as characters. And that tension is
registered throughout *Bleak House* as a tension within character
alone: Esther is presented as a split subject, divided from herself.
But narratological structures may appear as what we call psychological ones; the narratological and the psychological may be mutually determining. The detachment from and denial of knowledge
expressed here at the level of individual character reproduces the
structure of detachment and denial exemplified in the novel's
double narration. In other words, Esther's detached relationship to
her own knowledge, like that of those other fragmented characters
described above, may be seen as a version of the novel's more
general displacement of knowledge and responsibility – a displacement expressed most powerfully by the way in which the two
narratives, in the words of the character Vholes, 'divide the responsibility of knowing' (p. 672).

Knowledge – both its discovery and its ownership – is clearly a
problem in *Bleak House*. The word 'know' echoes throughout. 'I
know so much about so many characters', says Bucket (p. 782).
'Not to know that there is something wrong at the Dedlocks' is to
augur yourself unknown' (p. 842), the narrator claims. Says Bucket
to Esther, 'I know, I know, and would I put you wrong, do you
think? Inspector Bucket. Now you know me, don't you?' (p. 841).
And, of course, 'Jarndyce and Jarndyce drones on ... [N]o man
alive knows what it means' (p. 52). The world of Chancery and the
world of fashion, we learn early in the novel, are so separate that
neither knows the other; the world of fashion is 'wrapped up in too
much jeweller's cotton and fine wool, and cannot hear the rushing
of the larger worlds' (p. 55). But the narrator can 'pass from one to
the other, as the crow flies' (p. 55). As in *Dombey*, the third-person

narrator establishes his omniscience by moving between worlds that are kept distinct precisely to allow for such movement.

Each narrative, as I have suggested, provides a framework for and counterpart to the other. In contrast to Esther's narrative, the distant, disembodied third-person narrator easily assumes the position of what Lacan calls *le sujet supposé savoir*. Esther, on the other hand, has all the limitation a critic interested in first-person narration could hope to find; limitation is in fact her chief subject. She is indeed the subject presumed – primarily by herself – not to know.

But, as *David Copperfield* shows, the subject who presents him or herself as not knowing is not the same as the subject who doesn't know. *Bleak House* presents us with one place where knowledge appears to be and another where it does not. But the latter is, rather, a place where knowledge is asserted to be absent. Insisting upon her status as one who does not know, who does not even occupy the subject's position in her narrative, Esther works to efface her own knowledge. And her self-effacing narration serves both a narrative and a characterological purpose, enabling her to structure her narrative and her character without appearing deliberately to do so.

Though Esther is frequently more knowing than it seems her character 'should' be, her status as character is confirmed, for readers, by her insistence on her lack of knowledge. If, that is, Esther knows too much, her pathology insists that we forget or ignore her knowledge. As character, denying that she knows, Esther invites readers to feel that they know her better than she knows herself. For her discourse overflows with what is presented as unconscious material, assuming we understand the unconscious to be that which exceeds the subject's own knowledge or control. Our understanding of Esther's knowledge thus necessarily connects with the larger issues of knowledge and responsibility the novel raises.[4] And to explore that relationship more fully requires us to focus both on the way Esther's character is constructed by and founded in language, and on her relationship to her mother, who is essential to Esther's construction of herself as a subject who claims not to know.

In the essay 'Negation', Freud describes a characteristic structure whereby unconscious material emerges into discourse. The patient says, "'You ask who this person in the dream can have been. It was *not* my mother.'' We emend this: so it *was* his mother.'[5] Denial, according to Freud, permits a dissociation of intellect from affect that allows unconscious material to be spoken. 'Negation is a way of taking account of what is repressed; indeed, it is already a lifting of the repression, though not, of course, an acceptance of what is repressed ... The outcome of this is a kind of intellectual acceptance of the repressed, while at the same time what is essential to the repression persists' (pp. 235–6). Freud claims that such statements of negation – what Lacan, combining the terms 'denial' and 'negation', calls 'denegations' – derive from judgements about what the ego wishes to take into itself and what it wishes to reject. And judgement, the decision about what is 'good' or 'bad', is for Freud an extension of the pleasure principle. If we accept Freud's argument, then, intellectual judgement can be said to be the distant relation of pleasure or unpleasure. 'Good' and 'bad' signify what 'I should like to take ... into myself' and what I wish 'to keep ... out' (p. 237).

Denegation is a particularly prevalent form of rhetoric in *Bleak House*, presented to us ironically in the speech of such characters as Vholes and Skimpole. It is Vholes's distinctive habit, for instance, to assert his disinterest in Richard's case, on which he is employed. He exemplifies the novel's critique of 'duty', the attempt to dissociate interest from personal connections and feeling. Yet Vholes has 'interests' which he readily admits to even while he denies them: 'I have no interest in it,' he says of the case, 'except as a member of society and a father – *and* a son' (p. 672). In other words, he has nothing but interest in it – interest which, he means to say, is his own rather than Richard's. Attempting to distinguish between his interest and Richard's, however, Vholes succeeds rather in suggesting the extent to which the two are intertwined. The denial of interest does not, in *Bleak House*, mean disinterest, but usually its opposite. In fact, it is to the denial of interest that we can most successfully look for interest. In a variation on this theme, Bucket articulates the meaning of the mask of disinterestedness when he says, of Skimpole: 'Whenever a person proclaims to you "In worldly matters I'm a child", ... you have got that person's number, and it's Number One' (p. 832). For Bucket, the refusal of knowledge – like the refusal of interest – is just that: a refusal. Rather than signifying the absence of knowledge, it is a strategy for evading the responsibility that attends the ownership of knowledge.[6]

It is through her denegations that readers gain the sense that they know more about Esther than she knows about herself. When Esther says, 'As if this narrative were the narrative of *my life*!' or 'They said I was so gentle, but I am sure *they* were!', we 'emend', as

Freud does with his patient: so she *is* the subject. Esther's denegations signal her otherness to herself – the presence of material she
wishes to distance herself from – and even as they efface her, they
constitute her, marking her for us as a distinctive personality whose
most prominent feature is a very loud insistence on her own
insignificance. But they also comprise a narrative strategy that
enables Esther to construct her identity while – and by – constructing herself as a reflection of the gazes of others. What then is at
stake for Esther in the doubleness or denegation of her discourse,
the letting in of material she insists she keeps out?

Dickens gives Esther's divided subjectivity a fictional origin and
linguistic analogue in her godmother's characterisation of Esther's
relationship to her mother, which is, for a long time, all Esther
knows of her mother.[7] Mrs Rachael replies to Esther's question
about her origins with these words: 'Your mother, Esther, is your
disgrace, and you were hers' (p. 65). Her words identify Esther and
her mother rhetorically, making them mirror images of one
another. Esther immediately reproduces this stucture in connection
with the doll to which she confides her troubles: 'I was to no one
upon earth what Dolly was to me' (p. 65). According to this
reflexive and reflective structure, to exist is to exist *for* someone,
and to be nothing for someone is therefore to be a blank, an
absence. It is as 'nothing' that Esther is mirrored even by the doll
who is 'something' to her, the doll 'who used to sit ... staring at me
– or not so much at me, I think, as at nothing' (p. 62). Unseen by
her mother, Esther seems to herself to be absent, dead – a recognition she represents symbolically by burying the doll when she
departs for Bleak House. At the same time this burial and this sense
of herself as absence suggest that she also identifies with her mother
as the guilty absence, that she feels herself to be the disgrace
reflected by her mother's empty place.

Mrs Rachael's statement positions Esther ambiguously, as either
subject or object. As her mother's disgrace, she is either a separate
embodiment of disgrace or an attribute of her mother's. Thus she is,
again as Lacan argues of the mirror stage, both reflected by and
alienated from her mother's image. And the structure of Mrs
Rachael's statement allows for a play of identification and alienation, or similarity and difference, that enables Esther to structure
herself as subject by structuring herself as object, directing the
course of her narrative and articulating her own identity while
claiming that it is articulated by others.

In Mrs Rachael's statement, and those statements of Esther's which echo it throughout the novel, identity depends upon the reflexivity of subject and object: 'what this lady so curiously was to me, I was to her' (p. 372). Such sentences posit no origin; subject and object exist, suspended, only as reflections of one another. Moreover, this structure leaves open the possibility of substitution: 'this lady' may be someone other than the mother. And throughout her narrative, Esther replaces the object labelled 'disgrace' with good objects, shaping her rhetoric and her narrative so that she will be reflected by good objects rather than bad. Thus, while denying her position as subject, she transforms herself. Through a strategy of self-effacement, merely reporting what she sees in others or what others say about her, she deliberately constructs her own reflection.

She does so because she comes into existence as a subject divided between innocence and guilt, and because the reflective structure of her character – its play of identification and alienation – accommodates both. As soon as she hears Mrs Rachael's statement, Esther feels a desire 'to repair the fault I had been born with (of which I confessedly felt guilty and yet innocent)' (p. 65). Her goal then becomes 'to do some good to some one, and win some love to myself if I could' (p. 65). In other words, Esther's goal is the separation of herself from the bad object – her mother – and from that part of herself which is identified with her mother. And she will accomplish this goal by seeking out love in return for goodness, by substituting good objects for the bad object that is her mother. It is this production of good images which gives us the proliferation of Esther-doubles in the novel – Caddy, Charley, and, most important, Ada. Yet even as Esther transforms the object, and hence herself as subject, the structure of her discourse remains unchanged. Esther's denegations are thus double in more than one way. They both contain and do not contain her mother, and they are an acknowledgement of the guilty self as well as a protestation of innocence, a refusal to make any claim whatsoever. Esther Summerson will be only what others say she is, the object for whom others are subjects. And while her asserted absence from the subject's position displays her continued need to deny what is 'other' to her, it also defines her as acted upon rather than acting, an innocent object of the determinations of others.

The rhetorical structure governing Esther's narrative thus strikingly reproduces the way she constructs, or construes, her identity. She is to others what they are to her; she speaks not of herself but of others. She is, as Flaubert said of the novelist (and as I have said of the omniscient narrator), everywhere and nowhere at once. Denegation allows the speaker to have it both ways: to be present and yet absent, letting herself in even as she insists on her desire to keep herself out. Denegation *is* the structure of Esther's identity, a structure 'given' to her by others (as the scene with Mrs Rachael almost allegorically enacts) in the same sense that, according to Lacan, language constitutes the unconscious. For the doubleness of denegation is also the doubleness of language, which both names and refuses to name, structuring the subject even as the positions it articulates – such as 'I' and 'you' – refer to no one in particular, thus leaving open the possibility of movement and substitution.[8]

Esther comes into existence for herself already structured by what Lacan calls the symbolic: by language, morality, and the law. Feeling herself to be both guilty and innocent, she fashions her narrative to confirm her as the latter but not the former. And the subject–object confusion described above enables her to do so. Though her discourse possesses an imaginary quality in that she seems unable to distinguish herself from those around her, that inability serves her purpose, allowing her to deny the unpleasurable self. At the end of her narrative she has not lost the tendency to see herself reflected everywhere. Rather, she has succeeded in constructing a world which reflects only the self she wishes to see. But that ideal self nevertheless continues to reveal, in the structure of her discourse, what has presumably been expunged from it. Esther's narrative thus reflects the conflict necessitated by the taking of a place within the social world, for, empowered as narrator to construct an identity for herself, she can do so only by choosing one identity and rejecting another. Paradoxically, then, the construction of identity here requires effacement, the repression of identity. And where David Copperfield's self-effacements reflect his centrality as middle-class male subject, the complexities inherent in Esther's self-construction exemplify the tension between empowerment and disempowerment characteristic of Victorian middle-class femininity. As Jane Gallop observes, 'women's traditional place in culture [is] neither subject nor object but disturbingly both. Woman's ambiguous cultural place may be precisely the standpoint from which it is possible to muddle the subject/object distinction.'[9] And because for Esther self-construction requires self-effacement, any attempt to align the two narratives with the categories of the personal and the impersonal breaks down. For that difference already exists within her.

The split between the two narratives, as I suggested earlier, might seem easily to be resolved by such a division. Indeed, a distinction between the personal and the impersonal is the one the usual account of first- and third-person requires us to make. The novel further structures the difference between its two narratives as one of limitation and knowledge, and as the difference between 'the eye of affection' and 'the eye of business' (p. 607), to use the novel's own words. But both narratives blur the distinctions between knowledge that belongs to the self and knowledge that is the property of others. Both narrators 'efface' themselves, in different ways and to different degrees, but ultimately for the same purpose: to locate elsewhere, as narrators fantasmatically can, what 'belongs' to the self.

The third-person narrative displays the kind of detached, impersonal interest in the secrets of others typical of characters such as Tulkinghorn and Bucket, while Esther, as we know, has a personal reason to feel 'interested about my mama' (p. 63). Corresponding to the first narrative's impersonality is the idea of 'duty', the impersonal performance of tasks which prompts individuals to neglect such values as friendship and family, and which, John Lucas argues, is at the heart of Dickens's critique of society in this novel: '[M]uch of the horror of the social situation that Dickens presents in *Bleak House* is caused by people doing their duty.'[10] Strangely, however, the novel presents 'duty' as looking very much like the personal. Thus the Bagnets, observing Bucket as, unbeknownst to them, he takes George Rouncewell into custody, remark that Bucket 'almost clings to George like, and seems to be really fond of him' (p. 733). And thus Esther, according to Jarndyce, would have sacrificed her love for Woodcourt to 'a sense of duty and affection ... so completely, so entirely, so religiously, that you should never suspect it, though you watched her night and day' (p. 914). Indeed, the terms in which Esther expresses her decision to accompany Bucket on his search for Lady Dedlock fluctuate madly between the personal and the impersonal: 'It seemed to become personally important to myself that the truth should be discovered', she says. 'In a word, I felt as if it were my duty and obligation to go with them' (p. 759). 'Myself', in this sentence, remains strangely distant from the self; it is a third-person self, a self Esther does not seem to know. And feeling is distanced, 'about' duty and obligation ('*as if* it were my duty and obligation') rather than their object, which, in any case, is not Lady Dedlock but 'myself'. Lady Dedlock is the impersonal solution to a mystery which 'seems' to concern Esther personally; it is as the location of 'truth' that she must be sought out.

Personal knowledge in *Bleak House* can thus be said to take a peculiarly impersonal form. Esther responds to her own personal interests with busyness. After a reference to Woodcourt, she finds herself 'humming all the tunes I knew; and ... working and working in a desperate manner, and I talked and talked, morning, noon, and night' (p. 742). 'I had only to be busy and forget it' (p. 561), she says of her lost looks. Talk – what Esther calls 'prosing, prosing' – is relief and release, but it is also repression. It is what takes over, as Lady Dedlock fears, when the subject is gone ('Is it the town talk yet?' [p. 632]), and it also participates in doing away with, or re-inventing, the subject. The connection between busyness and busi-ness tells us much about the relationship between the two narratives, between 'the eye of affection' and 'the eye of business'. Business, in the third-person narrative, is the name for interest in others' personal affairs; busyness is what Esther turns to when any-thing that immediately concerns her nears the surface of the text. Esther is 'full of business' (p. 173), and she is so, I would argue, because about herself she is 'content to know no more' (p. 149). The chief business of English law is, of course, to make business for itself, and that business creates a smooth surface which overlays 'the roughness of the suitors' lives and deaths' (p. 399) – the same smooth surface, of course, that covers Tulkinghorn and Bucket.

Esther's narrative, of course, never attains such smoothness; her language always displays itself as a mechanism of repression. She disowns 'personal' knowledge: the secret of her birth possesses the peculiar status of being about her – constituting her – and yet never belonging to her. It is free-floating knowledge which others possess for her and which, after Mrs Rachael's outburst, she does not want to possess. For when Esther finally comes face-to-face with her mother – to take possession, it seems, of her secret – her impulse is to distance herself from her mother and from the secret, as if she were only in the business of keeping the secrets of others. Like Tulkinghorn and Jarndyce, Esther becomes the keeper of someone else's secret, a secret she can keep because she has in fact truly given it away. I have said that Esther's unconscious 'speaks' in her denials: what she denies at this point is that 'the secret' is hers. 'If the secret had been mine', she says, 'I must have confided it to Ada ... But it was not mine; and I did not feel that I had a right to tell it' (p. 573). To Woodcourt, she says, 'I need wish to keep no secret of my own from you; if I keep any, it is another's' (p. 861). Her feeling for Lady Dedlock seems to be primarily one of obligation and duty – 'my duty was to bless and receive her' (p. 565) – and the keeping of the secret a duty performed for another: 'My present duty appeared to be plain' (p. 573).[11]

The reflexivity of Esther's rhetoric breaks down when she describes her meeting with her mother. Though the two have been identified in a number of ways – by sentences in which subject and object mirror one another, by the scarred face which links Esther to her mother's sexual guilt, and by the wearing of veils – when the two finally meet, Esther denies, and her scarred face enables her to deny, the existence of any resemblance between them.

The scarred face has been recognised by many readers as symbolic of Lady Dedlock's sexual crime.[12] Esther's disfiguration, like David Copperfield's marked face, signals the construction of the self by another: the mark is a metaphor for a character's status as object for a narrator. But Esther's scar has another function. Introducing difference where there had been similarity, it allows her to deny her identification with her mother. After her illness, when Esther observes her face in the mirror, the language of familiarity merges with that of separation: 'At first, my face was so strange to me. ... Very soon it became more familiar, and then I knew the extent of the alteration in it better than I had done at first' (p. 559). And when Lady Dedlock reveals herself to Esther, Esther responds with an astounding expression of her need to differentiate herself from the figure she most resembles:

> I felt, through all my tumult of emotion, a burst of gratitude to the providence of God that I was so changed as that I never could disgrace her by any trace of likeness; as that nobody could ever now look at me, and look at her, and remotely think of any near tie between us.
>
> (p. 565)

Here, as in Mrs Rachael's statement, the question of who disgraces whom remains ambiguous; the 'tie' reveals each to be potentially the other's disgrace. Esther's disfiguration and the veil that covers it signal her ambivalent status as both character and narrator, at once like and unlike her mother. As character, she shares her mother's 'disfigurement'; as narrator, she has the power to efface it, shifting the scar's significance solely to her mother. (And it is significant that her scarred face – like her unscarred face – is never really described. We as readers never 'see' Esther.)

As the novel progresses, Esther's narrative, in conjunction with the impersonal detectives of the third-person narrative, externalises and displaces the secret of Esther's origin, the plot underscoring this conjunction when she joins Bucket in pursuit of Lady Dedlock.[13] The 'other' narrative's impersonal approach to Lady Dedlock's secret may make the revelation of the secret seem 'impersonal and inevitable', as John Frazee writes, but Esther's narrative finally does the same.[14] Esther's personal history is ultimately defined only as her mother's secret; where she had looked for likeness she is now grateful to perceive difference. And this is not simply a refusal to recognise whatever similarity might exist between her mother and herself, a refusal we might locate at an unconscious level. Esther's narrative is constructed so that, when she and her mother finally meet, recognition is in fact problematic because likeness has actually been erased. Denial thus takes place not just at an unconscious level within the narrative, but is built into the narrative's structure. After Esther's illness, her very appearance constitutes a denial of her mother. Indeed, we might say that this is the very function of her illness. If Esther feels 'guilty and yet innocent', the structure of her narrative allows her to do so, enabling her to differentiate herself from the bad object while not assigning to her the responsibility for doing so.

Esther's initial response to her meeting with her mother is the sense that 'the blame and shame were all in me' (p. 570). But she soon asserts her innocence in a way that she has been unable to throughout her entire narrative: 'I knew I was as innocent of my birth as a queen of hers; and that before my Heavenly Father I should not be punished for birth, nor a queen rewarded for it' (p. 571). The discovery of her parentage is at once a realisation and a terrible unrealisation of the family romance. Esther discovers that she is of noble parentage only to find that her mother's nobility is damaged beyond repair. Associating her own birth with that of royalty, she finds herself blameless, and is able to do so, it seems, because the 'blame and shame' have found their proper object.

Esther's relationship to her mother evokes a fear of the loss of distinctions similar to Sir Leicester's anxiety about the loss of distinctions between social classes – his fear that 'the floodgates of society are burst open' (p. 628). In fact, the novel's famed emphasis on connection between social classes fails entirely when it comes to Esther's relationship with her mother. The novel achieves social coherence not by inclusiveness but through the elimination of dif-

ference; Esther comes into her own as a member of the social structure, and of a family, by eliminating the image in which she did not
want to see herself reflected.

Responsibility has long been considered a major theme of *Bleak
House*, but the novel's structure, in which a subject presents herself
as object, makes it difficult to connect knowledge and responsibility
at the level of narrative. The end of Esther's narrative stresses
'sameness', asserting the persistence of the conditions that preceded
Lady Dedlock's irruption into the placid life of Bleak House.
Jarndyce is 'what he has ever been'; Esther keeps 'all her old names'
and her seat in the chair by his side, 'just the same' (p. 934). Her
true origins revealed and thereby, it seems, expunged, Esther is
installed in a family she has found on her own. And just as the end
of her narrative reinforces her continued dependence on others for a
view of herself ('The people even praise Me as the doctor's wife ...
They like Me for his sake, as I do everything I do in life for his
sake' [p. 935]), so too does it continue to obscure the extent to
which she plays a role in the construction of her narrative – or,
what is the same thing, in the determination of those who will sur-
round her at its end. Nowhere does the novel say, for instance, that
Esther 'passively colludes' with Bucket to pursue Lady Dedlock to
her death.[15] And yet it says so everywhere in the language of
denegation, which would kill the mother by denial – in the dreamlike recognition scene, for instance, in which Esther essentially
claims, 'It was *not* my mother.' As in the structure of denegation
itself, at the end of Esther's narrative we are caught between intellect and affect, or consciousness and unconsciousness: between
seeing Esther as she sees herself – as an object of the gazes of others,
merely reporting what they say about her – and acknowledging that
she has played some role in the construction of those gazes, and
hence of her own identity.

Constituting as it does a subject who does not know herself,
denegation may be seen as integral to the fiction of Esther's consciousness – the fiction that Esther *is* a consciousness. By means of
denegation, a subject presumed not to know can in fact know, and
can relay to readers what they need to know without seeming to be
a mere mouthpiece for the author, without ever seeming 'out of
character'. Thus Esther can chastise Skimpole as long as she seems
in awe of him; she can suggest that she distrusts Richard because
she at the same time announces her distrust of herself for doing
so.[16] Presenting herself as alienated from her own knowledge,

Esther cannot be held responsible for what she knows or says. Her denials are essential to the sense we have of her as a passive construction, a character who is not responsible for what she knows. Similarly, knowledge in the third-person narrative emanates from no specific source. Seeing is done by objects: 'Mirrors reflect' (p. 210), 'fire watches' (p. 78), the house 'stares' (p. 817), and the sunshine 'looks' (p. 203), as does the 'wintry morning' (p. 418). A view of Lady Dedlock comes, ventriloquistically, from 'authorities' of 'the world of fashion' (p. 57). Indeed, of the 'conductor' of the opinions dispersed throughout the third-person narrative, we might say what the narrator himself says of the Lord Chancellor's 'very little counsel': 'Everybody looks for him. Nobody can see him' (p. 54). Thus while *Bleak House* makes responsibility one of its central thematic issues; that same issue is, at the level of narration, the novel's essentially unsolvable (and unspeakable) problem. In its two narratives, the novel asserts the impossibility of fixing responsibility for knowledge. It is a structure that, to quote the words of that sinister but perspicacious character Vholes once again, 'divides the responsibility of knowing'.

Reporting what he knows of Richard's troubled situation in order to divide this responsibility, Vholes acts, he says, in neither his personal nor his professional capacity: he wants specifically to do something which 'can be charged to nobody' (p. 672). Between the personal and the impersonal resides 'nobody'. And it is between Esther's unspeakable personal desire to separate herself from her mother, and the professional duty which has the novel's detectives seeking her out, that Lady Dedlock's death takes place – a death that, serving personal and impersonal interests, is also chargeable to nobody. Just as the novel divides the responsibility of knowing between its two narratives, so too is knowledge divided within individual subjects, in what we commonly understand to be the division between consciousness and unconsciousness. And if the responsibility of knowing is divided, where are we to locate the subject who knows?

It is tempting – and many critics have been tempted – to make Esther the source of *Bleak House*'s general anxiety about knowledge. Indeed, it is tempting precisely because the novel offers us Esther's personal history, I would argue, as an answer to the omniscient narrative's obsessive concern with knowledge and secrecy. Esther's story provides a source for the omniscient narrative's anxiety about knowledge; indeed, we might say that her narrative in fact exists in order to do so. For as psychoanalytic criticism of the novel has demonstrated, the omniscient narration's obsession with secrecy and anxiety about knowledge may be traced to the blocking of Esther's curiosity about her mother.[17] Unlike Tulkinghorn and Bucket, that is, Esther has a personal reason for being interested in her mother: 'I had never heard of my papa either, but I felt more interested about my mama' (p. 63). In another birthday scene imbued with feelings of emptiness and alienation, of something missing at the centre, Esther's sense both of her difference from others and of her similarity to her mother is reinforced by the striking reciprocity of Mrs Rachael's comment. Since Esther's curiosity is met with this explosion of wrath and a warning about disgrace, Esther understands only that it is dangerous to ask about her origins and might be still more dangerous to receive an answer. And she substitutes for the knowledge she cannot get incessant talk about her inability to find out, as well as a sense of herself as full of secrets: '[H]ow often I repeated to the doll the story of my birthday' (p. 65).

> I busily stitched away, and told her every one of my secrets. ... It almost makes me cry to think what a relief it used to be to me, when I came home from school of a day, to run upstairs to my room, and say, 'O you dear faithful Dolly, I knew you would be expecting me!' and then to sit down on the floor ... and tell her at all I had noticed since we parted.
>
> (p. 62)

Esther's world becomes full of secrets she is forbidden to investigate, and her 'noticing way', a response to this, may be seen as the source of the unmotivated curiosity that many of the novel's characters manifest.

Esther's personal history, in other words, can stand as the source for the other narrative's anxieties about knowledge. But if we argue that her history performs this function, can we not also see the situation in reverse? That is, if we regard the subject's case history as the source of a more diffuse anxiety about knowledge, might we not also consider that anxiety to be the source of what appears in the novel as the subject – as 'case history' or individual psychology? Esther's story 'contains' the anxiety about knowledge that the other narrative displays; as personal history, her secret can be known, contained, expunged. But if an answer to supposedly objective conditions can be localised in the individual subject, it is also the case that the subject has been constructed to serve precisely that function: to fall ill and be cured, in a process that keeps society from seeing itself as needing curing. For just as Esther's narrative may be said to provide an origin for the concerns of the novel as a whole, so too does the novel's 'Other' produce the subject as an effect of its concerns: 'The consistent subject is the place to which the representations of ideology are directed: Duty, Morality, and Law all depend on this category of subject for their functioning, and all contribute as institutions to its production.'[18] Each voice is what the other is not. Esther may be said to derive from, or to be the effect of, the 'Other' narrative, just as it may be said to derive from her.

The subject lives, as Rosemary Coward and John Ellis put it, an 'imaginary wholeness': 'Ideologies set in place the individual as though he were this subject: the individual produces himself in this imaginary wholeness, this imaginary reflection of himself as the author of his actions' (p. 76). In the reading presented here, the imaginary quality of Esther's narrative becomes visible. Her narrative positions her within the social whole, but the structure of her narrative reveals that her position depends on a denial of difference. Omniscience is similarly, as I have been arguing, an imaginary wholeness – one whose imaginary quality is more difficult to perceive because it typically provides us no place to stand outside it. In *Bleak House*, however, it does provide us with such a place, not only in what is offered as the subject's personal history but also in the space between the two narratives, suggesting thereby the other perspectives we have not been offered as well as the way each narrative derives its significance from the other. Rather than seeing omniscience merely as an effect or derivation of individual psychology, then, we can say that omniscience gains its power from the very notion of individual psychology, which it constructs and on which it depends. Omniscience and first-person exist only as reflexes of one another. We can thus use the opportunity afforded by the novel's double narration to do what omniscience cannot do: to stand in the space between what is constructed as the subject and the impersonal agency which seems to construct it. The imaginary wholeness of each will appear imaginary only from such a position.

David Copperfield's and Esther Summerson's narratives illustrate that the construction of the social subject paradoxically requires self-effacement – that as some aspects of identity are constructed and confirmed through narrative, others must be disavowed. But the difference in gender of these two narrators has consequences for the form and substance of their construction. In both novels Dickens balances self-effacement against what is, in cultural terms, self-fulfilment. And yet differences between David's and Esther's characteristic evasions of knowledge and responsibility are registered in the success with which each conveys an effect or illusion of fulfilment, in the extent to which, we might say, self-effacement is concealed by self-inscription. Where David consciously assumes his position as narrator and progresses toward the full assumption of his father's name, Esther ends as 'the doctor's wife', all the while insisting upon her tangential status. Where the construction of the social self always requires denial, the Victorian angelic ideal takes denial as its principle, making even a fiction of fulfilment difficult to maintain.

Both narratives trace a movement from an apprehension of the self as 'nobody' to the occupying of a position as 'somebody', and in both cases that movement entails loss as well as gain: for Esther, the loss of the self identified with Lady Dedlock; for David, the sacrifice of numerous characters with whom the narrator refuses to acknowledge his identification. As characters, both come into existence as scars, or marks; as narrators, both work to efface this markedness. In doing so, however, they reveal the way they are ineluctably shaped by the linguistic and cultural systems they inhabit.

From Audrey Jaffe, *Vanishing Points: Dickens, Narrative and the Subject of Omniscience* (Berkeley, CA, 1991), pp. 128–149.

NOTES

[*Bleak House* succeeded *David Copperfield*, where Dickens for almost the first time wrote not as the omniscient narrator but as the character David, a character describing his childhood for part of the time. In doing so, the text focused particularly on the problem of omniscience: on what the child knows. Audrey Jaffe argues that writing narrative, whether first person or as the omniscient narrator 'involves the desire to take up a position outside the self' – a fantasy which contrasts with Esther's stated modesty about her self. And indeed, by the end, Audrey Jaffe argues, Esther 'has succeeded in constructing a world which reflects only the self she wishes to see' (p. 170). This fits with the dream of omniscience, another name for which is the power of ideology, into which the subject is fitted or fits himself or herself; this recalls what Althusser says about ideology, that by it 'men represent their real conditions to themselves in imaginary form' ('Ideology and

Ideological State Apparatuses', *Lenin and Philosophy* [London, 1971]
p. 153).

Audrey Jaffe's approach deconstructs the distinction between the omniscient narrator and the first person narrator by showing the act of narrating
to be a dream of possessing the world, without accepting responsibility for
knowledge (the word 'responsibility' goes back to Robbins's essay [no. 6]).
But it is a dream dependent for its existence on the split subject which Jaffe
discusses (see also the Introduction, pp. 13–17). Narrative cannot exist
without the split subject, indeed. If the 'omniscient', present-tense narrative
is concerned with secrecy and discovery, Esther's 'case-history' offers a
reason why it should be, by showing her own blocking of information
about her mother. But such blocking comes about from the way that the
subject is constructed: it is not spontaneous, but comes about from the
subject's placement in the symbolic order, or, better, within ideology.
Audrey Jaffe quotes from the Penguin edition (1971). Ed.]

1. I do not mean that the omniscient narrative cannot deal with material
   also appearing in Esther's narrative; of course, it does. But the elaboration of Esther's point of view is given to us as something the omniscient narrative cannot contain within itself, and which therefore needs
   to be located elsewhere.

   I use the term 'omniscient' for this narrative not because I believe
   that it 'is' omniscient, but because I believe that Dickens meant it to be
   taken as such. It is no more or less 'omniscient' than any of the other
   narratives discussed here.

2. See Jacques Derrida, *Of Grammatology*, trans. Gayatri Spivak
   (Baltimore, 1976), pp. 141–57.

3. There is little agreement about the nature of and relationship between
   Bleak House's two narratives. Catherine Belsey states bluntly, 'Neither
   is omniscient', without arguing the point. J. Hillis Miller writes that
   'both narrators hide as much as they reveal' (though 'hiding' does not
   obviate omniscience). For Ellen Serlen the impersonal narration is an
   objective, impersonal eye representing what we are meant to understand as the 'real' world; for John Lucas, who seems to consider the
   narrator a person, 'the narrator's poised and comprehensive knowledge give him an authority we do not feel ourselves in a position to
   challenge'. Taylor Stoehr, however, claims that the third-person narrator only possesses knowledge of the present. And while Serlen finds
   Esther's narrative obviously unreliable, for W. J. Harvey, Esther 'offers
   us stability, a point of rest in a flickering and bewildering world, the
   promise of some guidance through the labyrinth'. G. Armour Craig
   finds that the two narratives are separated by 'a gulf ... greater than
   can be bridged by any connection', though many critics seem able to
   discuss the difference between the same events as reported in each narrative. Together, writes Peter Garrett, the two narratives give us a
   sense of 'alternate versions of meaning ... the sense that every event or

relationship is subject to opposed interpretations'. Catherine Belsey, *Critical Practice* (London, 1980), p. 80; J. Hillis Miller, introduction to Penguin edition of *Bleak House* (Harmondsworth, 1971), p. 13 [p. 31, above]; John Lucas, *The Melancholy Man* (London, 1970), p. 211; Ellen Serlen, 'The Two Worlds of *Bleak House*', *English Litorary History*, 43 (1976), 551–66; Taylor Stoehr, *Dickens: The Dreamer's Stance* p. 147; W. J. Harvey, 'Chance and Design in *Bleak House*', in Gross and Pearson (eds), *Dickens and the Twentieth Century* (Toronto, 1962), p. 152; G. Armour Craig, 'The Unpoetic Compromise', in Jacob Korg (ed.), *Twentieth-Century Interpretations of Bleak House* (Englewood Cliffs, NJ, p. 1968), p. 60; and Peter Garrett, *The Victorian Multiplot Novel*, p. 59.

4. On Esther's strategic use of repression, see John Kucich, *Repression in Victorian Fiction* (Berkeley and Los Angeles, 1987), pp. 252–70.

5. Sigmund Freud, 'Negation', in *The Standard Edition of the Complete Psychological Works of Sigmund Freud*, ed. James Strachey, 24 vols (London, 1966), vol. 19, p. 235. Subsequent references included in text.

6. The relationship between interest and knowledge here is the same as that between pleasure/unpleasure and judgement in Freud's structure. We 'know' what we have an interest in; impersonal knowledge is a transformation of personal interest.

7. Alex Zwerdling writes that 'her godmother's words ... become the most powerful determinant of her adult personality and life choices'. See his 'Esther Summerson Rehabilitated', *PMLA*, 88 (1973), 430.

8. See for details E. Benveniste, 'Relations of Person in the Verb', in *Problems of General Linguistics*, pp. 195–204.

9. Jane Gallop, *Reading Lacan* (Ithaca, NY, 1985), p. 15.

10. Lucas, *The Melancholy Man*, p. 214.

11. I am not suggesting that Esther should own her mother's secret, but only that she inevitably does. As Gordon Hirsch points out, '[G]uilt and responsibility ... for [a] parent's sexual vagaries, are not so easily put aside ... Esther, once acknowledged as Lady Dedlock's illegitimate daughter, would not so easily escape from the social consequences of the sins of her parents, regardless of how innocent she may feel herself to be.' See 'The Mysteries in Bleak House: A Psychoanalytic Study', *Dickens Studies Annual*, 4 (1975), 137.
    Karen Chase discusses Esther's use of personal pronouns, as well as the shift from 'my' to 'the' that occurs between Lady Dedlock and Tulkinghorn in ch. 48. ('It is no longer your secret', says Tulkinghorn.) Chase's general point is that the third-person narrative is characterised by the impersonal form and Esther's by the personal. For instance, she

cites the change from 'the mother of the dead child' to 'it was my mother, cold and dead' when Esther and Bucket discover Lady Dedlock's body. Yet she does not discuss Esther's use of impersonal forms, and it would also seem important to note that Esther can acknowledge her relationship to her mother only in the past tense: 'It *was* my mother.' See *Eros and Psyche* (New York, 1984), pp. 115–17.

12. Christine van Boheemen-Saaf writes that Esther's disease 'is on a symbolic level related to the unbridled sexuality of Esther's parents; and "smallpox" is indeed close enough to "pox" to assume a sexual connotation': 'The Universe Makes an Indifferent Parent', in Joseph H. Smith and William Kerrigan (eds), *Interpreting Lacan* (New Haven, CT, 1983), p. 245. [See pp. 54–64 – Ed.]

13. This collapse is represented in Dickens's number plans for the novel by the phrase 'Mr Bucket and Esther'. See the Penguin edition of *Bleak House*, p. 950.

14. John P. Frazee, 'The Character of Esther and the Narrative Structure of Bleak House', *Studies in the Novel*, 17 (1985), 325.

15. These are Virginia Blain's words: 'Double Vision and the Double Standard in Bleak House: A Feminist Perspective', in Harold Bloom (ed.), *Modern Critical Interpretations: Bleak House* (New York, 1987), p. 155. [See pp. 65–86 – Ed.]

16. Suzanne Graver discusses Esther's inability to reconcile her critical sense with the Victorian womanly ideal in 'Writing in a "Womanly" Way and the Double Vision of *Bleak House*', *Dickens Quarterly*, 4 (1987), 3–14.

17. As Gordon Hirsch writes, '*Bleak House* deserves to be considered one of Dickens's first achievements precisely because its formal design as a mystery so successfully expresses and attempts to work through its latent content, its concern with the investigation of the mysteries associated with parental sexuality.' 'The Mysteries in *Bleak House*', p. 152.

18. Rosalind Coward and John Ellis, *Language and Materialism* (London, 1977), p. 76. See also Alan Sheridan's 'Translator's Note', in *Ecrits*: 'the subject, in Lacan's sense, is himself an effect of the symbolic' (p. ix).

8

Re-reading *Bleak House*: The Chronicle of a 'Little Body' and its Perverse Defence

KATHERINE CUMMINGS

Structurally speaking, *Bleak House* is a twin narrative. It faces in two directions (past and present); it incorporates two worlds (private and public); and it is told in two voices, one of which is serious, often pained, mimetic or realistic, the other parodic, playful, and deliberately artificial. Their mixture produces uncanny and undecidable effects. Not the least of these is the evocation of a second, postmodernist, frame of reference, which others have referred to as copy-writing and is here copied over as (g)host writing, parody, and perversion, all three being characteristic of a spurious narrative or orphan text. My own writing will necessarily follow the same procedure. It begins accordingly, not with Dickens and *Bleak House*, but with other authors to whom it looks for (a) copy, 'writing over' – describing, yet (as is inevitable in any translation), distorting/disguising – their texts.

Those signed by Derrida, Lacan, and Irigaray introduce mimesis or copy-writing. The three cite no other writing in or of texts. Playing upon the coincidence of 'seme' and 'semen', Derrida entitles the second(hand) script 'dissemination', opposing it to 'insemination' and the fiction of a licit paternity. The last is a narrative whose signification or value lies within as genetic inheritance, fixed by the father who signs. In contrast, copy-writing lacks resolution or authority. 'A nonviable seed', it designates 'everything in sperm that overflows wastefully.' Unable to name its father, the bastard('s) script cannot account for origin or author, reproduce a legitimate or proper meaning, which precedes and informs the production of the text, nor follow a single intention, a straight paternal line. In fact, it often lacks, or seems to lack, such anchor points or (paternal) metaphors as will arrest the erratic course of (narrative) desire, limit the play of metonomy, and affix a provisional meaning, signification, or sense. In other words, the orphaned narrative runs awry, 'toward indulgence in pleasures without paternity'.[1] Such pleasures include deferral, illicit plotting, and perversion. These pleasures throw a wrench in the ideological machine of the text, thereby jamming its production of gendered subjects.

All three pleasures are attributes of the 'little' stylist who assumes other signatures and names apart from that of Esther Summerson. Fading in and out of *Bleak House*, Dickens's second narrator suffers, is seduced but also seduces; even more, she simulates, this nomadic daughter, or plays. In theoretical parlance, Esther is, then, a split subject, and contradiction her métier. [...]

Esther is decidedly uncomfortable with the act of writing, and her history is also – in fact, more so – perverse. It is not in keeping with her character to put herself forward, to tell the story of her life, as if a woman's life could be a history and women historical subjects with something significant to say. Indeed, the act of history making causes Esther all sorts of trouble – not the external hardships endured by Richardson's women, to be sure – but internal anguish 'just the same' (ch. 67, p. 769). The Victorian's problem is that she wants to be a heroine – precisely, an exceptional daughter who has negotiated woman's Oedipal journey successfully so that 'passivity now has the upper hand'.[2] Yet that she writes and what she writes breach the Oedipal contract, distinguishing Esther from the exceptional daughter and her feminine fate. Partially because she is already an outcast by virtue of her illegitimate birth, this second deviation from sociocultural expectations causes Esther intense pain. But pain represents only one of her registers; she finds pleasure in acting – writing, mimicking, 'let[ting] go of her self' besides.[3]

Thus, in Esther we are offered two opposing views of perversion, as it were. One is in the nature of a moral judgement, belonging to her censor.[4] In the names of textual, sexual, and social law and order, perversion is roundly condemned. The other view of perversion is in the nature of a celebration. For Little Esther is fond of digressing, regressing, and excessing; she parodies femininity, makes us laugh at fathers, and thus imagines for us an alternative women's history, whose conditions differ from those under which the writer lives. Her 'elsewhere' is never simply a utopic there and then, however; it is also 'the elsewhere of discourse here and now'.[5] There are alternatives to be found in one narrator's (language) gaming and another's masquerading, but also and more inclusively in the ideological contradictions of the novel and/or its failure to provide a coherent reading of events.

Unlike what might be called master narratives, or scripts that seek to exert their 'own' authority by faithfully reproducing their fathers' names, the orphan text that is coproduced by Esther and her nameless other makes an art of non-mastery itself. Picking up strays, their story will repeat and double back upon itself, starting over: setting off in *more* directions *than one*.[6] Its odd shape has been dictated by 'a number of separate instincts ..., which independently of one another have pursued a certain pleasure as their sole ... aim'.[7] One other detour through Freud, then Derrida, leads me back to *Bleak House* with its orphans, copies, Krooked plots, and arrest.

[In a cut passage, Katherine Cummings examines Freud's 'Beyond the Pleasure Principle' with its discussion of the death-drive, emphasising the 'da' of the boy's (Ernst – not named in Freud's text) Fort/da game (see p. 25), played in the absence of the father ('da') (who will come back) and the mother (who has died). 'Da' evokes the (grand)father – Freud, and puns on 'Derrida', another father who discusses 'Beyond the Pleasure Principle' in *The Post Card: From Socrates to Freud and Beyond* (Chicago, 1987). Freud speaks for his grandson, 'ghosting' him; and 'Ernst's game can also be read as an autobiography of Freud ... a description of his own writing' (Derrida, quoted Cummings, p. 197).]

In beginning, Esther comes into her own as an orphan who means to be (a) copy, and copy(ist) is essentially what she remains. Because her assumption of the 'feminine role' is altogether too perfect, becoming woman is 'already to convert a form of subordination into' parody – an 'affirmation' of difference within the heart of the same.[8] Like Freud's text, Esther's narrative is equally recollective; hence, as a rule, she proceeds by turning up other orphans, ghosts, and copy-writers, along with 'nameless' fathers from the

past. In fact, the whole plot of *Bleak House* resembles the representation of the other orphan's activity, for it is also digressive and/or
perverse, producing at least two readings, each responding to one of
two moments in the child's game. One of them will celebrate the
pleasure of copying without arrest, emphasising the movement of
metonomy. The other will mourn the absence of an *authority* or
paternal metaphor and the subsequent spread of artifice and confusion. Where the first mode of reading recalls Freud's (theory of)
deferral and repetition in the *Pleasure Principle*, along with
Derrida's reproductions of this and other texts, the second brings
up Freud's representation of reality, Lacan's *nom du père*, and
Dickens's Nemo, the no name father.

It looks as if the latter ghostwrites (for) both narrators in *Bleak
House*. Certainly, Nemo copies for others, while our view of him is
of the other: the copyist being altogether anonymous, but also an
outlaw, a spectre, and a host. When *Bleak House* opens, Nemo has
disappeared; not long after, this (non)father will die yet live on as
always in writing. We catch sight of him here and there, contaminating various 'characters' in the book. While disease is Nemo's
element, so also is disorder or confusion. He has copied for Kenge
and Carboy and later Snagsby, for instance, assuming separate signatures (or putting on a 'new' identity) in every case. Because all
contact with the writer is mediated by an alias, moreover, he comes
across as a copy of someone else's 'real' address. Although born
with the proper name of Hawdon, that is, in these pages Dickens's
copy-writer will almost always pass for 'no one', or rather for the
translation's original, which is the Latin 'Nemo'. A dead language
and a foreign signifier tell the story of Esther's da insofar as he has
become a living ghost.

If names are decisive (and in *Bleak House* they seem to be), then
the other pair of writers are 'just the same'. One remains altogether
nameless, for instance, while the second proves to be self-effacing.
As it happens, Esther's (loss of) identity is doubly related to the
name(s) of the father – to Nemo, no doubt, but also and more
explicitly to John Jarndyce, the Guardian (ch. 8, p. 90), who occupies the missing father's place. Nemo's generative function has
merited the close attention of Michael Ragussis; and in 'The
Ghostly Signs of *Bleak House*', he explicitly places the non-father at
the centre of the novel's preoccupation with naming and the daughter's lack of a 'proper name'.[9] Dickens's play papa will repeat the
orphan's real da, transforming as he translates. Hence, from the

beginning, Jarndyce refuses to call Esther by her proper name; instead, he turns to literature for copy. His choices of names include Dame Durden, Old Woman, Mother Shipton, and Cobweb (ch. 8, p. 90), all of which are curious selections. For, however different they sound, in principle their subject remains the same. They are all different representations of one figure, we are told, who is recognisable as a witch or a hag.[10] Either figure belongs to a broader category of miscreants that tend to identify Esther with the outcast – in other words, with a metaphor for (the paternal pseudo-name of) 'no one'.

The metaphor has material effects. To begin with, Esther's most intimate friends all seem to have forgotten her real title, although they have little trouble in remembering her father's nicknames. In fact, so persistently is she addressed as 'Little Woman', 'Dame Durden', and the like that the original Esther would fade completely into some sort of paternal trope were it not for her writing. As it is, she disappears and comes back again – first and foremost in the biographies of the other orphans who make up her autographic text. Its writing is thus a kind of mirror game: the salient difference between her play and Ernst's being that Esther takes as much pleasure in rematerialising elsewhere as she does in vanishing from her viewers' sight.

ORPHANS, HOSTS AND (OEDIPAL) GHOSTS

As a group, the novel's mini-biographies are admittedly a collaborative effort, since some episodes are penned directly by Summerson and some by Dickens's other hand. Whatever their point of origin, however, the orphan scripts ask to be read both as a testament to Esther – or (unrealised) possibilities in her own life story – and what Derrida has called a 'living description of ... writing in the mimist's book'. Consequently, orphan narratives will introduce nearly all of Dickens's themes (including paternity, absence, and confusion), along with many of its devices (the most notable being metonomy and/or perversion).

Leaving aside for the moment the major characters – Esther, Ada, and Richard – none of whom has 'real' parents, I count three complete orphans: Jo, Guster, and Phil Squod. Traceable to no one, they come from unnamed parents, are introduced by the book's anonymous author, and reappear in the course of both narratives as signs (that things have) gone seriously astray. Jo, for instance, is compelled to 'move on' and obliges by moving in circles. Guster is impelled to move off: she falls into fits or wanders in wits, typically at Mrs Snagsby's instigation. Finally, Phil must move 'round', 'tacking off at objects he wants to lay hold of instead of *going straight* to them' (emphasis added). His course 'has left a smear all round ..., conventionally called "Phil's mark"' (ch. 21, p. 272); it is an implicit remark upon the original 'stain' and perverse turns of the narrative – a twisted plot, as we shall see, in more ways than one. For the moment, it is enough to observe that discussion of 'Phil's Mark' follows an account of the Smallweed Family's designs upon Trooper George and Captain Hawdon, whom we recognise as the copy-writer's original, while immediately anticipating the vagabond's scene of origin. Thus, '"You were found in a doorway, weren't you?"' George asks. '"Gutter," says Phil. "Watchman tumbled over me"' (p. 272)

Each of these strays is unmistakably a missing person as well. By definition, all have lost their origin. In addition, Guster and Jo are also missing patronyms, places, and thus significance, not to mention (the capacity to impose) sense.

The female orphan 'holds her place precariously', which is precisely what Garret Stewart has said of Esther.[11] More specifically, Guster is a servant liable to fits, hence firing. And, like the narrator, she is a subject 'fading', who disappears and comes again under a foreign address.[12] 'Supposed to have been christened Augusta', Dickens's character appears astray within the 'name of Guster'. Indeed, Cook's Courtiers all remark that this metonym 'ought to be the name of Mrs Snagsby' (ch. 10, p. 117).

Unlike Guster, Jo actually holds no place at all – unless, perhaps, it is the empty place of Nemo's adopted son. His is the patronym of a 'Nobodaddy' (from) whose *sematary* plot Jo strays only to return. In the second half of the book, Nemo's signature will leave the cemetery with him as the pox which Jo carries and with which he (un)erringly infects Esther Summerson. Hereafter, the non-name of the father is engraved on the daughter's scarred face.

Phil Squod's case is similar. What he's kept in name, he has paid for in number and person. Since beginning, he has lost significant pieces of himself and the definitive part of his age. It's 'something with an eight in it', he's sure. 'It can't be eighty. Nor yet eighteen. It's betwixt 'em, somewheres', in the muddle of middles, where it's 'queer, wery queer' (ch. 26, pp. 326–7).[13]

These lines of Phil Squod's act as Post Script: coming after Esther's narrative of origins, they remind us of her position or lack of a definitive place. It is this lack which points back to her parents, or rather to their 'unnatural' substitutes, one of whom is Barbary and the other Jarndyce – or Jaundice as its pronunciation should suggest.

Barbary conceals the details of Esther's origin but not the matter of her niece's disgrace. Insinuating that there has been a sexual 'stain' in Esther's past, she forecasts the return of the 'father's sins' in the life of his daughter. Moreover, in telling her tales, Barbary will provide a pretext for what I have earlier alluded to as the text's 'dissemination'.

Jarndyce differs markedly from the 'unnatural woman'. He is open hearted, generous – philanthropic, as eager to avoid unpleasure as the aunt is to produce pain. Despite their visible differences, however, both figures bear a certain resemblance, as they are implicated in repression and perversion by the text: Barbary, in the second, by her acts of sadism and Jarndyce by sexual proposals made to Esther, hence by a desire which calls to mind Freud's incestuous father. Above all, they are keepers of secrets, and when it comes to repression, these substitute parents are virtual kin. Hence, for other motives than Barbary's, Jarndyce also resists revealing what little he knows of Esther's origin. Instead, he attempts to father the orphan himself, initially by repressing or forgetting the daughter's given name of 'Esther', while substituting coinages of his 'own'. Later, he further (con)fuses familial relations by introducing a marriage proposal – as it happens, 'two of them'. After first proposing himself as Esther's husband, that is, Jarndyce next proposes (the man who) Woodcourt in his place.

It's no wonder that Esther appears in a muddle, then, and that her story bears the mark of her strain. Not only do tale and teller announce their 'difficulty in beginning' (ch. 3, p. 17) but the two equally trail off in supposition, unable – or just possibly unwilling – to come to a satisfactory end. Once again, Esther's 'predicament' is reproduced in the 'chronicles' of all the novel's orphans, none of whom can arrive at a conclusion or give an account of what they are, since they don't know where they have been or – what amounts to the same thing – where and how to begin.[14]

The orphan problem is taken over and repeated by the subjects in Chancery, for whom questions of origin and paternity become particularly pressing, largely because the convincing reconstruction of a case history will directly determine the success or failure of their suit. As the chief claimants in the central case of Jarndyce versus Jarndyce, Esther's cousins Richard and Ada exemplify the plaintiff's need for narrativity, which Richard acts upon and converts to demand. What he is after are the original facts on Jarndyce and a straightforward presentation of the family case. But the origin of the affair has been lost in translation; Chancery copy, representing quite chancy copy, now stands in its place. Thus, Richard finds only duplications and legal complications, which make a 'joke' out of Jarndyce (ch. 1, p. 8) and ghosts out of those like Richard who follow the case.

Though it receives more of Esther's attention, Richard's narrative experience is hardly unique. On the contrary, his plight is one with that of the other Chancery 'children', whose paternal names are Gridley and Flite. Both petitioners are mad, and like so many others they are also partial orphans (in law): Flite losing her father, family, health, and sanity all in Chancery (ch. 35, pp. 440–1), Gridley the same 'possessions' and more. First he loses his father, twice. Gridley is orphaned once by his parent's death, then, as if a single orphaning were incomplete, a second time by legal dispute. As with all disputations in *Bleak House*, the Gridley suit compulsively returns/turns around the original 'issue' so that what began as a matter of property has since turned into the problem of establishing a licit paternity. No more than the novel, does the suit have 'the sense of an ending'; on the contrary, legitimacy is suspended indefinitely, as lawyers spend lifetimes in debating whether the plaintiff is or is not his 'father's son' (ch. 15, p. 193). Continuances are only one of the orphan's problems, however. There is yet a second difficulty, which, in its relation to legitimate naming, duplicates the first. Once he's involved in the Chanc(er)y process of proving paternity, that is, Gridley all but loses his identity to the generic 'man from Shropshire' (ch. 15, p. 192) – the improper name by which he is legally addressed. All of these initial losses are in time reframed and repeated elsewhere in Gridley's subsequent loss of temper, wits, and life.

Finally, there are the book's domestic orphans. One of the most significant is Charley Neckett, who is taken in by Jarndyce after her own father's death. Her surrogate father makes Charley over into a 'Token' of love, then passes her along as a 'present' for Esther (ch. 23, p. 299). Next there are the Jellyby children and Skimpole daughters, whose fathers may as well be dead. Certainly, they are out of place in paternal positions, especially those prescribed for Victorians.

Jellyby perverts paternity besides its complement, potency; and in twisting around these and other conventions, he strays from what is proper in a Dickensian script. Contrary to masculine convention, that is, Esther's Jellyby has the habit of always going limp. Withdrawing from all conversation and drooping his head in despair, Jellyby commits Dickens's unpardonable sin by submitting to the misrule and confusion of a wife (ch. 30, pp. 373–7). Skimpole represents a more potent principle of disorder, evidently. We catch him breeding confusion in the family home, for instance, and, on more than one occasion, mixing up the genealogical line. In his own terms and evidently on them, Harold is no father of daughters, then, but rather 'the youngest' in the family's childhood romance (ch. 43, p. 526).

This father and his story have evidently gone awry. To begin with, Harold reappears beside himself as 'the Skimpole' (ch. 6, p. 66), while appearing alongside Leigh Hunt and Esther Summerson as their parody or perversion.[15] Skimpole also stands outside common laws of responsibility and fair exchange, though perfectly within the Law of Equity or Same: he is, perhaps, its ideal copy or metonymic case. He is also something of a vanishing figure, given to abrupt disappearances and reappearances that call to mind the other orphans' da. Neither present nor absent, the nominal father of Jo and Esther has been described as (g)hostlike: 'living on'. [...]

On one hand there are ghosts (especially ghostly papas) and on the other (fathers who are) hosts. Both (da's) 'return endlessly' in the course of the narrative – are virtually 'always there', then, or about to be there. Turveydrop is in every way a parasitic father. A '"model" of Deportment', the narrator calls him (ch. 14, p. 171), and mentions how he is living on his son. But the father is never simply a parasite in the orphan's text, he is also – in his own fashion – a host. The Regent and his reign survive in Old Turveydrop's appointments, for instance, and in the perverse naming of Young Mr T., 'Prince' – a metonym that reproduces a period, as the boy's father intended, but also 'sounds like a dog' (ch. 14, p. 169), as Caddy says. The Regency, to our ears, rings the same. More significantly, the 'arch' parasite Skimpole lives on (in) Hunt and Esther, and with the help of Equity and its 'respectable' spectacle Vholes, he nonchalantly 'makes a meal of' Richard in the end.

A family ghost walks the battlements at Chesney Wold, and s/he paces so that Lady Dedlock cannot help but hear (ch. 8, p. 85). With her family history, it's no wonder. 'Separated: joined. There are two of them, absolutely different', separated by sex and centuries and yet fused, folded over in each other; within the (m)other lies a 'crypt', from out of which the ghost 'comes haunting'.

An aside from George's mother furnishes the 'original' ghost story.[16] In it the history of Hamlet's haunting is repeated perversely as Lady Dedlock schemes to betray her husband (Sir Morbury) and king (Charles I). Other points of resemblance between the Dedlock family fortunes and Hamlet's depend upon the teller's word choice and, more, the tendency of her signifiers to be unruly: to involve different characters which *indirectly* start saying something other than what they were first heard to say. Thus, while Mrs Rouncewell tells how the Lady eavesdrops, the story's plot line and setting speak of poison drops that were introduced into the sleeping king's ear. Not, it would seem, by the lord's lady but by her lover who enacts her wish. Later in the tale, Lady Dedlock will lame the men's horses and try to *turn aside their designs*. Instead, the lady is *diverted*, 'lamed in the hip' (ch. 8, p. 84) – and the sexual innuendo insists – by her husband or perhaps his 'favourite horse' (p. 84). Thereafter, she walks haltingly like a silent, accusing spectre until she falls, vowing to *return, overturn*, in a word, *pervert* the Dedlock line.

Her ghost 'signifies and preserves the other', the Nemo who lives on – copying. Thus, Lady Dedlock perverts, turns aside his line, giving birth to a nameless bastard who will in turn take her turn (pardon these re-turns) upon the Ghost Walk (ch. 36, p. 454), until she overturns the mother and ensures the Dedlock decline.

On the night following Esther's reunion with her mother, then, and her discovery of the circumstances surrounding her birth, Esther takes the place of the family ghost by 'coming back to haunt' a duplicate path, which is appropriately placed beneath the original walk. As she passes here, her 'echoing footsteps' recall 'a dreadful truth in the legend of the Ghost's Walk', which is 'that it was I who was to bring calamity upon the stately house' (p. 454). And s/he does, though this 's/he' is not simply or singly Esther, but heteronomous – more than one. I count the 'family ghost' or phantasm of the (m)other's guilt, but also Tulkinghorn, Hortense, Bucket, Smallweed, the Chadbands, and Mrs Snagsby, all of whom diversely *conspire* against Lady Dedlock, with the result that her *plot* ends beside her husband's – coming too early, at the improper time.

In a reading of *Beyond the Pleasure Principle*, Peter Brooks has suggested that the narrative's 'subplot stands as one means of warding off the danger of short-circuit, assuring that the main plot will continue through to the right end'.[17] The relation between the two plots is repeated with emphasis in *Bleak House*, where the mother dies and the daughter 'lives on' *beyond* to frame a new beginning from her ending, which is 'supposing—' (ch. 67, p. 770). Esther's non-end leaves her readers guessing, introduces further complications, is productive, then, of other stories – *l'arrêt de mort*. In their effect, her final words inscribe an 'elsewhere': quite possibly a feminine space, but certainly another zone that is foreign to the drawn boundaries of man's masterplot, the 'right end' having been reimagined as the non-end, after all.

Cook's Court remarks a second family spectre. This spook, 'name of' Peffer, crosses Hamlet with Nemo in a comic compound (of) ghost (writing). Like the Dedlock ghost, Peffer is introduced by the novel's anonymous hand or ghostwriter, but unlike the spectre, Peffer is fully phantasm or writing (d)effect, appearing first in the fading shop sign of PEFFER and there adding a second ghostly signature to the narrator's first. Those of Hamlet indirectly, via dramatic allusion, and Nemo directly, or explicitly as referent, immediately follow. Like the displaced figure of 'Peffer', who literally disappears from his proper place only to reappear in another (ch. 10, p. 116), these ghosts come back to haunt – not the father, Peffer, but Snagsby, the 'ex-centric' Oedipal 'son *in-law*'.

'PEFFER', then, is set beside, and aside, by a son or rather (since all things – most things – happen indirectly in *Bleak House*) by the smoke that metonomy substitutes for him. This 'smoke ... had so wreathed itself around Peffer's name and clung to his dwelling place that the affectionate parasite quite overpowered the parent tree' (ch. 10, p. 116). Or so it seems. But in fact, this *da* is no more *fort* than the others; instead, Peffer disappears, then comes again 'until admonished to return by the crowing of the sanguine cock' (p. 116).[18]

Peffer's admonishment immediately recalls Hamlet and is about to call up Nemo beside(s). As it happens, twice. Thus, not only will Chadband associate Dickens's spectre with 'a story of a Cock and of a Bull' (ch. 25, p. 322), but the narrator (whom we take for another sort of ghost writer) will more pointedly eulogise the copier

in allusions to 'an avenging ghost' (ch. 11, p. 137). Their similitude
is soon extended. For like Nemo, Peffer copies and is copied
diversely. After dying, both da's are accordingly converted into
copy – the first, by a 'comic vocalist'/novelist called 'Little *Swills*' or
named nothing at all (ch. 10, p. 116 and ch. 11, pp. 130–6). It is
this Swills who now provides the context of legatees and litigation –
of an inheritance, in other words, that haunts. In the cases of Nemo
and Peffer, 'there are two' figures who stand to inherit the most:
one being the aspiring apprentice, son-Snagsby, and the second, the
ephebe Summerson.[19] The guilty haunting of Snagsby repeats the
more painful episodes in Esther's life (story) with pleasure, while
oddly recapitulating her position as the presumptive writer of a
non-Oedipal/Oedipal text: non-Oedipal, in part, because sport is
made of Freud's 'original' figures and serio-tragic events in the
name of the perverse; non Oedipal, on the whole, because the
writing ends with an enigma and not its resolution; but Oedipal,
nonetheless, in its persistent returns to the father as source.

The Snagsby plot originates, as Esther's does, in the family – and
more precisely in a familiar romance. Its subjects include an appren-
tice-son, a master-father, and a niece-daughter, while the dramatic
tension is provided by Snagsby's aspiration to be a partner and/or a
father. In the present case, that is a Peffer in (the) law. What
happens is that Dickens's aspirant succeeds to daughter and partner
simultaneously. Soon after the daughter has become a Snagsby,
however, the Peffer begins to fade.

As framed, the story of Snagsby is recognisably Oedipal, therefore. But Oedipal, we are made to notice, with a difference, since all
of the unconscious 'tokens' in the original drama (Freud's/Esther's)
have been rearranged or 'laid out' ex-centrically with *jeu d'esprit*.
The most significant displacement in the second(hand) scene is also
the most decidably Oedipal and occurs when Snagsby takes Peffer's
place. Little good it does the flesh-and-blood Snagsby, however,
whose triumph is configured in the shop's legend and is limited to
existing in (the) legend itself. Indeed, the son's takeover has been
altogether metaphorical; there's a murder here, but it's been staged
in name only, precisely in the dramatic writing of SNAGSBY onto
the sign that once held PEFFER alone.

We have only to set SNAGSBY beside Snagsby in order to see
that the little man of the fiction can be no match for his characters
or script. And that, of course, is the writer's point. Apart from what
is momentarily made of a Snagsby by some copy-writing, there is

no one there but an 'emphatically ... retiring and unassuming man' (ch. 10, p. 117). Dickens's other Snagsby wakes up and 'finds himself in a crisis of nightmare' (ch. 25, p. 316). He is haunted by a Nemo and further hounded by a wife, who is after all a Peffer living on.

In fact, 'Mrs Snagsby is so perpetually on the alert, that the house becomes ghostly with creaking boards and rustling garments. The 'prentices think somebody may have been murdered there' (ch. 25, p. 317). And Snagsby, 'he is doubtful of his being awake and out – doubtful of the reality of the streets through which he goes' (ch. 22, p. 284). He thinks – whatever the crime – that the criminal must have been he (ch. 33, p. 407). Meanwhile, 'Mrs Snagsby sees it all', and all there is of it is a muddle about paternity. In a slippery exchange of glances, she then looks at Jo, who 'looks at Mr Snagsby', who 'looks at him'. Immediately after, 'she is seized with an in*spira*tion ... It is as clear as crystal that Mr Snagsby is that boy's father' (ch. 25, pp. 317–18, emphasis added). She is sure of it.

Readers, however, are bound to see things differently. We are certain that Mr Snagsby cannot be the man. For some time now we have been thinking that the name of the boy's father must be 'no one', in point of figure if not in fact. Our conviction is called for by the plot of *Bleak House*, which is (dis)organised by figures of metonymy and/or the structure of perversion. J. Hillis Miller makes a similar observation in his Introduction to the novel, though his copy of the narrative and translation of its structure depart substantially from mine. Essentially, Miller finds that 'metaphor and metonymy' constitute the 'deep grammatical armature' of *Bleak House* [p. 32, above], while his reading implicitly privileges a disturbing metonymy. Miller's use of this trope as a narrative principle, which 'presupposes a similarity or causality between things presented as contiguous and thereby makes story-telling possible' [p. 32], and my different use of the metonym and metonymy as principles of unrest, which *subvert* any storyline and work to make storytelling impossible, originate in Roman Jakobson and diversely reflect subsequent (post)structuralist descriptions of language systems. Generally, the latter represent metonymy as the displacement of one signifier by another along the horizontal or diachronic axis of the signifying chain. Metonymy's skid further formalises what I read (through Lacan and Brooks) as the narrative's suspension of sense: its endless substitution of one signifier or metonym for another, that is, without the possibility of arrest.[20]

According to the novel's law of metonomy, Nemo will substitute for Jo's loss of an originating signifier and the original facts of the orphan's birth. Not only does he identify (with) the boy as outcast, but he shares what *little* he has to share and so becomes a kind of father. Without the name. Nemo never utters the word 'father', that is, nor does Jo, who cannot pronounce it – even in imitation. Hence, Ragussis will argue that 'while repeating the prayer "Our Father" after Woodcourt, the orphan without any Christian sign stops short at a particularly relevant point: "Hallowed be – thy—" (ch. 47, p. 572). ... Our Father stands for that symbolic silence where the name should be but is not'.[21] In *Bleak House*, the orphan's vacant space stands for Nemo and, more, for the nameless metonym and countless metonyms that are put in place of the (paternal) metaphor or the name of the Father, the original of whom seems to be Hawdon.

Nonetheless, what Jo can name 'points to' part of the unnamed problem. Nemo, he says, 'wos wery good to me, wery good to me indeed, he wos', and he asks to be 'berried' 'along with' the *non père* or put *beside* him (ch. 47, p. 571). The orphan's conclusions are more than Summerson can say directly of Hawdon and much like what Jo also says of Snagsby. The repetition causes trouble for the stationer, we know, whom it subjects to the da's ghost-effect. In another context, Derrida has described how the (g)host 'comes haunting out of the Unconscious of the other ... He is not an effect of repression "belonging" to the subject he comes to haunt with all kinds of ventriloquism; he is rather "proper" to a parental un-conscious. Coming back to haunt [la revenance] is not a return of the repressed'.[22]

In the orphan's book, one of the first 'signs' of a ghost will be the return of letters. And letters is a signifier that carries more than one sense. One of the first is the common 'missive', whose transcription is here bound up with fathers, family secrets, and the perverse. Early on we will come across identical letters that are directed by the legal firm of Kenge and Carboy in response to Esther's Greenleaf narratives. Although the lawyers' letters have been written on behalf of/in the name of John Jarndyce, they all have been penned by the hand of Nemo, the copy-writer, who is a second ghostwriter in the Greenleaf exchange where Kenge and Carboy (in writing for Jarndyce) are the first. We must suppose, then, that Esther receives letters from her own father under his sub-stitute's address. Yet all letters in *Bleak House* are also simply that:

letters. As alphabetical 'signs', they are made for making sense or nonsense – depending.

Some of the more (non)sensical are the letters that Jo returns – turns around or scrambles. I think especially of the twist that is given to a proper name when the orphan calls his second benefactor 'Mr Sangsby' (ch. 47, p. 567). Jo's inversion of the second two letters produces both the stationer and 'his' ghost, 'Sangsby' returning 'Snagsby' even as it names 'no one'. There is something about calling that elicits a response, nonetheless, so that here even the non-signature summons someone by the name of 'Nemo', precisely.

The Snagsby law of exchange rephrases the orphan's slip of the tongue, since the law also invests in secrecy, while trading in illicit currency as well. Not surprisingly, then, one of the stationer's most distinctive 'tokens' is the half crown, which is given to Jo furtively with the understanding that the donor be unnamed. The exchange proves more effective than we might expect, in that Jo can keep safe a secret, while so, it seems, can trading in a text. This orphan(ed) intelligence and trading conspire to displace and so efface 'Snagsby' with 'Sangsby' in Jo's mind and half crown 'tokens' in our own. Much like Nemo, then, Mr Sangsby/Snagsby 'haunts' (ch. 32, p. 393) and is haunted in turn. In their haunting both are very like 'the t'other one' (ch. 31, p. 381), in particular, they resemble Summerson, which prompts Jo to count 'there [are] *three* of 'em then?' (ch. 31, p. 383).

A KROOK'S PLOT OR POACHING ON THE FATHER'S PRESERVE

All of these duplicates motivate a 'return to an earlier' site in the text. For from the beginning, the name of 'Nemo' has pointed repeatedly to Esther: to copying as constitutive of the orphan and copy-writing as another name for a perverse narrative, otherwise an outsider's biography or orphan's text.

[A large cut has been made in the text here, dealing with instances of 'copying' in *Bleak House*, and their parodic and perverse nature, and including discussions of the repetitions/doublings in the names 'Ada' and 'Jarndyce and Jarndyce' and ranging through comments on the text's minor characters.]

But let me try to be more methodical and precise; these copies are having disturbing effects. One of them is to call all copies 'illegitimate'; another is to recall copying (with) 'pleasure'. Both callings summon the narrative I, by which I allude to a common alias for Esther Summerson. She copies her narrative from 'life', yet fears the copy may well be illicit and her writing a perverse attempt to out-father her father or grand-father herself. Hence her difficulty in beginning again and again.

This explanation hardly seems better, though; only a minimal improvement upon the first. What I need here is the introduction of other writing to slow the pace, extend the narrative, and recompose – by restating – the orphan's case.

It is often said, then, that Esther's narrative earnestly imitates life, where the anonymous narrative playfully imitates art. Many cite their difference in Esther's favour. Thus, they find her record of events a necessary supplement to the anonym's whose exposé of society and aim of social change are limited by the artificiality of the writerly voice. Artifice may delight the reader, they'll argue, but it also operates to distance her or him. In consequence, s/he is not moved pathetically to act, nor is s/he inspired to change.

My conclusions are somewhat different. To begin with, I take Esther's 'life' as shorthand for a complex of fictions, among them contemporary representations of duty, denial, and earnestness. Nonetheless, I concur that hers remains the more sincere(ly) (mimetic) work and the other's the more playful artifice. However, since I view both hands as alternate, discontinuous representations of one subject (which is not the same as one person but marks what I have called an orphan function) and since I detect traces of the other hand – indeed, other hands – in those sections that are implicitly/ explicitly signed by the one, I end with a less resolute text. This orphan chronicle 'exposes incoherences, omissions, absences and transgressions which in turn reveal the inability of the language of ideology to create coherence.'[23] Finally, I do not believe that playful language or comedy cripples criticism as a rule, or I would not have written as I have. Still, as worked out within the orphan narrative of *Bleak House*, Dickens's comic practice perverts – turns aside and subverts – his critical programme. This is because the two writers and readers (at least this reader) are caught up in the pleasure of repetition. Moreover, they remain confused about how to read the book's exemplar and how to decipher inscriptions of 'illegitimacy' – does it fall within the domain of the reality or the pleasure principle?

This st(r)ain of illegitimacy touches nearly all of the characters I have cited, most of them with serio-comic consequence at their origin or birth. Some strays are likewise implicated in illicit returns. Smallwood and Skimpole, for instance, are explicitly associated with design and disguise for gain. So too is the little 'romantic' writer whose recollected 'life' has at least one utilitarian purpose, which is an attempt to 'win some love ... if I [Imago/Ideal] could' (ch. 3, p. 20).

It is difficult to decide to what degree the writing I is aware of her narrative's profitable coincidence, but it is not difficult to determine one of I's writing effects. That is, the exemplary 'young lady' cannot be taken seriously (simply/Skimpoley) as genuine but must also be read as artifice – and thus, the 'pattern' for a (dis)similar line of perverts, who mimic the father in a variety of ways.

And the trouble does not end here, in the critical portrayal of copy, but in its exuberant and playful returns – or rather, in between 'the two of them': that is, within the principle of reality and the principle of pleasure on the border of sense and nonsense. Both processes are at play in Esther's recollection of Jarndyce, whose case incorporates both Law and Father in the doublet 'dada'.

Esther's substitute dad clearly prefers the pleasure principle, perverse plots, and pleasures to the principle of reality, the last of which is thematised in the recurring figure of an easterly wind. The east wind invariably produces tension in Jarndyce, whose anxiety Esther successfully treats by constructing 'charming fictions'. Not only does her practice take over Skimpole's, but like his, it will contribute to the denial of the real.

The orphan's substitutions (of Jarndyce for Nemo, Esther for Skimpole, and fiction for fact) both increase the characters' yield of pleasure, since the copy generally improves upon the nature of its original in ways too numerous to note, and – as substitutes or metonyms – prolong (narrative) *jouissance* by promising that places and/or figures will continue to be exchanged and any end thereby displaced, differed, and deferred. But if metonymy thus inspires pleasure, it no less produces problems – always promoting confusion and disseminating disorder with ill effect upon conditions in the real.

Consequently, although he has the best or most benevolent of intentions, Esther's Guardian no less preserves the status quo of disease. In case we miss the charge, the writer repeats the accusation, playfully, in the articulation of Jarndyce's (common) name. Esther's (second) father also exemplifies disorder, however, which is responsible for my anachronistic 'dada'. Not surprisingly, perhaps, the doubled da recalls the none-too-singular Nemo, whom Mrs Snagsby further implicates in Babel(ing), when her tongue slips and names the copy-writer 'Nimrod' (ch. 11, p. 128).[24] With all of these coincidences, the father's fault is bound to look like more than a nominal coincidence. In fact, the errant parent is a central figure in the daughter's story and a substantive part of her plot. Despite Esther's express admiration of Jarndyce, then, her narrative will continue to hold him and particularly his position of separation or withdrawal indirectly responsible for the collapse of the social system and the chaos that is everywhere the law. In *Bleak House*, it is father who puts matters about muddles best. That is why John Jarndyce's alphabetical representation of Equity – with 'this counsel appearing for A and that ... appearing for B and so on through the whole alphabet ... constantly beginning over and over again so that nothing ever ends" (ch. 8, pp. 88–9) – occupies such a prominent place in I's reconstructive narrative. 'You have only to go and look to understand immediately that' his alphabet recapitulates the rubric of (g)host writing and the Krooked plot of Summerson's book. It is behind her now, this signature. Da.

From Katherine Cummings, *Telling Tales: The Hysteric's Seduction in Fiction and Theory* (Stanford, CA, 1991), pp. 191–229.

NOTES

[This is a short, heavily cut extract from a feminist reading of *Bleak House*, part of a longer playful argument about 'seduction' (and about who seduces who) using the French feminist theorists Luce Irigaray and Hélène Cixous, who in complex ways work with Lacan and Derrida, taking the binary division in sexual difference to be culturally constructed. The essay's main debt is to deconstruction, but in a way contrasting with Hillis Miller's. In a text so much concerned with paternity, it calls on Derrida's essay on Plato's *Phaedrus*, 'Plato's Pharmacy' (in *Disseminations* [Chicago, 1981]) which argues that writing is that which has no father, which exists in a freeplay which nonetheless the fathers need to give them an afterlife (Socrates in the *Phaedrus* in effect rubbishes writing, but he is dependent on it – he is only kept alive or in memory by Plato's text). If writing has no father, just as Esther has none, like so many other orphans in *Bleak House*, it has no responsibility to the concept of 'truth' phallocentrically maintained by patriarchy (see essay no. 2) but becomes parodic, double, playful, perverse.

This reading/writing of *Bleak House* is thus deliberately perverse, arguing for Esther 'seducing' by parodying femininity. Cummings plays upon the idea of the law-writer – which Michael Ragussis comments on – being a copy-writer, linking parody and copy (and the idea of copy brings into question the concept of the origin – that which the law-giver, the father, should be able to establish). Using an essay by Michael Ragussis (note 9), she puns on the copywriter being a ghostwriter, so that the text is full of the idea of haunting: the speech or writing of one subject being haunted by its other (as the feminine 'other' haunts masculine discourse). Esther writes in relation to an anterior writing of her father. Another text haunting Cummings's work is Maurice Blanchot's postmodern narrative (*récit*), *L'arrêt de mort* (1948 – translated as *Death Sentence* by Lydia Davis [New York, 1978]), which Derrida comments on in an essay called 'Living On'. This text also has two separate narratives, two women and a male narrator who moves between them: it makes life/death distinctions undecidable, and makes the notion of *return*, whether of the ghost (the revenant – that which turns back), or of writing (where there is the return of the repressed) basic to deconstruction and to this reading of *Bleak House*. Writing, in fact – that key concept of deconstruction – is an important 'return' in that it preserves life, as a form of 'living on'.

Another set of references to death in this essay comes from the psychoanalysts Nicholas Abraham and Maria Torok and their work on 'cryptonomy' in *The Wolfman's Magic Word* – which, put over-simply, involves the repression of material that the ego fears or censors. The ego 'encrypts' this material within itself – which makes the ego a tomb, but as with the best Gothic romances, a voice always comes out of the tomb: the repressed returns. In all these puns on haunting, Esther's writing also 'ghosts' the other narrative: perhaps both narratives are Esther's? Quotations are taken from the Norton critical edition of *Bleak House* (1977). Ed.]

1. See, for instance, Lacan's discussion of the letter [Jacques Lacan, *Ecrits: A Selection*, trans. Alan Sheridan (New York, 1977) – Ed.] in 'Agency of the Letter' (pp. 153–8) and 'Subversion of the Subject' (pp. 303–4). For Derrida, see 'Plato's Pharmacy', *Dissemination*, trans. Barbara Johnson (Chicago, 1981), pp. 149–52.

2. Sigmund Freud, *New Introductory Lectures on Psychoanalysis*, trans. James Strachey (New York, 1965), p. 128.

3. Hélène Cixous, 'The Laugh of the Medusa', trans. Keith Cohen and Paula Cohen, *Signs*, 1: 4 (1976), 875–93, p. 881.

4. I have referred to the woman's censor under the title of 'superego', but since this paternal precipitate stands in within the subject for patriarchal ideology, the latter will equally do.

5. Teresa de Lauretis, *Technologies of Gender: Essays on Theory, Film and Fiction* (Bloomington, IN, 1987), p. 25.

6. Luce Irigaray, *This Sex Which Is Not One*, trans. Catherine Porter with Carolyn Burke (Ithaca, NY, 1985), pp. 28–31.

7. Sigmund Freud, *Three Essays on the Theory of Sexuality*, trans. James Strachey (New York, 1975), p. 73.

8. Irigaray, 'Power of Discourse', *This Sex*, p. 76.

9. For Michael Ragussis, see his 'The Ghostly Signs of *Bleak House*', *Nineteenth-Century Fiction*, 34 (1979), 253–80. But see also Dianne Sadoff [*Monsters of Affection: Dickens, Eliot, and Bronte on Fatherhood* (Baltimore, MD, 1982) – Ed.], who have each differently defined Esther in relation to her problematic paternity. In *Monsters of Affection*, Sadoff works through what she sees as Dickens's preoccupation with origins, relying on the paternal metaphors of Jacques Lacan and Harold Bloom, along with the structure of Freud's primal scene. [Garrett] Stewart's 'The New Mortality of *Bleak House*' [*ELH*, 45 (1978), 443–87 – Ed.] more particularly poses the problem of Esther's positionality (and indirectly that of the other orphans) in the context of the narrator's place 'in the middest'; he finds that 'not knowing where she comes from, Esther can say neither who nor even whether she is' (p. 445). Like Ragussis, Sadoff, and Stewart, I am concerned about Esther's disappearance, the father's fault(s), and the daughter's pain. As they do not, however, I particularly emphasise the pleasure of Dickens's text and the design of copy-writing as well. More simply, to the Principle of Reality, I add the Principle of Pleasure.

10. See William Axton, 'Esther's Nicknames: A Study in Relevance', *Dickensian*, 62:3 (1966), 158–63.

11. Stewart also goes on to say that Esther's life is 'an eroded border between self and others' perception of it' ('New Mortality', p. 445). I recall this border and, even more, a Derridean one when suggesting that *Nemo* (among other figures) is his daughter's *Nemesis* – a ghost, then, who crosses over, 'coming back to haunt'. [Jacques Derrida, 'Living On: Border Lines', trans. James Hulbert, *Deconstruction and Criticism* (New York, 1979) pp. 162–7 – Ed.]

12. Lacan has coined the term 'fading' to describe an inevitable effect of representation. That effect positions the subject as 'a signifier for another signifier' within the substitutions of the entire signifying chain. Precisely because of these substitutions, the subject becomes a copy and occasionally, if she is a woman, an Ideal Image or an Other. Once reconstituted as a metaphor/metonym, s/he fades (from an original position) in the Real. [Jacques Lacan, *The Four Fundamental Concepts of Psycho-analysis*, trans. Alan Sheridan (New York, 1977), pp. 216–36 – Ed.]

13. Phil's finding is uncannily like Frank Kermode's, whose 'sense of an ending' (or for that matter an origin) is that it imposes sense on the nonsense of 'life in the middest'. [Frank Kermode, *The Sense of an Ending: Studies in the Theory of Fiction* (New York, 1967 – Ed.]

More recently, Peter Brooks has taken up Kermode's argument, developing the latter's position in ways that prove particularly germane to the original problem of paternity in *Bleak House*. In 'Fictions of the Wolfman' [Peter Brooks, 'Fictions of the Wolfman: Freud and Narrative Understanding', *Diacritics*, 9: 1 (1979), 72–81 – Ed.], Brooks links the rise of the detective story (and *Bleak House* is exemplarily this) to nineteenth-century historicism and both to 'the postulate that we can explain what we are only through finding out how we got that way, through plotting that story which traces effects to origins and enchains the events along the way' (p. 74). Brooks's description might serve equally for that of an Oedipal narrative, which, in the name of pleasure, is precisely the sort of narrative that the stray's story breaks faith with: representing just enough of it for the sequence to be identifiable, then letting go, moving on so that point of closure will be suspended indefinitely and Oedipus, confounded, will all but disappear.

14. My reference to chronicles presupposes Hayden White's description in 'The Value of Narrativity in the Representation of Reality'. [Hayden White, 'The Value of Narrativity in the Representation of Reality', in *On Narrative*, ed. W. J. T. Mitchell (Chicago, 1981) pp. 1–23 – Ed.] There, he defines the chronicle as lacking completeness and coherence; it does 'not so much "conclude"', as history does, but instead 'simply terminate[s]' without coming to an end (p. 16). If history is the story of Oedipus – a subject with an appointed destiny or fated end – then the chronicle, which predates historiography as we know it, is the legend of a time before (and, can we but manage the return, quite possibly a time again). This ahistoric period of fore-pleasure(s), as opposed to end-pleasure, of multiple instinctual aims and erotogenic zones, as opposed to *the* one of heterosexual reproduction (Sigmund Freud, *Three Essays on the Theory of Sexuality*, pp. 73–4) has been called a 'pre-Oedipal stage'. Stage: a phase doomed to extinction, but also, stage: an inner theatre of sorts where early perverse pleasures are preserved.

15. The parody of Leigh Hunt is unmistakable, so that citations of 'Skimpole' unerringly remark how Dickens 'turned away' (*pervertere*) from his original (friend before writing *Bleak House*). Esther's position is rather more complicated. On one hand, she represents a kind of touchstone, who speaks for Dickens with authority; on the other, her discourse occasionally copies and is infected by Skimpole's. His versions of Providence, for instance, appear before hers (ch. 16, pp. 194–5 and ch. 18, pp. 226–7) and reappear in hers (ch. 18, p. 228) so that Esther's voice is doubled, turned back upon itself in parody. In such moments, her perspective does not coincide with Dickens's, but perversely turning aside from yet another father, she envisions an 'elsewhere' or produces another view.

16. Coincidentally, George's phantasm makes his appearance in the remarkable likeness of his nephew Watt (ch. 7, p. 79). The boy is an attentive listener to his grandmother's tale, a felt presence in her scene, and a significant reminder of another rebellion, which is commonly known under its paternal name of Tyler.

17. Peter Brooks, 'Freud's Masterplot: Questions of Narrative', in *Literature and Psychoanalysis, The Question of Reading: Otherwise*, ed. Shoshana Felman (Baltimore, MD, 1980), p. 292.

18. These (dis)appearances are piling up; taken together they make me wonder whether someone in *Bleak House* isn't having fun with the father: playing him along, in effect, on a string.

19. For another extended comparison between Esther and Snagsby, see Lowry Pei, 'Mirrors, the Dead Child, Snagsby's Secret and Esther', *ELN*, 16 (1978), 144–56.

20. See, for instance, 'Agency of the Letter', where Lacan suggests that 'metaphor occurs at the precise point at which sense emerges from [the] non-sense' of metonymy (*Ecrits*, p. 158); see also Brooks, 'Freud's Masterplot' (pp. 280–3). But Irigaray and Gallop similarly cite the disruptive effects of metonymy, which they configure as a feminine operation initially at odds with the phallic metaphor (Irigaray, 'Mechanics of Fluids', *This Sex*, pp. 109–11; Jane Gallop, *Reading Lacan* [Ithaca, NY, 1985], pp. 124–7 – initially, because Gallop goes on to deconstruct the opposition between the two (pp. 131–2). Irigaray further affiliates metaphor with counting and metonymy with all that offers 'resistance to the countable' ('Mechanics', p. 111) or – as I prefer to think of it in *Bleak House* – with what (un)erringly messes up accounts.

21. Ragussis, 'Ghostly Signs', pp. 279–80.

22. Jacques Derrida, 'Fors', trans. Barbara Johnson, *Georgia Review*, 31: I (1977), 91. Coincidentally, the deconstructive writing of 'ghost effect' originated with the deceased poet-analyst, Nicolas Abraham, who reappears in Derrida's text as (g)host.

23. The phrase is Catherine Belsey's from her 'Constructing the Subject: Deconstructing the Text', *Feminist Criticism and Social Change*, ed. Deborah Rosenfelt and Judith Newton [(New York, 1985), p. 56 – Ed.], where she describes classical realism in general.

24. But see also Michael Ragussis, 'The Ghostly Signs of *Bleak House*' in *Acts of Naming: The Family Plot in Fiction* (New York, 1986), pp. 87–109, who discusses Mrs Snagsby's slip at length.

9

Esther's Will

TIMOTHY PELTASON

Some critics have described and praised and blamed Esther's self-denial, and Dickens's representation of it, on a variety of grounds.[1] I would like in this essay to trace out the counter-drama of Esther's growing self-assertion, arguing both for the power and interest of Esther's language and for the presence in Dickens of an alternative current of argument that stresses the importance not of transcending, but of discovering, the personal will.[2] Such a tracing must also include a substantial discussion of John Jarndyce, on Esther's account 'a superior being' (p. 934) and a moral exemplar, but an example she clearly does well not to follow – or to marry. Without claiming, or even wishing, to resolve all the contradictions of *Bleak House* and make all of its signs point in one direction, I do want to close at least part way the often-noted gap between the ideal of human character suggested by the hesitant, self-questioning heroes and heroines whom Dickens often seems to be recommending to us in his later novels and the alternative ideal, everywhere embodied in his novels, of his own superb and vital wilfulness.[3]

Every reader has noticed the relentlessness of Esther's self-depreciation, though not many have remarked the power and plausibility of Dickens's portrait of her or its relationship to a larger pathology of selflessness in the novel. This selflessness takes the form sometimes of a failure in vitality, as when Esther notes of Jo, weak and wandering with smallpox, that he 'was strangely unconcerned about himself, if I may say so strange a thing' (p. 488). The strangeness, of course, is that Esther should find it strange, for she too must struggle, both in sickness and in health, to be sufficiently interested in herself. Just before meeting Jo, the unwitting cause of her illness and of her meeting with Lady Dedlock – of her self-transformation and her self-discovery – Esther has had a premonition. 'I have always remembered since, that when we had stopped at the garden-gate to look up at the sky, and when we went upon our way, I had for a moment an undefinable impression of myself as being something different from what I then was' (pp. 484–5). This is at once premonitory of Esther's illness and typical of a removal from herself that defends against desire. [...] Both Esther's father and her mother are virtual suicides, and the novel presents one after another case study in the difficulty of combining goodness of heart with a sufficiently robust will to live. Selfishness and self-importance are apparently adequate motives for continued survival, but the good-hearted are often low on fuel or culpably timid. Even so generous and hearty a specimen as George Rouncewell has retreated from life and family, offering his own unworthiness as an excuse.

In Esther's case, those around her conspire in the process by which her selfhood is diffused, making arch play with Woodcourt's romantic interest in her (his flowers were left by 'Somebody') and, most memorably and repeatedly, by assigning her so many matronly nicknames 'that my own name soon became quite lost among them' (p. 148). Esther's 'self' thus becomes a function of the roles she plays in the household economy and her nicknames a conveniently transparent screen for her acknowledgement that she has, indeed, won the love of others. Esther finds it not only better, but far, far easier to give than to receive.

At its most extreme and self-censoring, Esther's inability to take things for herself verges on an inability to express any desire, or even to want anything. So perfect in contentment does she wish to be that she cannot bring herself, even at Jarndyce's invitation, to express any curiosity about her origins: 'I have nothing to ask you; nothing in the world' (p. 149). And later, when she encounters Allan Woodcourt after accepting Mr Jarndyce's marriage proposal, she strikes off this neat self-description: 'I have everything to be thankful for, and nothing in the world to desire' (p. 680). This would seem aggressive if it were not so clearly a kind of pep talk to herself; Esther's salvation is that the remark is so clearly untrue. To have nothing to desire would be to succumb to the death wish that she indulges briefly in her illness. But the story of Esther's narrative is the story of her progress in healthy self-love, and one function of her narrative is to express by whatever means the desires that she cannot otherwise acknowledge. It is when her desires are imperfectly suppressed that Esther's language comes most excitingly to life, possessed and energised by what can hardly be acknowledged, by her will to live and to have.

By the end of her first instalment, Esther is fixed as the tireless and compulsively generous attendant to the needs of others. Self-exiled to a supporting role in life, she reports without commentary an ambiguous remark by the Lord Chancellor in which he appears to cast her as the love-interest in the drama of Esther and Richard Carstone and Ada Clare. But Esther has also an odd and unaccountable strength. Timid, self-blaming, a kind of moral bully to herself, she cannot easily be bullied by others, and her removal from one kind of active life is also a form of power. Dizzy from the strangeness of her first, foggy day in London, she is, nevertheless, as conspicuously unawed by the Lord Chancellor as she is undeterred by the chaos of the Jellyby Household, which she encounters in chapter four.

In this first important venue for her ameliorative abilities, Esther reveals that her tentative solution to the difficulty of making a beginning is just to launch right in. She is ready for anything, as Mr Skimpole mock-enviously observes in the later case of Jo's arrival at Bleak House, and she has taken on the care of Peepy and Caddy Jellyby before her first night in London is through. But it is Caddy who also suggests an important limitation of Esther's readiness for anything in an exchange about the direction of their morning walk. When Esther responds to Caddy's inquiry by cheerfully declaring that she will go 'Anywhere, my dear', Caddy's sulky but shrewd assertion – 'Anywhere's nowhere' – is only partly answered by Esther's, 'Let us go somewhere, at any rate.' Esther's may be the best course in such a world of confusion. Like most of Dickens's admirable exponents of duty (a word she is quoting to Caddy very shortly after the exchange above) she owes something to the Carlyle (and to Goethe, whom he quotes) of *Sartor Resartus*: 'Let him who gropes painfully in darkness or uncertain light, and prays vehemently that the dawn may ripen unto day, lay this other precept well to heart, which to me was of invaluable service: "*Do the Duty which lies nearest thee*", which thou knowest to be a Duty! Thy second Duty will already have become clearer.'[4] But Esther and her companions lose their way in Chancery Lane – 'So, cousin ... We are never to get out of Chancery' is Richard's too cheerful and all too significant remark – and Caddy's point is made. A progress will require not just readiness, but direction.

Esther is soon enough out of London's maze and installed in Bleak House, where she quickly establishes herself as the loving centre of a well-ordered domestic system. Even at Bleak House, though, the limitations begin to declare themselves of a will that takes the form chiefly of willingness. The first and clearest such declaration is made by the story of Richard Carstone and his failure to find a suitable vocation. Not just Richard, but Skimpole, and the Honourable Bob Stables (who might have been a fine veterinarian if he had not been a Dedlock), and raft of Dedlock cousins, illustrate by negation the indispensability of a sense of vocation. When first queried about his choice of professions, Richard announces himself 'ready for anything' (p. 217), echoing the cheery, directionless 'Anywhere, my dear' of Esther's earlier response to Caddy. But he hasn't Esther's energy or persistence, and he soon speaks in an altered mood of his indifference between one profession and another, saying of medicine 'It's rather jog-trotty and humdrum. But it'll do as well as anything else' (p. 283). He has begun the long slide from Esther's brand of cheerful readiness to Harold Skimpole's, and on beyond it to a world-weariness that anticipates the levelling cynicism of another proud amateur, Henry Gowan of *Little Dorrit*. Skimpole has also trained as a doctor and has abandoned – has even, in the case of Jo, betrayed – his vocation. The figures of Allan Woodcourt, and, from *Little Dorrit*, of the significant minor character, Physician, indicate how grave a betrayal of promise both Skimpole and Richard have committed. Richard does not commit Skimpole's other sins, or Henry Gowan's either, and he never suffers the harsh judgement that Dickens and a sympathetic reader impose on Skimpole and Gowan. But he dramatises nevertheless the importance that Dickens attaches to vocation – to the concentration and dedication of purpose that come from choosing a life's work. Succumbing to the deathly allure of Chancery, Richard attends the will of others, rather than commanding a will of his own.

We need not believe that Esther is ever in any danger of emulating Richard in order to mark the occasional and disquieting congruences between his version and hers of a lack of forceful self-assertion. But they are there, even in the airy tribute to Esther's will that begins this essay. 'You are ready at all times to go anywhere and to do anything. Such is Will! I have no will ...' Ironies abound here, starting with Skimpole's disingenuous denial of what the reader soon recognises as his own powerful and focused will to survive. Bucket is characteristically penetrating on this point. 'Whenever a person proclaims to you "In worldly matters I'm a child", you consider that that person is only a-crying off from being held accountable, and that you have got that person's number, and it's Number One' (p. 832).[5] A further irony is that Esther's readiness for anything has extended even to the paying of Skimpole's debts. For Skimpole's own brand of selfish wilfulness depends absolutely upon the indiscriminately willing kindness of others, of Esther, of Richard, and, most important, of John Jarndyce.

John Jarndyce's character, in particular, and Esther's eerily and unwittingly ambiguous presentation of it, form a fascinating accompaniment to Esther's self-presentation and a significant part of Dickens's critique of the will. Jarndyce enters the novel as a bluff and hearty refugee from some earlier novel by Dickens, sounding more, in his first, unnamed appearance, like one of the Cheeryble brothers, or even like Lawrence Boythorn, than like his later self. He bestows plum-tarts, curses comically, and is provided with a tag phrase – 'Floored again!' – by which we may recognise him when he reappears at Bleak House. But this is soon dropped, as are two other of the tics that are on prominent display in his first, named appearance – an unwillingness to be thanked and a habit of recognising unpleasantness obliquely, by reference to the East Wind.

If Dickens quickly leaves behind this purely comic mode of representing Jarndyce, it is not because he solves or forgets the problems of conduct and character with which these comic behaviours are implicated. Jarndyce's unwillingness to be thanked blends easily into Esther's book-long celebration of a charity that gives without taking, a love that wants nothing in return. Described in this way, of course, Jarndyce's character is strikingly similar to Esther's, whose own unreadiness to take credit shades over into the uneasiness she feels upon receiving any tokens of love or esteem. Jarndyce's peculiar relation to desire, whether viewed idealisingly, as transcendence, or de-idealisingly, as unhealthy suppression, renders him more awkward at making proposals than Esther is at receiving them.

Jarndyce's conceit about the East Wind (central enough to Dickens's early conception of the novel that it figured in several of the titles that he considered for it), interpreted by Esther as a generous unwillingness to pass judgement on others, is yet another evidence of his willed separation from the world of human wills and desires. Dickens clearly endorses this generosity over the alternative represented by Esther's aunt, Miss Barbary, who cannot listen to the story of the woman taken in adultery, but must rise up herself in wrathful judgement. And yet Jarndyce's inability to assign blame is less a helpless recognition of complexity and intractability (like Stephen Blackpool's 'It's aw' a muddle', in *Hard Times*, or Plornish the plasterer's conclusion in *Little Dorrit* that his tangled affairs are 'Nobody's fault') than a culpable evasion. A charity that extends itself equally to Esther and Skimpole, to Mrs Jellyby, Mrs Pardiggle, and Charley Neckett, dramatises once again the necessity of direction and discrimination.

One way in which the novel induces our uneasiness about Jarndyce's character is precisely by making him the voice of moral admonition. When Esther calls Jarndyce 'a superior being', she arouses a natural, fallen impulse in the reader to question his exalted status and to see through or around him. Jarndyce himself arouses such an impulse when he moralises to and about Richard and others on the importance of vocation. In so doing, he offers a view that the rest of the novel unquestionably supports, but offers it with a complacency and an apparent lack of self-awareness that begs for comment. Jarndyce himself follows no profession save for a kind of free-lance philanthropy, sometimes admirable in its effects, sometimes not, always well-motivated, but no different in kind from the timidly, guiltily proffered half-crowns of Mr Snagsby. Jarndyce's questions about Mrs Jellyby at his first meeting with Esther and Ada suggest that he is conducting an enquiry into the available forms of charity, but he gets no further than the Dickensian first principle that charity begins in the heart and then the home and radiates outwards. He seems neither to answer nor to ask how these principles are to be translated into action, so that his speeches on vocation, clearly endorsed by the rest of the novel, nevertheless beg to be turned against him. What does he do? the reader reasonably asks. To what calling does he devote himself with the energy and single-mindedness that he commends to Richard? Similarly, when he lectures Richard on the evils of Chancery and presents himself to Gridley as a model of resistance to its lures, he is faultlessly generous in his judgements, but oddly silent on a crucial difference between his situation and theirs – he has plenty of money and is thus spared both the need to find a calling and the temptation of the call of chancery. If Jarndyce is right to abandon the delusional search for a true and final judgement from the court of Chancery, he is something less than right, and something less than fulfilled, in his failure to embody his good-heartedness in work. For all his admirable role in bettering the lives of those around him, the novel compels us to ask whether he has discovered even for himself a mode of living that Dickens recommends.

Esther Summerson does more and does better. Charting a course through the densely peopled world of *Bleak House*, Esther gathers to herself plausible simulacra of the family and community her illegitimacy have at first barred her from, dramatising the fact that there are other choices and commitments to make than those of vocation, other forms that the concentration of energies can take. Good-heartedness collects and focuses itself not just in paid work, but in the acts of will that are required to form an intimacy, to fall in love, to make a home or a family.

In his remarkable essay on *Bleak House*, D. A. Miller has demonstrated how porous the division between the private and the public is in the novel. In Dickens's copiously documented case against Chancery practice, the public and institutional world of the law repeatedly invades and destroys the private world of the family and the still more private world of the psyche. Even away from Chancery, the public contaminates the private whenever a disastrously flawed judgement about the welfare of the public, like those of Mrs Jellyby or Mrs Pardiggle, is simultaneously a disastrously flawed judgement about the welfare of the family. Both D. A. Miller and J. Hillis Miller, before him, are particularly alert to the subtler and more pervasive ways that the very practice of copious documentation brings worryingly home to the novel-reader the dangerous excesses of Chancery. Esther herself is on several occasions 'a pattern' young lady, the heart of a well-functioning 'system'; her rage for order, her famous self-suppressions, and, most of all, her restless nervous energy can plausibly be viewed as the privatised extensions both of the regulatory functions and the busyness of the public world that Dickens deplores.[6]

But this only makes her occasional triumphs of self-expression and her general efficiency all the more remarkable and significant. On the one hand, the family is undefended from a discouraging variety of forms of exploitation – the Jarndyce and Gridley and Flite families are destroyed by Chancery; the Bucket family is entirely absorbed in police-work; the Vholes family is a marketing device. On the other, families are made as well as unmade in *Bleak House*, and the energy that goes into making them is an energy directed outwards, from the self into the world. Jarndyce and

Esther work together to make the families of the two Bleak Houses, families whose success outweighs, if it does not obscure, the anomalies of their constitution. And in spite of the sometimes queasy-making power that Jarndyce exercises over her will at crucial moments, Esther emerges as the more appropriately wilful of the two, as the one who is ready, finally, to acknowledge and to gratify her own desires.

Esther's initial unwillingness to acknowledge either her desire or her desirability leads to some peculiar displacements of feeling. When Mr Guppy first proposes to her, she rejects him quickly and self-assuredly, then busies herself at her desk, feeling 'so composed and cheerful that I thought I had quite dismissed this unexpected incident'.

> But, when I went upstairs to my own room, I surprised myself by beginning to laugh about it, and then surprised myself still more by beginning to cry about it. In short, I was in a flutter for a little while; and felt as if an old chord had been more coarsely touched than it ever had been since the days of the dear old doll, long buried in the garden.
>
> (p. 178)

This is one of several occasions in the novel when Esther's busyness takes on a slightly desperate quality, and on each of these occasions the source of her not-quite-mastered anxiety is in some degree erotic. She need not be tempted by Guppy's proposal in order to be flustered by the role in which it casts her. The mere possibility of entering into a relationship of mutually acknowledged desire returns her to the dear, but unresponsive, doll of her childhood: 'And so she used to sit propped up in a great arm-chair, with her beautiful complexion and rosy lips, staring at me – or not so much at me, I think, as at nothing –' (p. 62). The doll, buried by Esther when she leaves her godmother's house, just as she will later burn Allan Woodcourt's flowers to begin a new life as the betrothed of John Jarndyce, is at once an emblem of love, of its necessary one-sidedness, and of Esther's wilful suppression of her own desires.

Another erotic occasion, and a curious and beautiful episode in the history of Esther's career in love, is the moment when Esther first meets Ada after she has been disfigured by smallpox. Esther's first anxiety throughout her illness has been that Ada should be protected from infection. Ada wants to take care of Esther, Esther wants to take care of Ada, and Esther, typically, wins this competition of generosity, a competition that we never really see from

Ada's side, as she remains throughout the novel a mere sketch. But Esther indulges herself, too, by denying Ada her company even after her recovery. 'I hope it was not a poor thing in me to wish to be a little more used to my altered self, before I met the eyes of the dear girl I longed so ardently to see; but it is the truth. I did' (p. 549). Esther has not met even her own gaze – she has yet to look in the mirror – and she has just before her a series of highly charged encounters, little dramas of mutual acknowledgement between herself and her new face in the mirror, between herself and Lady Dedlock, though she does not yet know about this one, and between herself and Ada.

This last she defers until she has travelled to Mr Boythorn's for a period of rest and restoration. When Ada is at last to arrive, Esther grows frantic with anxiety, first walking out early to meet her, then rushing back, then finally caught by surprise and flustered into hiding. 'I was not in this slight distress because I at all repined', Esther explains to the reader, 'I am quite certain I did not, that day – but, I thought, would she be wholly prepared? When she first saw me, might she not be a little shocked and disappointed?' (p. 572). Here, as elsewhere in the novel, Esther lends out to others anxieties that she cannot acknowledge in herself, and her meeting with Ada will afford her another opportunity to meet her new self. She will look at Ada's face as she has looked, a few pages earlier, at the face in the mirror, a face that encouraged her when she saw 'how placidly it looked at me' (p. 559). And she will find out again how altered she is by looking into the mirror, this time the mirror of her beloved's eyes. In the event Ada (or is it Esther?) passes the test triumphantly: 'The old dear look, all love, all fondness, all affection. Nothing else in it – no nothing, nothing!' (p. 573). It is Ada's finest and most vivid moment in the novel:

> O how happy I was, down upon the floor, with my sweet beautiful girl down upon the floor too, holding my scarred face to her lovely cheek, bathing it with tears and kisses, rocking me to and fro like a child, calling me by every tender name that she could think of, and pressing me to her faithful heart.
>
> (p. 573)

For all the erotic energy with which Esther invests this episode – her nervous excitement, the charged drama of approach and avoidance, and this last, rapturous embrace – it does not seem to be an exploration, conscious or otherwise, of the possibilities of lesbian desire: at least, not unless lesbian desire is figured regressively as immaturity and narcissism. Two other powerful currents of feeling flow through this ecstatic moment and help to explain what otherwise might seem its surplus of affect.

First there is its unremarked proximity (unremarked by Esther anyway) to another overwhelming moment, to Esther's discovery that Lady Dedlock is her mother. Esther's embrace with Ada comes at the end of a chapter in which she has seen her own, scarred face for the first time. And then, a few pages later, she encounters Lady Dedlock unexpectedly and suddenly sees 'a something in her face that I had pined for and dreamed of when I was a little child' (p. 563). Esther has seen Lady Dedlock's face once before and felt on that occasion that it was 'like a broken glass to me, in which I saw scraps of old remembrances' (p. 304). This time, the drama of recognition goes forward to its natural conclusion, and Esther and her mother have the one emotionally wrenching encounter of their lives.

What is striking about this encounter is how little scope it offers to Esther's own needs and desires and, thus, how little it partakes of the special power and interest of Esther's language at its finest. Lady Dedlock is the featured performer, and the performance is pure melodrama. Esther meanwhile operates entirely in the mode of overcompensating generosity. Thus, her first thought, after Lady Dedlock has briefly 'compassionated' her and begged her forgiveness, is one of near-literal self-effacement: 'I felt, through all my tumult of emotion, a burst of gratitude to the providence of God that I was so changed as that I never could disgrace her by any trace of likeness; as that nobody could ever now look at me, and look at her, and remotely think of any near tie between us' (p. 565).

This peculiar and excessive reaction sets the tone for the whole encounter, which focuses exclusively on Lady Dedlock's sufferings and in which Esther accepts Lady Dedlock's valuation of events without commentary or any sign of inward dissent. 'She put into my hands a letter she had written for my reading only; and said, when I had read it, and destroyed it – but not so much for her sake, since she asked nothing, as for her husband's and my own – I must evermore consider her as dead' (p. 566). Esther does not ask, nor is the reader encouraged by any obvious sign to ask, how it is for Esther's sake that she must be abandoned a second time by the mother she has just met.

We are to assume, I suppose, that Lady Dedlock is protecting Esther from the stain of publicly acknowledged illegitimacy.

Throughout his novels, Dickens treats his fallen women – or at least he has his fallen women treat themselves – as if their sins barred them forever from the society of all decent people. But there are also decent people in these novels – Sir Leicester Dedlock and Esther among them – who clearly disagree, though without ever formulating an explicit criticism of the rigid moral orthodoxy from which they are dissenters. 'My duty', says Esther, 'was to bless her and receive her, though the whole world turned from her, and ... I only asked her leave to do it' (p. 565). To ask why Lady Dedlock does not flout public opinion and offer to Esther the mother-love she claims to feel is to go beyond the bounds of Esther's imagination, and apparently of Dickens's, and off into the regions of a novel we probably don't care to read and of the extra-literary space where Lady Macbeth's children are numbered. But it is also to mark the critically relevant limitations of this central scene and to take some measure of the pent-up emotional needs that burst forth elsewhere in Esther's narrative.

In this encounter with her mother, those needs are not a topic. Lady Dedlock was 'nearly frantic' (p. 566) during Esther's illness, and she is nearly frantic in this encounter, too, repeatedly asking the forgiveness of her 'injured child' (p. 568). But she does not inquire at all into the extent of Esther's injuries or ask what her life has been, and she leaves her with this last, self-regarding display:

> 'My child, my child!' she said. 'For the last time! These kisses for the last time! These arms upon my neck for the last time! We shall meet no more. To hope to do what I seek to do, I must be what I have been so long. Such is my reward and doom. If you hear of Lady Dedlock, brilliant, prosperous, and flattered, think of your wretched mother, conscience-stricken, underneath that mask! Think that the reality is in her suffering, in her useless remorse, in her murdering within her breast the only love and truth of which it is capable! And then forgive her, if you can; and cry to Heaven to forgive her, which it never can!'
>
> (p. 568)

She is her sister's sister – 'We held one another for a little space yet, but she was so firm, that she took my hands away' – and this scene eerily echoes the one to which Esther, in her own imagination, soon returns, the scene in which Miss Barbary refuses her embrace and first tells her of the sin that Heaven cannot forgive. And after each of these scenes, Esther doubts her right to be alive: 'I ... felt so sensible of filling a place in her house which ought to have been empty' (p. 66); 'So strangely did I hold my place in this world, that, until within a short time back, I had never, to my own mother's knowledge, breathed – had been buried – had never been endowed with life – had never borne a name' (p. 569). When she thinks of her mother, Esther feels a 'terror of myself' (pp. 569, 571, and again on p. 647), and she succumbs for a moment to the belief 'that it was wrong, and not intended, that I should then be alive' (p. 569).

With the morning, and with letters from Ada and John Jarndyce, comes 'a better condition', described at first in these rather pat terms: 'For I saw very well that I could not have been intended to die, or I should never have lived; not to say should never have been reserved for such a happy life. I saw very well how many things had worked together, for my welfare' (p. 571). The real drama of recovery and rebirth is not enacted until just after this pious paragraph, in all of Esther's nervous agitation about her reunion with Ada, and in the embrace that is the more moving and extraordinary when it is seen as the fulfilment of all that was unaccomplished and unattempted in Esther's interview with her mother. For it is only in Ada's embrace, at last and for a moment, that Esther can cease to be the comforter and caregiver and receive the loving ministrations of a mother. The eruption of feeling in that passage, with Ada 'holding my scarred face to her lovely cheek, bathing it with tears and kisses, rocking me to and fro like a child', is not from the seat of sexual desire, but from the unfulfilled longings of the child.

I have said that two currents of feeling flow through this passage, the first from Esther's special needs as an unloved child. The second comes from a tendency in Esther I have already remarked, to cast Ada as a kind of alternative self, projecting onto her anxieties and desires that Esther cannot acknowledge, and conferring on her a privilege of desiring and being desired that Esther will not claim. 'How does my own Pride look?' (p. 497) Esther asks Charley from her sickbed, and she begins a later chapter with this arresting clause: 'One morning, when I had done jingling about with my baskets of keys, as my beauty and I were walking round and round the garden' (p. 670). Ada is the justly proud self, the beautiful self, an identification that Esther's scars only confirm. Esther can love and admire Ada, can see her loved and admired, without apology or awkwardness. For the reader, Ada is shadow to Esther's substance, but for Esther, it is Ada who represents her in the substantial, public world of wills and desires.

The special psychic uses to which Esther puts Ada are nowhere more evident than in the course of her engagement to John Jarndyce. Although Esther does not permit herself to regret this engagement, she permits Ada to regret it for her. 'It came into my head', Esther says, when she sees that Ada is hiding something from her – in fact, her secret marriage to Richard – 'that she was a little grieved – for me – by what I had told her about Bleak House' (p. 742). How this came into her head, Esther cannot imagine: 'I was not grieved for myself; I was quite contented and quite happy.' And when she asks 'What could I do to reassure my darling ... and show her that I had no such feelings?' she answers with a resolution 'to be doubly diligent and gay' and sets about reassuring herself with the busyness that is so frequently the sign of her own quickened and unacknowledged desires: 'So I went about the house, humming all the tunes I knew; and I sat working and working in a desperate manner, and I talked and talked, morning, noon, and night' (p. 742).

It is appropriate that Ada's marriage to Richard is the proximate, if concealed, cause of this flutter, for Esther has made Ada's romantic and sexual nature a symbol of her own. How else to make sense of the strange and beautiful moment in which Esther decides to accept Jarndyce's proposal and then to destroy the flowers that Allan Woodcourt has once given her? But first she steals in to the room where Ada is sleeping:

> It was weak in me, I know, and I could have no reason for crying; but I dropped a tear upon her dear face, and another, and another. Weaker than that, I took the withered flowers out, and put them for a moment to her lips. I thought about her love for Richard; though, indeed, the flowers had nothing to do with that. Then I took them into my own room, and burned them at the candle, and they were dust in an instant.
>
> (p. 669)

Putting the flowers to Ada's lips, Esther says goodbye to the romantic ambitions that only the beautiful self can ever have entertained. Through Ada, her licensed emissary in the world of youthful, romantic desire, Esther renounces her place in the world. But in the rest of this chapter, 'The Letter and the Answer', Esther makes a touchingly muted, but still significant, gesture in the direction of reclaiming this place.

The previous chapter has ended with Esther's revelation to Jarndyce of her true parentage and with Esther wondering 'How could I ever be busy enough, how could I ever be good enough, how in my little way could I ever hope to be forgetful enough of my self, devoted enough to [Mr Jarndyce], and useful enough to others, to show him how I blessed and honoured him' (pp. 662–3). Jarndyce will show her a way, but he is so concerned not to take advantage of Esther's gratitude that he mediates and moderates his proposal until it has no romantic conviction at all, none of the face-to-face urgency of romantic desire. He first warns Esther that he has something on his mind, then asks if he may write to her about it, then asks her to look into his face and be sure that she sees no sign there of any suppression of feeling or that his 'old protecting manner' (p. 665) could ever change. Only then does he say that Esther can send Charley to him for the letter and, at that, not for a week, in spite of Esther's protestations that she believes and trusts him.

Once before in the novel Jarndyce has sent Charley to Esther with a message of love, when she first appears as Esther's maid. 'If you please, miss, I'm a present to you, with Mr Jarndyce's love' (p. 389). And again, 'If you please, miss, I am a little present with his love, and it was all done for the love of you. Me and Tom was to be sure to remember it' (p. 390). To give one person to another is an act of godlike power – or, at least, of fatherly presumption – and Jarndyce will do it again, when he gives Esther to Woodcourt at the end of the novel. But Jarndyce is neither a god nor a father and in making his charity to Charley a function of his love for Esther, he disturbingly blends caritas and eros and reveals the suppressed human desire that is often at work behind paternalistic benevolence. The benevolence is real, in this case, but the blend is an awkward one. When Jarndyce later tells Esther of 'the old dream I dreamed when you were very young, of making you my wife some day' (p. 913), he unsettles us once again – just how young is very young? – by bringing together the two kinds of love, the fatherly and the erotic. Jarndyce himself has been unsettled by this; his feelings for Esther have been a clearly signalled 'trouble' to him (pp. 289, 291) since early in the novel.

Jarndyce resolves his trouble by attempting to suppress completely his own desires, but this leads to other deformities of behaviour, such as the desireless marriage proposal of 'The Letter and the Answer'. When the week has elapsed, Esther sends Charley promptly for the letter, which asks her not if she will be Jarndyce's wife but, in another mediating gesture, 'would I be the mistress of

Bleak House' (p. 666). 'It was not a love letter', Esther goes on to say, but a letter full of love, written in Jarndyce's 'kind protecting manner', and assuring her 'that I would gain nothing by such a marriage, and lose nothing by rejecting it; for no new relation would enhance the tenderness in which he held me' (p. 666). Presenting his case 'as if he were indeed my responsible guardian, impartially representing the proposal of a friend' (p. 667), Jarndyce tries to purge his proposal of the taint of self-interest. But to be utterly without self-interest, if it is not a hypocritical pretence, as is often the case when Dickens's characters regard themselves in the third person, is some other and subtler form of failure in living. When George Rouncewell is accused of murder and refuses to engage a lawyer in his own defence, in spite of Jarndyce's earnest advice that he do so, he embarrasses Jarndyce by confronting him with the lived consequences of his own precepts. Jarndyce's rather lame effort to distinguish between criminal law and equity hardly mitigates the awkwardness of his new position, and he finds himself suddenly and peculiarly an advocate for the law.[7] More peculiarly, the novel suggests that he is right. At least, Trooper George is surely wrong to hold his own life so cheap. His principled refusal to fight for his life is consistent with the mistaken principle that has kept him for years from seeing his mother, on the grounds that he is unworthy. This failure to value himself is really a failure in generosity, as is his later insistence on being 'scratched' from his mother's will, a gesture of self-effacement that puts his own compulsive modesty before his mother's pleasure in giving. It is the perfect Jarndycean gesture – refusing to be named in a will – now exposed as both a denial of self and a refusal of relatedness. For the question of wills is ultimately a question of relationship between generations, a question that the novel puts to Jarndyce by raising, only to deny, the possibility of his having a sexual life.

Returning now to the terms of Jarndyce's proposal to Esther, we may reasonably ask what sort of will is behind it and what sort of relationship it proposes. Telling Esther that she would 'gain nothing by such a marriage, and lose nothing by rejecting it', and that 'no new relation could enhance the tenderness in which he held' her, Jarndyce offers, if not a sexless marriage, at least a sexless proposal. In his effort to suppress all guilty self-assertion, Jarndyce asks for nothing and offers nothing.

But Esther's response is quite different. She begins by thinking that she will marry Jarndyce in order to thank him, and then, overwhelmed as always by the proximity of desire, she cries for the loss of something that she cannot name even to herself as the possibility of a full romantic and sexual life with Woodcourt. She feels 'as if something for which there was no name or distinct idea were indefinitely lost to me. I was very happy, very thankful, very hopeful, but I cried very much' (p. 668). Chastising herself into a better mood, she pronounces what sounds like a terminal sentence: 'And so Esther, my dear, you are happy for life' (p. 668).

But she also struggles to engage her own self-interest in this inner discussion: 'I thought all at once, if my guardian had married some one else, how should I have felt, and what should I have done! That would have been a change indeed' (p. 668). And then, when she has determined to accept Jarndyce's proposal and burned Woodcourt's flowers, she is ready to meet Jarndyce in a new and eager way and to alter the terms of their relationship. Renouncing Woodcourt, she has not renounced desire. I must quote at length from the quietly vibrant passage that ends this chapter in order to capture the sense of Esther's timid urgency and of Jarndyce's frustrating failure of response.

> On entering the breakfast-room next morning, I found my guardian just as usual; quite as frank, as open, and free. There being not the least constraint in his manner, there was none (or I think there was none) in mine. I was with him several times in the course of the morning, in and out, when there was no one there; and I thought it not unlikely that he might speak to me about the letter; but he did not say a word.
>
> So, on the next morning, and the next, and for at least a week; over which time Mr Skimpole prolonged his stay, I expected, every day, that my guardian might speak to me about the letter; but he never did.
>
> I thought then, growing uneasy, that I ought to write an answer. I tried over and over again in my own room at night, but I could not write an answer that at all began like a good answer; so I thought each night I would wait one more day. And I waited seven more days, and he never said a word.
>
> (p. 669)

Esther determines at last that she must act, and she comes down 'on purpose' to ask Jarndyce when he would like an answer to his letter. Even then, with Esther before him, he will betray no eagerness and blandly asks her if Charley will bring him the answer:

> 'No, I have brought it myself, Guardian', I returned.
> I put my two arms round his neck and kissed him; and he said was this the mistress of Bleak House; and I said yes; and it made no

difference presently, and we all went out together, and I said nothing
to my precious pet about it.

(p. 670)

'It made no difference presently.' But surely Esther's decision
ought to make a difference, a difference that she tries to signal by
coming forward frankly to kiss Jarndyce, her 'two arms' indicating
the fullness and directness of this embrace. Her later anxieties about
the engagement – the anxieties that she can acknowledge only by
projecting them onto Ada – are a manifestation of her regrets over
Woodcourt, but also of her regret that her relationship with
Jarndyce has not changed its character. When Ada's marriage to
Richard has been revealed, Esther is liberated to express her parallel
desires, albeit in her own special mode of timid self-criticism. 'Bleak
House is thinning fast', Jarndyce remarks to her:

> 'But its mistress remains, Guardian.' Though I was timid about
> saying it, I ventured because of the sorrowful tone in which he had
> spoken. 'She will do all she can to make it happy', said I.
> 'She will succeed, my love!'
> The letter had made no difference between us, except that the seat
> by his side had come to be mine; it made none now. He turned his old
> bright fatherly look upon me, laid his hand on my hand in his old
> way, and said again, 'She will succeed, my dear. Nevertheless, Bleak
> House is thinning fast, O little woman!'
> I was sorry presently that this was all we said about that. I was
> rather disappointed. I feared I might not quite have been all I had
> meant to be, since the letter and the answer.

(p. 757)

By now, Jarndyce has begun the process of self-examination that
will lead him eventually to surrender Esther to Woodcourt, and it is
difficult to say whether selflessness or sexual fear is the right name
for his resistance to Esther's advances here. Her bafflement at the
end of 'The Letter and the Answer' has ripened into disappoint-
ment, in a passage whose tone and pace and significant wording
echo the earlier one. The letter has 'made no difference' in her relations with Jarndyce, and Esther has been frustrated in the transition
to a fuller, more sexualised relationship, a transition that she is
gamely, touchingly ready to make. In all the months of her engagement to Jarndyce, Esther tells us, the fact of their being engaged is
mentioned only twice, each time by her (p. 893). On the second of
these occasions, as on the first, she announces her eagerness to be

adequate to Jarndyce's desires, but Jarndyce has by now conceived and executed his plan for a second Bleak House, and he holds her in the old 'protecting manner' (p. 893), even as she kisses him 'just as I had done on the day when I brought my answer' (p. 894). Jarndyce's plan – simply to give Esther to Woodcourt without consulting or preparing her – is as unsettling as Esther's rapt, unquestioning acquiescence in it, and it is easy to imagine a future time when scholars attempt to explain away the peculiarity of this last gesture of benevolence by calling it a religious allegory, like Chaucer's *The Clerk's Tale*. Esther's faith and obedience have already been tested, in the night-time ride with Mr Bucket, when he carries her back towards London, away from her fleeing mother, she agitatedly thinks, but without telling her of his suspicion that her mother and Jenny have changed clothes. His silence on this point is arbitrary, but Esther keeps faith and is rewarded with his good opinion and with the tragic satisfaction of being the first to approach and to touch her mother's dead body at the gates of the pauper graveyard. Jarndyce tests her faith, too, sending her off on a journey to the new Bleak House, but without telling her where or why she is going. And he explains to her, after Woodcourt has materialised to receive her, that she has passed another test unawares by sacrificing her love to duty 'so perfectly, so entirely, so religiously' (p. 914) that Mrs Woodcourt could detect nothing of the effort that this sacrifice must have cost her. By suppressing her desire perfectly, Jarndyce seems to say, Esther has earned the right to have it gratified.

But we are surely close enough to know, as those future scholars may not be, that no religious allegory or anthropological reduction of 'the Victorian mind' can explain away the human strangeness of these events. And we have five hundred pages of testimony from the Griselda of this tale to demonstrate that she is not merely an allegory of obedience and self-sacrifice, but a struggling and desirous soul. 'What do I sacrifice?' Jarndyce asks as he deeds Esther to Allan Woodcourt, 'Nothing, nothing' (p. 915). But Jarndyce himself has just told us that he knows the hidden costs of an apparently free and full sacrifice, and his own sufferings can be inferred. In Esther's case, no inference is required, for we have seen her psychic economy in operation, seen the imperfectly suppressed desires that are the mark of her emergent will, a will to live, to love and be loved, to want and then to have.

Esther remains herself, and her triumphs are muted ones. She is not so wilful or self-assertive as to protest Jarndyce's presumption when he assures Woodcourt that she is 'a willing gift' (p. 915), a phrase that conflates her will with his own. Instead, the displaced erotic and assertive energy of this bizarre episode bursts forth in her excessive and near-heretical exaltations of Jarndyce – the new Bleak House is a new Eden, Jarndyce is haloed in light, and, at the climax, 'He rose, and raised me with him' (p. 915). And in the last pages of the book, she can only come close to the frankly self-admiring assertion that she is beautiful and worthy of the love she receives, an assertion that hovers beyond the margins of her last, interrupted sentence.

The new family that she has made, furthermore, is a melange of invented relationships – a willed and created thing, but a troublingly indeterminate one. Esther is a second mother to Ada's son, Ada is something else, as hard to specify as ever, to her, and Jarndyce – 'To Ada and her pretty boy, he is the fondest father' – but not really – and 'to me, he is what he has ever been, and what name can I give to that?' (p. 934). Awed as ever by Jarndyce's goodness, Esther invokes the ineffability topos, but, at the same time, focuses the reader's uneasiness about him. Esther has all of her old names, too, and there is no decisive emergence of her own name from among them. On the last half-page of the novel, Allan calls her 'My precious little woman', 'my dear', 'my busy bee', and 'My dear Dame Durden' – and never Esther. She has seemed to others to be ready for the renunciation of desire and for the new relationship with Jarndyce that 'made no difference' from the old. But Esther has asserted herself even so, laying claim to the affections of 'the unknown friend to whom I write' (p. 932), the same friend to whom she has confided her desires, however tentatively, and to whom she has dared to reveal her undeterred readiness for the human relationship that makes a difference.

Dickens has explicitly entered my narrative less often than he might have, in testimony to the achieved integrity of his creation, Esther Summerson. What an act of ventriloquism and art it is for the burstingly vital Dickens to have impersonated Esther Summerson for dozens of chapters and twenty months. But the distance between the two of them is not so great as it first appears. The force of self that I have looked for in Esther, under the names of the will and of desire, is coincident with the force that has created her and that goes by other names in the alternate narrative that I have scanted in my effort to bring Esther forward. The bafflement of desire in one narrative is the bafflement of imagination in the other, and the bafflement of the will in both. Think of Snagsby's 'meditative and poetical' (p. 181) musings, of the something in poor Guster 'that possibly might have been imagination' (p. 201), but has been distorted into fits, of Phil Squod's longings – 'I see the marshes once' (p. 420) – or of the stunted fancies of the Smallweeds. *Bleak House* is full of frustrated and displaced energies. Even Tulkinghorn, savouring his good port, has a secret sensuousness that offers the beginnings of an explanation for his apparently motiveless malignity.

But the healthy imagination is not just more free than all these. It is more generously interested in the world, a faculty of perception and penetration, as well as of free creation, focused and directed, as well as extravagant. The characters in *Bleak House* who most closely resemble their creator are the strange pair of Bucket and Esther Summerson, two penetrating observers. The one, Mr Bucket, who is never off duty and who even in the desperate all-night chase after Lady Dedlock is 'kept fresh by a certain enjoyment of the work in which he was engaged' (p. 837), is a guilty acknowledgement of how amorally curious and self-delighting the professional observer can be. And then there is Esther, who tells us in the first page of her narrative that she 'had always a rather noticing way' (p. 62), but also that her understanding is quickened by her affection; Esther, who represents the imagination as a power of sympathy, but also, and more embarrassingly, as a restless energy born of an unappeasable need.

From *English Literary History*, 59 (1991), 671–91.

NOTES

[This essay picks up on a Dickensian theme – lack of will – that was first noted by Lionel Trilling in 1953 in discussing *Little Dorrit*. By it, Peltason returns to the impotence of John Jarndyce (especially with reference to his philanthropy) and so many of the other figures of *Bleak House*, hobbled as they are by the 'will' of the old Jarndyce that speaks to future generations, patriarchally, from beyond the tomb as the voice of the primal father (so Freud discusses this in his *Totem and Taboo*). In contrast to such a 'will', that of John Jarndyce, in asking Esther to become mistress of Bleak House, is importantly sexless, non-generational, and denying Esther her own will, which may be interpreted as her sexual desire. ('Will' of course also puns on its older meaning – familiar in Shakespeare – of the will as phallic.) Perhaps Peltason is too quick to dismiss the idea of something lesbian in the Esther–Ada relationship, because his essay importantly reads the quiet assertiveness of Esther – her will to power – as being inseparable from the sexual, just as when he pairs Bucket and Esther together at the end as a composite portrait of Dickens. Esther's comment about her 'rather noticing way' not only makes her a detective, and aligns her with Bucket's amorality, but it also recalls the point that the detective, in classic psychoanalytic theorisations, is a voyeur, whose interest is in the primal scene, in the importance of the founding nature of the sexual, a knowledge systematically repressed (yet by that token produced) in her narrative. Quotations come from the Penguin 1971 edition. Ed.]

1. The most frankly evaluative, and negative, account of Dickens's portrayal of Esther, and one which I have kept in mind as a challenge throughout the writing of this essay, is from the influential book by Robert Garis, *The Dickens Theater* (Oxford, 1965). A central argument for Esther's success as a character on which I have relied is from Q. D. Leavis's chapter on *Bleak House*, in F. R. Leavis and Q. D. Leavis, *Dickens the Novelist* (New York, 1970) especially pages 154–60. I have also found extremely helpful and interesting Robert Newsom's pages on the uncanny in *Dickens on the Romantic Side of Familiar Things: 'Bleak House' and the Novel Tradition* (New York, 1977). A short bibliography of 'Esther studies' would also include William F. Axton. 'The Trouble with Esther', *Modern Language Quarterly*, 26 (1965), 545–57; Alex Zwerdling, 'Esther Summerson Rehabilitated', *PMLA*, 88 (1973), 429–39; Judith Wilt, 'Confusion and Consciousness in Dickens's Esther', *Nineteenth Century Fiction*, 32 (1977), 285–309; Suzanne Graver, 'Writing in a "Womanly" Way and the Double Vision of *Bleak House*', *Dickens Quarterly*, 4 (1987), 3–15; and Helena Michie, 'Who is This in Pain': Scarring, Disfigurement, and Female Identity in *Bleak House* and *Our Mutual Friend*', *Novel*, 22 (1989) 199–212.

2. The 'will' denominates a loose and baggy category in the philosophical and literary discussions of the last two centuries, and I won't be discovering in Dickens or concocting for myself a complicated, finely discriminated terminology of wills, but simply using the term in a variety of ways that I hope are responsibly answerable to Dickens's uses of it. For a more rigorous and panoramic account, see Michael G. Cooke, *The Romantic Will* (New Haven, CT, 1976), which offers warrant for the sense of the will as a kind of life-force, coincident with or underlying the imagination. Another line of argument, which would invoke Blake and Lawrence, uses the will as the name for a narrowing, more negatively viewed form of self-assertion. See Margery Sabin's chapter on *Women in Love* in *The Dialect of the Tribe: Speech and Community in Modern Fiction* (Oxford, 1987); and, with particular reference to Dickens, Leavis (note 1), pp. 229, 231. For a sense close to my own of Dickens's portrayal of the will in *Bleak House*, see J. Hillis Miller,

Charles Dickens: The World of His Novels, (Cambridge MA, 1958), pp. 217–19. The pun on 'will' was first noted, I think, by Joseph Fradin in 'Will and Society in *Bleak House*', *PMLA*, 81 (1966), 95–109. To my surprise, I don't find that it's been much noted since.

3. The central accounts of Dickensian self-contradiction in *Bleak House* are by Garis (note 1), who, for all his evident pleasure in the novel, finds it chiefly an index of failure in control and execution; by J. Hillis Miller, in his introduction to the Penguin *Bleak House* (Harmondsworth, 1971); and by D. A. Miller in 'Discipline in Different Voices: Bureaucracy, Police, Family, and *Bleak House*', in *The Novel and the Police* (Berkeley CA, 1988). I differ from Garis in finding these self-contradictions mostly assimilable to a coherent account of Dickens's conscious purposes in the novel. I differ from J. H. Miller's deconstructive reading and D. A. Miller's Foucauldian one in finding them assimilable to a more conventional definition of novelistic 'richness' and a more conventional account of the demands that novels make on readers. After their salutary (and certainly not identical) de-familiarisations of the experience of reading *Bleak House*, I have hoped to accomplish a salutary re-familiarisation, by seeing how far a psychologistic account of Esther's speech and motives and behaviour may go towards explaining and justifying, even celebrating, the undeniable peculiarities of *Bleak House*.

4. Thomas Carlyle, *Sartor Resartus*, ed. C. F. Harrold (New York, 1937), 196.

5. Dickens liked this joke enough to offer another version of it in *Hard Times*, where Tom Gradgrind is said to have been turned, by his father's educational system, into 'that not unheard of triumph of calculation that is always at work on the number one'. The linkage of Skimpole to Tom Gradgrind is no more unlikely than the linkage of both Gradgrinds to James Harthouse, a linkage that *Hard Times* insists upon and that is merely another way of reinforcing the connection between utilitarian calculation and dandyism as forms of the denial of responsibility. Turveydrop and Henry Gowan would fill out the picture.

6. On the 'enormous length' of *Bleak House* as a replication of the 'monstrous length' of *Jarndyce* v. *Jarndyce*, see D. A. Miller [p. 109, above – Ed.] On the internalisation of social suppressions and instabilities into family life and on the way Esther's psyche reproduces the mechanisms of policing, see D. A. Miller, pp. [117–19, above]. J. Hillis Miller, in his introduction to the Penguin *Bleak House* (note 3), [p. 49, above], remarks the ways that both Esther's and Jarndyce's behaviour reproduce some of the worrying features of Chancery practice, and remarks, in particular, Esther's participation in a vocabulary of 'system' and 'pattern' that has such ominous implications elsewhere in the novel. Garis (note 1), pp. 130–4, notes the ways that even 'good work' in the

novel – his examples are Charley Neckett, Phil Squod, and, at greatest length, John Rouncewell – is made to appear mechanical and systematic.

7. Garis (note 1), pp. 128–9, notes the awkwardness of Jarndyce's position, and of Dickens's, in this encounter.

10

Losing One's Place: Displacement and Domesticity in Dickens's *Bleak House*

KEVIN McLAUGHLIN

Like most good novels, Dickens's *Bleak House* invites us to consider its composition as a version of its theme: in this case, reading the novel involves following the logic of a narrative whose formal realisation turns on the consolidating of a family or a *house*. This association of the novel with domesticity is hardly limited to *Bleak House*. On the contrary, it shapes a whole strain of eighteenth- and nineteenth-century British novels that organise themselves by analogy to the home. Indeed, the formal ideal of domesticity may well be a fundamental literary *myth* linking, for instance, modern English novels to ancient Greek drama and epic.[1] And if the founding of a household may be considered the plot of plots in Western literature (or at least in one major strand of it – the 'comic'), it is not surprising that theoretical attempts to identify the fundamental newness of the novel have generally focused on the theme of displacement or homelessness. One thinks here of the tradition of 'philosophical' criticism, culminating in Lukács's *Theory of the Novel*, that has sought to think of the novel as the genre of 'transcendental homelessness'. Much of the critical debate about novels like *Bleak House* can be seen in terms of this conflict between the domestic analogy that organises the novel and the various figures of displacement that continue to guide important novel criticism.

Let us step back for a moment from the question of domesticity in literature and literary studies. For the home is not at all the exclusive domain of novels and literature. It is no accident, for example, that economics takes its name from the Greek word for household (*oikos*), or that politics is traditionally divided into 'domestic' and 'foreign'. Social theory in the broadest sense is indeed fundamentally marked by domestic form. Evidence of this basically defining, delimiting character of the home in Western culture can be found in its early Indo-European root *dem-*, which, according to Emile Benveniste, was used in a wide range of contexts to mean the delineation of inside and outside.[2] Some anthropological and linguistic research even indicates that the home may be the primal social form – the figure of form in the social domain. However, despite its fundamental importance in the social sciences, this formal or aesthetic feature of the home seems to remain largely taken for granted by social scientists. While economists may talk a great deal about households, for instance, rarely do they stop and reflect on the figurative character of the household itself – on the household as instituting a certain kind of form in the social world.[3]

This, I would argue, is precisely the question raised by a reading of a novel like *Bleak House*.[4] By addressing itself to the special reflection on domestic form in Dickens's novel, such a reading examines what may be considered the fundamental, and relatively unexplored, ground of the social sciences. I will begin my reading of *Bleak House* by analysing the crucial formal link in Dickens's novel between the home and the subject. To identify the special character of this link I will begin by comparing subjectivity in *Bleak House* to the 'self-estranged subject' of Hegel's *Phenomenology of the Spirit*. Having noted the perhaps surprising resemblance between these two subjects, I will then go on to show how on an institutional level, and specifically with regard to the home, Dickens's novel departs from Hegel's model. Since the 'philosophical' identification of the novel with 'homelessness' has in part derived from Hegel's description of the 'self-estranged subject', an analysis of subjectivity in *Bleak House* suggests the ongoing relevance of this speculative tradition for the study of social and institutional questions in nineteenth-century novels. A careful examination of domesticity in Dickens's novel also demonstrates, however, the need to refuse to grant priority to philosophy in these matters.

As in economics and politics, in novels the home is a source of definition and order. *Bleak House* opens with the threat posed to the institution of the home by the radical disorder of official legal institutions, specifically Chancery Court (itself 'at the heart' of an indefinite 'fog' and 'mud' in which even the most basic physical elements – earth, water, air – have lost their identity). Most damaging about the Court's challenge to domestic order, it seems, are the consequences it holds for individual subjects, who turn to the Court, rather than to hearth and home, for order; throughout the novel, we are introduced to characters who are effectively destroyed as subjects by the disorder of the Court. Most striking perhaps is Richard Carstone, whose indecision and procrastination reproduce on a subjective and individual level the institutional chaos of Chancery. By contrast, the possibility of a different mode of subjectivity – one that is bound to a more suitable institutional context than that to which Richard binds himself – is elaborated through the character of Esther Summerson, whose autobiographical account is interwoven with the novel's third-person narrative. Before analysing Esther as a subject, it should be noted that she is, from at least two perspectives, a paradigmatic autobiographical subject: Esther is both homeless and a woman.[5] For if, as Lukács has argued, the novel is founded on an interrogation of the 'homeless' biographical subject, then in the British novel this interrogation unfolds most prominently in connection with the female subject. Like narrators from Pamela to Jane Eyre, Esther occupies what is, as several commentators have shown, the highly ambiguous position of housekeeper or governess of Bleak House (i.e. she is neither wife, nor daughter, nor merely hired hand).[6] And, as with Jane Eyre, this ambiguity is heightened in Esther's case by her clouded family history. Thus, throughout most of the novel, uncertain of her family origins and unsure of her role at Bleak House, Esther leaves unanswered a marriage proposal by the fatherly John Jarndyce, her employer and benefactor. Through the character of Esther, then, the question of the subject is crucially linked to the question of the home and vice versa, just as the novel itself is in a formal sense profoundly connected to Esther's 'autobiography', which measures and delimits the narrative of *Bleak House*.

But what kind of subject is Esther?[7] This can perhaps best be answered through a reading of a key scene in the novel, one which might be called Esther's 'mirror stage'. At this point, Esther is recovering from a life-threatening fever which she and her helper, Charley, have caught from the crossing-sweeper, Jo, whom they had tried, unsuccessfully, to nurse back to health.[8] In other words, the disease had been acquired through what the novel holds up as a positive form of 'philanthropy' (a central theme of *Bleak House*). Thus, Esther's fever originates in an act involving contact and immediacy – one *communicates* contagious diseases – as opposed to what Dickens's third-person narrator ridicules throughout *Bleak House* as 'telescopic philanthropy' – that of Mrs Jelleyby, for instance, whose philanthropy operates from a distance, by *telecommunication*, we might say (the ceaseless letter-writing on behalf of African natives of Borrioboola-Gha). Esther survives the fever, but it disfigures her. Because of this, Charley has removed the looking glass from the room where Esther had been quarantined. In the following passage, however, she has gone to recuperate at Mr Boythorn's house where she finds herself in a room with a mirror. Esther's narrative runs as follows:

> I had not yet looked in the glass, and had never asked to have my own restored to me. I know this to be a weakness which must be overcome; but I had always said to myself that I would begin afresh, when I got to where I was now. Therefore I had wanted to be alone, and therefore I said, now alone, in my own room, 'Esther, if you are to be happy, if you are to have any right to pray to be true-hearted, you must keep your word, my dear.' I was quite resolved to keep it; but I sat down for a little while first, to reflect upon all my blessings. And then I said my prayers, and thought a little more. My hair had not been cut off, though it had been in danger more than once. It was long and thick. I let it down, and shook it out, and went up to the glass upon the dressing-table. There was a little muslin curtain drawn across it. I drew it back: and stood for a moment looking through such a veil of my own hair, that I could see nothing else. Then I put my hair aside, and looked at the reflection in the mirror, encouraged by seeing how placidly it looked at me. I was very much changed – O very, very much. At first, my face was so strange to me, that I think I should have put my hands before it and started back, but for the encouragement I have mentioned. Very soon it became more familiar, and then I knew the extent of the alteration in it better than I had done at first. It was not like what I had expected; but I had expected nothing definite, and I dare say anything definite would have surprised me. I had never been a beauty, and had never thought myself one; but I had been very different from this.[9]

What we have in this passage is a scene remarkably similar to the one characterised by the section of Hegel's *Phenomenology of the Spirit* entitled 'Self-Estranged Spirit, Education' (*Der sich entfremdete Geist. Die Bildung*) – the recognition or production of oneself as different or *fremd*, precisely 'strange', as Esther puts it: 'my face was so strange', she says.[10] Esther makes herself here the object of her own knowledge. This gesture is in a sense exemplary of her discourse throughout *Bleak House*. Esther's narrative begins in the novel, for instance, by emphasising, albeit unknowingly, self-knowledge: 'I have a great deal of difficulty in beginning to write my portion of these pages', she starts, 'for I know I am not clever' (p. 62). And her narrative ends the novel on an elliptical, reflexive note with the remark that her family 'can very well do without much beauty in me – even supposing –' (p. 935). Appropriately, then, in our passage here Esther starts by underlining her awareness of her own 'weakness' and then, even more to the point, describes a dialogue with herself that, as we learn later in the passage, was a key factor in enabling her to face her new self in the mirror (she 'started back' at first, she reports, then remembered her own 'encouragement' – encouragement derived, it seems, from her 'placid' reflection in the mirror, from her 'reflection' on her 'blessings' and also presumably from the hortatory promise she makes to herself of 'beginning afresh'). By presenting this dialogue with herself, Esther stages the reflexive gesture that founds her autobiographical narrative and the question of subjectivity which is its theme. Or, to phrase it in the grammatical terms favoured by Hegel, Esther makes herself the subject and the predicate of her narrative.[11] After she goes through with it, after she faces her disfigured self-image, it becomes 'more familiar', as she puts it, through the knowledge of its disfiguration or 'alteration'. And, in keeping with the dialectical character of this passage, Esther writes that, though her self-image was 'unexpected', the fact that it was unexpected was not. What was really unexpected, it turns out, was 'anything definite'. And rightly so, since it is indeed the persistent indefiniteness of Esther's self-image – the self-difference she notes in the final sentence of this passage – that drives her narrative forward to its last elliptical phrase.

In this passage, however, another important dimension of this indefiniteness is invoked, specifically through the figure of the veil (in fact there are two veils present – the 'muslin curtain' and the 'veil of [Esther's] own hair'). In confronting a veil before her own reflection (in veiling herself), Esther meets in effect a figure of her own mother, whose identity is still unknown to her at this point in the novel. For the figure of the veil is repeatedly associated in *Bleak House* with Lady Dedlock, who has worn a veil in a key scene earlier in the novel, in which she visits the half-buried corpse of her former lover, Captain Hawdon, in the company of the crossing-sweeper Jo. In fact, Lady Dedlock is veiled in several respects in the novel. Her expression, for instance, is described as veiled – she conceals her thoughts behind a shroud-like veil suggested by her name (Dedlock). But this veiled expression is the sign of another veiling in the novel – namely, the false shroud figuratively placed over the baby she conceived with Captain Hawdon (Esther). Lady Dedlock had been deceived by her sister into believing that the baby had died at birth. When Esther sees the veil of her own hair in this passage, then, it is in fact a particular aspect of her own identity – her relation to her mother, Lady Dedlock – that is veiled, that presents itself as a veil. But if in viewing this veil, Esther sees and does not see her mother, she is, in drawing it back, brought into a similar kind of confrontation with her father. For what Esther unwittingly sees in her disfigured face is in fact, as we know from her retrospective narration, a trace of her dead father – the mark of a disease that has travelled to her by way of Jo from Tom-all-Alone's, where the corpse of her father (Captain Hawdon) lies half-buried.

The implications of all this mirroring become clearer several pages later in an exchange between Lady Dedlock and Esther. Lady Dedlock has discovered some time previously that Esther is her daughter. With this knowledge she approaches Esther. She is carrying a handkerchief that Esther had placed over another dead baby – that of a local brickmaker – earlier in the novel. Esther's account runs as follows:

> I cannot tell in any words what the state of my mind was, when I saw in her [Lady Dedlock's] hand my handkerchief, with which I had covered the dead baby. I looked at her; but I could not see her, I could not hear her, I could not draw my breath. The beating of my heart was so violent and wild, that I felt as if my life were breaking away from me. But when she caught me to her breast, kissed me, wept over me, compassionated me, and called me back to myself; when she fell on her knees and cried to me, 'O my child, my child, I am your wicked and unhappy mother! O try to forgive me!' – when I saw her at my feet on the bare earth in her great agony of mind, I felt, through all my tumult of emotion, a burst of gratitude to the providence of God that I was so changed as that I never could disgrace her by any trace of likeness; as that nobody could ever now look at me, and look at her, and remotely think of any near tie between us.
>
> (p. 565)

Here, the character of Esther's self-recognition, the issue of her identity as a subject, is somewhat clarified. At the beginning of this scene she is in darkness (she 'could not see [Lady Dedlock]'); she does not know her relation to Lady Dedlock, she does not know herself, we might say (Lady Dedlock 'calls [her] back to [herself]'). Accordingly, in the course of the passage Esther discovers who she is – she is the daughter of Lady Dedlock. But what is most emphasised in this passage from Esther's account is once again the disfiguration of the disease that sets her apart from her mother, for whom she has in fact been mistaken several times in the novel (including, obsessively, by Jo). If this passage begins with the strange terror of recognition (or of resemblance) that Esther feels at the sight of, as she says, 'my handkerchief in her hand', then the scene closes with the relief and 'gratitude' caused by the realisation that her disfiguration has destroyed 'any trace of likeness'. In other words, a resolution to the question of Esther's identity comes to her as a threat (to her and to Lady Dedlock); its approach makes her feel, as she says, 'as if my life were breaking from me'. It follows then that preserving this 'life', the life of her subject, we might say, depends on another kind of break – the breaking action of the subject dramatised in these two passages as Esther is set apart first from herself and then from her mother.

But why, we might ask, should this return of Esther's familial origins at a crucial stage in her subjective development come in the form of the breaking and disfiguration of a contagious disease? Here it is useful to elaborate a bit further the parallel to Hegel's 'self-estranged subject', which is also characterised by a certain contagion. Turning briefly to the passage from the *Phenomenology* on 'self-estranged spirit', we find ourselves in the historical situation of irony which, we recall, Lukács identifies with the novel as a genre. At this point in the development described in the *Phenomenology*, a crucial disjunction has emerged between individual and universal, the latter of which is represented by the mere conventionality or legality of Roman culture (the individual as 'legal entity', we might say). This artificial legality cannot contain spirit's self-estrangement (irony), which Hegel describes as essentially linguistic in character ('This estrangement though occurs alone in *language*, which appears here in its essential meaning').[12] It is this situation that generates the process of *Bildung* – the dynamic movement of self-estranged spirit as it assumes and discards conventional forms. The proliferating exchanges between individual ('*Ich*') and general that make up *Bildung* are characterised as follows:

The *I* is *this* I – but likewise *universal*; its appearance is likewise imme-diately the depropriation and the disappearance of *this* I and thereby its remaining in its universality. The *I* that expresses itself is *appre-hended*; it is an illumination [*Ansteckung*] in which it goes over imme-diately into the unity with that for which it exists and is universal self-consciousness. – That it is *apprehended*, therein does its *existence* itself immediately *fade away*; this its otherness is taken back into itself; and just this is its existence, as self-conscious *Now*, as it is there not to be there and through this disappearance to be there. This disappear-ance is thus itself its remaining; it is its own self-knowing and its self-knowing as that which has gone over into another self – that which has been apprehended and is universal.

(p. 376)

Such is the mode of being specific to *Bildung*, the *language* of self-estranged spirit. Here, appearing (*Erscheinen*) is a disappearing (*Verschwinden*) or, as Hegel suggestively puts it, a depropriation (*Entäusserung*); being heard or perceived (*vernommen werden*) is fading away (*verhallt werden*); being there (*Da-sein*) is not to be there (*nicht da zu sein*). It is precisely this dis-appearing, this absence, Hegel explains, that constitutes being there (*da zu sein*), or remaining (*Bleiben*). Thus *Bildung* is '*eine Ansteckung*': an illumi-nation or a lighting (as of a fire) that is a going out, and in fact a 'going over' (*übergehen*) into a specific mode of universal self-consciousness. Even if this illuminating process belongs to the Enlightenment (*Auklärung*) within Hegel's historical scheme, it cannot help but bring to mind the self-cancelling movement of *Aufhebung* itself that guides the *Bildung* of *Geist* as narrated by the *Phenomenology*. Indeed, the essentially linguistic character of self-estranged spirit's *Ansteckung* also recalls the description of specula-tive reason as such, which is likewise presented in terms of language in the 'Preface' – the 'subject' and 'predicate' of the 'speculative sen-tence'. The wider effects of this similarity between the illumination of self-estranged spirit and the movement of spirit as such seriously complicates the seemingly straightforward historical pattern of the *Phenomenology*.

But what concerns us most here is the resemblance self-estranged spirit bears to Esther, and in particular the mode of self-conscious-ness they seem to share. Both involve the recognition of self as 'strange'. But beyond that, enlightenment is also associated in both cases with contagion. In the *Phenomenology* this association is appropriately conveyed by the word *Ansteckung*, which means not just illumination or lighting but also infection. *Bildung*, the

Enlightenment stage of the spirit's self-recognition, is characterised by mimesis, the contagious effects of which Hegel demonstrates in his famous reading of Diderot's portrait of Rameau's nephew. It is undoubtedly this mimetic component of *Bildung* that accounts for the contaminated character of the self-estranged subject's recognition, which is not pure illumination but illumination combined with infection (*Ansteckung*). And indeed one could hardly select a more appropriate figure for infection than the potentially limitless multiplication of mimesis, which is since Plato the anti-philosophical contagion *par excellence*.[13]

Even more interesting than this traditional 'philosophical' blend of mimesis and Enlightenment in Hegel's inventive use of the word *Ansteckung* here is the link it suggests between this entire constellation and domesticity. For as it turns out, the metaphorical mixture of illumination and contagion available in the German word *Ansteckung* is itself based on a domestic analogy. The signification contagion or infection derives from the common use of the word *Ansteckung* to describe the setting of houses on fire: a contagion spreads like a fire from house to house.[14] Thus, *Ansteckung* is in a very precise sense a figure of homelessness. What puts an end to the spread suggested by this figure is a process of conversion, whereby the contagious house-fire of self-estrangement becomes subject to a purer flame – *Geist*, which, as Hegel tells us in this same section, is a 'consuming flame'.[15] *Geist*, it seems, will not proceed in a way comparable to an exchange between discrete households, the contaminating economic connotations of *Aufhebung* notwithstanding. Indeed, it is precisely this new movement of light and fire as it 'destroys' the 'solid ground' of mere 'formal thinking' that the *Phenomenology* conceives as the instituting of *Geist*, which in its continuous unfolding through history consumes all other institutions.[16] And it is such an emphatic movement, itself a form of 'transcendental homelessness' (as distinct from the mere homelessness of *Ansteckung*), that oversees the self-estranged subject of the *Phenomenology*.

With Hegel in mind, then, let us return to this question in *Bleak House*. We can now see that there is a similar association of contagion, self-consciousness and domesticity in Esther's case. It is as though a contagion emerges out of the failure of her parents to consummate their marriage, a contagion that reaches her at the centre of her autobiographical *Bildungsroman*, which in fact nearly destroys the crucial possibility for a new healthy household which would be called 'Bleak House'. What is more, we now find another important similarity to Hegel's self-estranged subject in Esther's narrative. As with the former, for whom Hegel says 'it is the power of language as something which performs that which is to be performed',[17] for Esther self-recognition is intimately connected to language and especially, in her case, to writing. Esther 'realises' herself as a subject (a development which leads eventually to the writing of her narrative) through a process of differentiation, as we said – the disfiguration caused by the disease that has travelled to her from her father, Captain Hawdon, marks her as different from her mother, Lady Dedlock. Crucial here of course is the role of Hawdon as a source of writing in the novel, as the scribe whose writing insistently returns first to Lady Dedlock and then to Esther. If Hawdon's ghost travels to his daughter by way of the contagion carried by the illiterate Jo and leaves its mark on her, it is also conveyed to his wife in the form of marks – the legal documents presented to Lady Dedlock early in the novel, in which she is shocked to recognise the hand of her lost lover. The important difference here is that while Esther bears the disfiguring marks of Hawdon's ghost – marks which, as we have suggested, determine her as a subject – Lady Dedlock is determined conversely by her inability to bear the return of Hawdon's traces which eventually include not just his legal hand but also the physical trace of their union, Esther herself. Thus, the prominence of writing in the drama of Esther's self-realisation seems to underline once again its surprisingly detailed similarity to Hegel's presentation of self-estrangement.

But when we shift from the subjective to the institutional level, *Bleak House* parts company with the *Phenomenology*. For the institution that ultimately intervenes and determines self-estranged subjectivity in Dickens's novel differs decisively from the continuous, absolute institution of *Geist*. *Bleak House* seems to carry over and transform on the institutional level of the home precisely the displacement or 'homelessness' that *Geist* would go beyond or 'transcend'. Since, as we noted at the outset, Dickens's novel organises itself by analogy to the home, it is not surprising that we can best begin to get a sense of this difference near the end of *Bleak House* – where the question of how the novel will end coincides with the question of the institution of Bleak House itself as a home. As we move toward this point in the novel, various questions are resolved (more or less), but, in spite of Esther's agreement to become 'the mistress of Bleak House', as Jarndyce's written marriage proposal somewhat ambiguously asks, this central question persists: will Esther become Jarndyce's wife and thereby complete the household of Bleak House? Of course this question too is eventually answered, but more interesting than the answer itself is the way in which it is given. In the end, John Jarndyce imposes a solution (he 'gives' Esther to the young physician, Allan Woodcourt), and he does so in a scene of legislation which differs dramatically from the continuity and immanence that characterises the conversion of the self-estranged subject into *Geist* in Hegel's *Bildungsroman*. Indeed, what is perhaps most striking about this scene is the manner in which it insistently calls attention to the abruptness and even violence associated with instituting Bleak House. For, there is clearly something *unheimlich* about *Bleak House*; Jarndyce builds another house, also named Bleak House which is, interestingly enough, a mirror image of the original Bleak House (p. 912). Here, in other words, by means of the kind of strong, distorting interpretation of a written document quite at home in the perverse institutional setting of Chancery, Esther does in fact become the 'mistress of Bleak House', though in a different house and with a different husband (namely, Woodcourt). In other words, the final scenes of the novel suggest that in order for Bleak House to become realised or completed, in order for it to become itself, it must be moved or doubled – self-estranged through a process of mimetic reproduction. So, we might say that if Esther's status as a subject in the novel is founded by disfiguration, Bleak House's status as an institution (a home) is founded by displacement. In *Bleak House*, in other words, both the subject and the domestic institution that determines it present themselves in a decisive and abrupt movement which calls attention to itself as such.[18]

Critical discussion has yet to account sufficiently for this dynamic, transformative aspect of the home in a novel like *Bleak House*. A suggestive illustration of the difficulties involved in doing so is offered by one of the most insightful recent 'new historical' approaches to Victorian literature and culture – the work of D. A. Miller on disciplinary institutions and the novel in the period. In an essay on *Bleak House* which can, I think, be regarded as representative of this work, Miller addresses the issue of domesticity in a way that indicates the limitations of such approaches. And though it is never made explicit, his argument here seems to reach further than *Bleak House* to pose an indirect response to what we invoked at the outset as the traditional 'philosophical' reading of the novel in general as the genre of homelessness.[19] In short, Miller's essay attempts to establish a perspective beyond the conflict with which we began between the domestic analogy that organises a novel like *Bleak House* and a certain critical stress on displacement. From his perspective, the question of whether the novel achieves or fails to achieve an aesthetic ideal of domestic form would give way to what appears to be a new question. Opposing what he considers a certain typical post-structuralist emphasis on the 'gaps' in the domestic ideology of a novel like *Bleak House*,[20] Miller argues that such gaps should 'be understood – not in the old-fashioned way, as a failure of organic form, nor even in the new-fashioned way, as the success of a failure of organic form – but, in the broader context of institutional requirements and cultural needs, as the novel's own "work ethic", its imposing refusal of rest and employment.'[21] It is Miller's contention that precisely by representing the threats posed to the home and by exposing the 'gaps' in its domestic ideology Dickens's novel in fact exhorts its readers to shore up the domestic institution. This rhetorical feature of Victorian novels like *Bleak House* is characteristic, Miller says, of institutions generally in what Michel Foucault calls 'disciplinary society'.[22] Or, as Miller puts it, discipline 'reforms' the novel much as it does other institutions at the time (the prison, the school, the hospital, etc.).[23]

Miller argues for a view of the nineteenth-century novel as demonstrating a certain special effect of discipline – that of total surveillance, of the mode of surveillance Foucault identifies with Bentham's plan for a circular prison, the Panopticon.[24] Indeed Miller finds this mode at work in various places in *Bleak House*: in the totalising detective and surveillance abilities of Inspector Bucket as he tracks down the murderer of the barrister, Mr Tulkinghorn, who himself represents a less effective mode of surveillance in the novel; in Chancery Court whose power, Miller writes, 'does not impose itself by physical coercion ... [but rather] relies on being voluntarily assumed by its subjects, who, seduced by it, addicted to it, internalise the requirements for maintaining its hold';[25] in the 'novel's own representational practice', which is seen to expose willingly the similarity of its own massive, seemingly limitless perspective and length to the totalising bureaucracy of Chancery Court. But, not surprisingly, Miller proposes that the key thematisation of disciplinary power in *Bleak House* comes in what we have been considering its crucial institutional reflection on the home.

Here Miller concludes that Dickens's novel encourages 'that one hold one's place' in a home which, he says, maintains itself 'by becoming its own house of correction'.[26] Thus, Miller implicitly offers a significant reinterpretation of the novel's traditional association with the home: *Bleak House* shows how the nineteenth-century novel is only incompletely regarded as the genre of homelessness; for, seen from the wider perspective of discipline, Dickens's novel represents the possibility or threat of homelessness by showing the home's instability, but it offers this representation as a call for institutional stability. In this sense, all the self-estrangement and displacement in the novel itself takes place, in Miller's view, in the continuous, overarching presence – or *spirit* – of 'discipline'. *Bleak House*, then, is to be regarded as a demonstration of how homelessness in the novel is always subliminally placed within the confines of a larger structure or 'economy' of power – the big house, so to speak, of disciplinary power where one is warned to 'hold one's place'.

But are we not again neglecting the special dynamic character of the home in *Bleak House*? For, while Miller correctly emphasises that the displaced subject in the novel always ultimately finds itself in a particular institutional setting, he acts as though this institutional setting itself were fixed and constant – as though the displacements of the subject were from one pre-existent place to another, from room to room, so to speak, within the great house of disciplinary power.[27] But in fact, as we have seen, this is precisely not what happens in *Bleak House*. For crucial to the domestic institution in Dickens's novel is that it *moves* – it displaces itself and brings about a decidedly new place. In view of this important fact, it is hard to see how *Bleak House* can be understood to advise that 'one hold one's place'. In fact, the dead end of holding one's place is made explicit in the counter-example of Lady Dedlock, who attempts unsuccessfully to avoid losing her 'fashionable' place at Chesney World by concealing the disturbing evidence of Captain Hawdon's irrepressible return; just as, in a parallel way, the Dedlock household, true to its name, seeks in vain to maintain itself as an institution by excluding altogether the sort of tremors this shocking evidence would set off.[28] Indeed, the emphatically written character of the evidence in the case of Captain Hawdon's handwriting seems to stress that, with regard to the home as to the novel itself, one can only hold one's place when one stops reading. The practice of reading, including the practice of reading a novel, precludes that one hold one's place, since reading itself requires precisely that one keep moving. It is exactly here that the special link of the subject and the home to the novel in *Bleak House* begins to disclose itself. Put simply, Dickens's novel appears to suggest that the subject, the home, and the novel all share a movement which resembles reading – an activity or practice in which holding a place means abruptly and repeatedly losing one.

But, to recall our initial question, what is the significance of this abruptness – of the special aesthetic or figurative dimension of a household that is instituted through displacement? Here it may be useful to return again to the analogy we began with between the home and the novel. For one way to describe the manner in which Bleak House is instituted in Dickens's novel is as an interpretation, in the broad sense of the Latin *interpres* meaning mediator, negotiator, broker, or even translator. And, to be sure, the readers of *Bleak House* share all these roles with Mr Jarndyce in the novel – as we shuttle back and forth between plot lines attempting to arrive at some form of coherence. But what of the crucial scene in the novel where Jarndyce intervenes abruptly to found Bleak House as a household? Interestingly, as we have seen, it is here that it becomes difficult to speak of mere brokering between two already established places. Could it be that as readers of Dickens's novel we find ourselves faced with an analogous problem – with the absence of an already available place where *Bleak House* could be somehow realised? It seems hard to say what such a 'place' would be like, except that, following the example of Dickens's novel, it would have to come about through an act of displacement, a refiguration that would constitute some sort of new image of the novel itself. But whatever this 'new place' might be, it seems clear that it cannot be a question here of merely finding one that is already 'there'; it must, in other words, be a matter of something other than simple brokering between, say, Dickens's novel and Foucault or even Hegel. And yet one cannot help thinking here of the compulsively oversimplified subject of aesthetics, particularly of Kant's definition of aesthetic judgement, as occurring only in the absence of *a priori* general principles.[29] By inviting such a thought with regard to the home and – by analogy – to itself, Dickens's *Bleak House* seems to open the possibility of a wider reflection on the link between aesthetic and institutional questions in the nineteenth-century novel that has yet to be fully explored.

From *Modern Language Notes*, 108 (1993), 875–90.

NOTES

[This last essay recalls the importance of the 'house' part of the novel's title. Dickens's Preface speaks of 'familiar things' – which obviously pertain to the household, but McLaughlin reverts to the novel as the form whose subject is homelessness, and to Hegelian self-estrangement, the unfamiliar in the familiar (the uncanny), the source of irony. Esther's knowledge of her origins comes through an illumination which is also an infection (*Ansteckung* – as Hegel describes this). McLaughlin connects this discovery, which displaces Esther (as well as disfigures her) to the idea of homelessness, and then uses D. A. Miller's essay (no. 4) to argue that it is this sense of homelessness which is corrected by the disciplinary technologies of the nineteenth century, which are replicated in the novel form itself. (The logic of Miller's argument would make the eighteenth-century novel [Fielding, Smollett, Sterne especially] less disciplinary than the more professionalised nineteenth-century novel: the implications of this need weighing when it comes to considering the form of Dicken's texts: especially remembering both George Eliot's distaste for them for their non-realism, and Henry James's criticism of them for their lack of organic form.) McLaughlin finds it important that *Bleak House* ends with a shift of place: the novel moves on, accepts displacement. The essay suggests that the text is not outside disciplinarity – household rules that apply to bourgeois society and which license even aesthetic judgements, which seem to be unprompted – but that it also subtly changes these in a way that McLaughlin suggests opens the way to rethink the relationship between the text and what the text points to, and those founding disciplinary determinants provided by ideology which seem so permanent. Ed.]

1. On the household in the Homeric world, see James M. Redfield, 'The Economic Man', *Approaches to Homer*, ed. Carl A. Rubino and Cynthia W. Shelmerdine (Austin, TX, 1983), pp. 218–47.

2. On the transformations in usage of the term 'home' leading to the spatial or 'territorial' signification, see Emile Benveniste, *Le Vocabulaire des institutions indo-européennes*, Vol. 1 (Paris 1969), pp. 293–307. In keeping with the etymological roots of economics, the Victorian household does indeed seem to have been managed according to contemporary business principles. See Asa Briggs, *Victorian Things* (London, 1988), pp. 218–20 and J. A. Banks, *Prosperity and Parenthood: A Study of Family Planning among the Victorian Middle Classes* (London, 1954), pp. 12–47.

3. The same could be said of the term 'state' in political theory, which is itself regularly thought of in domestic terms – the 'homeland'. For an examination of the connections between politics and domesticity in ancient Greece, see Jean- Pierre Vernant, 'Espace et organisation politique en Grèce ancienne', *Mythe et pensée chez les grecs* (Paris, 1966), pp. 159–95 (especially pp. 161–3).

4. I say 'a novel like *Bleak House*' to indicate that Dickens's novel is part of a tradition of novelistic treatments of domesticity that dominates the genre and extends, say, from Richardson's *Pamela* through the novels of Jane Austen, Charlotte Brontë, and George Eliot. See Nancy Armstrong, *Desire and Domestic Fiction: A Political History of the Novel* (New York and Oxford, 1987), pp. 59–95.

5. On the paradigmatic character of the female subject in the British novel, see Armstrong, *Desire and Domestic Fiction*, pp. 20–2.

6. See M. Jeanne Peterson, 'The Victorian Governess: Status Incongruence in Family and Society', *Suffer and Be Still: Women in the Victorian Age*, ed. Martha Vicinus (Bloomington, IN, 1972), pp. 3–19. On the influence of Brontë's *Jane Eyre* on Dickens's Esther, see Ellen Moers, '*Bleak House*, The Agitating Women', *Dickensian*, 69 (1973), 13–24.

7. Here, in other words, in the belief that the question of the mode of subjectivity represented by Esther has not yet been exhausted, I return to what is, to be sure, an institutionally determined subject: precisely that 'contradictory, discursive category [of subjectivity] ... Foucault analysed', which some recent Victorian critics would move beyond. See, for instance, Regenia Gagnier, *Subjectivities: A History of Self-Representation in Britain, 1832–1920* (New York and Oxford, 1991), pp. 8–10.

8. In addition to its thematic centrality in *Bleak House*, contagious disease was a topic to which Dickens repeatedly turned in *Household Words*. See, for instance, 'Healthy by Act of Parliament', *Household Words*, 1: 20 (10 August 1850), 460–3.

9. Charles Dickens, *Bleak House* (New York, 1971). pp. 558–9. All subsequent references to *Bleak House* will be made to this edition with page numbers given in parentheses following the citation in the body of the essay.

10. See, for instance, Georg Wilhelm Friedrich Hegel, *Phänomenologie des Geistes*, Theorie-Werkausgabe, Vol. 3 (Frankfurt am Main, 1969–71), pp. 363–4: 'Or self-consciousness is only *something*, it only has *reality*, insofar as it estranges itself.' All translations from Hegel are my own.

11. This is what Hegel calls the arrival of the second or 'knowing subject' (*das wissende Ich*) in the position of the first, or 'logico-grammatical subject' (*Phänomenologie des Geistes*, 58). For an interesting reading of this key passage, see Andrzej Warminski, *Readings in Interpretation* (Minneapolis, 1987), pp. 168ff.

12. Hegel, *Phänomenologie des Geistes*, p. 376.

13. Indeed one could argue that the same basic kind of controlled mimesis analysed here in the *Phenomenology* is also the aim of Socrates's

theory of *Bildung* or pedagogy. See *Republic*, Book III, 394d–398b. This, as usual with the *Phenomenology*, discloses another example of the profoundly and self-consciously mimetic character of Hegel's text, which is itself a *Bildungsroman*.

14. *Trübners Deutsches Wörterbuch* (Berlin, 1939), for instance, gives the following explanation: 'The leaping-over of smoke and flames from the burning house to the endangered neighbour yields in our language in the sixteenth century its particular image for infectious diseases [*ansteckende Krankheit*]'. *Trübners* further notes the frequency of this usage among the German *Klassiker*, who 'loved figurative formulations', citing among others, Wieland and Schiller.

15. The German here is: 'verzehrende Flamme', Hegel, *Phänomenologie des Geistes*, pp. 366–7. This is in keeping with the surpassing authority of the state, over and above that of the family, in Hegel's philosophy. See George Armstrong Kelley, *Idealism, Politics and History: Sources of Hegelian Thought* (New York), 1978), pp. 347–8 and Jean Hyppolite, *Genise et structure de la Phinomenologie de l'Esprit de Hegel* (Paris 1946), pp. 326–37.

16. See Hegel, *Phänomenologie des Geistes*, pp. 58–60. On this purgative or cathartic force of *Geist* in Hegel, see Peter Szondi, *Poetik und Geschichtsphilosophie*, Studienausgabe der Vorlesungen, Vol. 1 (Frankfurt am Main, 1974), pp. 323–4; and also Jacques Derrida, *De l'esprit: Heidegger et la question* (Paris, 1987), pp. 157–9.

17. Hegel, *Phänomenologie des Geistes*, p. 376.

18. A closer examination of the passage in question would further reveal the violence associated with this instituting movement: both with respect to Mr Jarndyce's imperious legislation ('Hear me, my love', he says to Esther, 'but do not speak. It is for me to speak now.') and Esther's reception of it ('I was cold, and I trembled violently', she reports). See *Bleak House*, pp. 911–14.

19. Indeed this essay, entitled 'Discipline in Different Voices: Bureaucracy, Police, Family, and *Bleak House*', which originally appeared in the inaugural issue of *Representations* 1: 1 (February, 1983), 59–89, has since become the central chapter of Miller's larger study of the Victorian novel, *The Novel and the Police* (Berkeley, 1988).

20. Miller associates this reading specifically with J. Hillis Miller's introduction to *Bleak House* (New York, 1971) [essay 1 – Ed.]

21. Miller, 'Discipline', p. [120, above].

22. The portion of Foucault's analysis of 'disciplinary society' most relevant to Miller's discussion is in *Discipline and Punish* (New York, 1979), pp. 195–228.

23. Miller, *The Novel and the Police*, p. 17.

24. Bentham's Panopticon envisions a circular prison in which fully visible inmates would think themselves under constant surveillance by unseen guards in a central watchtower. See Foucault, *Discipline*, p. 200.

25. Miller, 'Discipline', p. [89, above].

26. Ibid., p. 83.

27. Indeed, the illusion of permanence is a central feature of the Panopticon, according to Foucault. For instance: 'Hence the major effect of the Panopticon: to induce in the inmate a state of conscious and permanent visibility that assures the automatic functioning of power. So to arrange things that the surveillance is permanent in its effects, even if it is discontinuous in its action' (*Discipline and Punish*, p. 201).

28. Even the death of Richard Carstone in the novel seems to originate less in his losing his place in the sophistry and deferrals of the Chancery suit than in his attempt to establish a firm position in its shifting discursive sand.

29. Immanuel Kant, *Kritik der Urteilskraft* (Frankfurt am Main, 1974). See, for example, 'Vorrede' and 'Einleitung', especially Section IV. An example of current anti-Liberalist reduction is Gagnier, *Subjectivities*, pp. 15–18. This view of Kant's aesthetics derives from Pierre Bourdieu, *La Distinction: critique sociale du jugement* (Paris, 1979), pp. 574–83. For readings which illuminate the more complex, conflictual character of institutional and cultural form in Kant, see Samuel Weber, *Institution and Interpretation* (Minneapolis, 1987), pp. 138–52 and Peter Fenves, *A Peculiar Fate: Metaphysics and World-History in Kant* (Ithaca, NY and London, 1991), pp. 258–85.

Further Reading

Bleak House was published in 20 monthly instalments (the last being a double-number), each with two ilustrations by 'Phiz', from March 1852 to September 1853, and then straightaway issued in volume form. Most of the current editions, such as the Penguin version of 1971, print the last edition of the novel issued in Dickens's lifetime (1868): the new Penguin edition, introduced by Nicola Bradbury (1996), uses the first, as will the Clarendon Dickens edition (not yet available). The Norton Critical edition (New York: W. W. Norton, 1977) ed. George Ford and Sylvère Monod, uses the first edition, that of 1853. Bradbury's new edition appeared too late for me to consult, but it is obviously very relevant.

For monographs on the novel I take the date of the original Casebook as a cut-off point. The Macmillan Casebook on *Bleak House*, ed. A. E. Dyson, appeared in 1969, with essays by Humphry House, John Butt and Kathleen Tillotson, Edgar Johnson, J. Hillis Miller (from his monograph on Dickens of 1958), Monroe Engel, C. B. Cox, Mark Spilka, W. J. Harvey, Taylor Stoehr and Dyson himself. Since then there have been other book-length studies of the novel: by Robert Newsom, *Dickens on the Romantic Side of Familiar Things: Bleak House and the Novel Tradition* (New York: Columbia University Press, 1977); by Graham Storey (Cambridge University Press, 1987); by Jeremy Hawthorn (London: Macmillan, 1987), Harold Bloom's collection of essays (New York: Chelsea House, 1987), Elliot L. Gilbert (ed.), *Critical Essays on Charles Dickens's Bleak House* (Boston: G. K. Hall, 1989), Pam Morris, *Bleak House* (Open Guides to Literature, Milton Keynes: Open University Press, 1993). Susan Shatto's *A Companion to Bleak House* (London: Unwin Hyman, 1988) is useful for its annotations of the text. Many of these volumes contain useful Bibliographies. Further bibliographic help should be obtained from *The Year's Work in English Studies*, and from such journals as *The Dickensian* (1905 onwards), *Dickens Studies Annual* (1971 onwards) and *Dickens Quarterly* (1984 onwards). Further relevant suggestions will be found in the companion Macmillan New Casebooks: Roger D. Sell (ed.), *Great Expectations* (1994) and John Peck (ed.), *David Copperfield* and *Hard Times* (1995), as well as John Peck (ed.), *Middlemarch* (1992), the New

Casebook on the Victorian text which is as long, as canonical and as different from *Bleak House* as may be imagined.

On Dickens, the *Life* by John Forster is the essential primary source, though there are many modern biographies, perhaps the best being Fred Kaplan, *Dickens: a Biography* (London, Sceptre, 1989). The *Letters* (ed. Clarendon Press, 1965 onwards) are essential reading to supplement Forster with a sense of Dickens's day-to-day activities. Volumes 6 and 7 deal with the period of *Bleak House*.

There are backgrounds to the text in Dickens's writings in *Household Words* (1850–9): see 'A Detective Police Party' and 'Three Detective Anecdotes', all in 1850; 'On Duty with Inspector Field' (1851) and 'Down with the Tide' (1853) all now in *Reprinted Pieces* (the first renamed 'The Detective Police') and, with W. H. Wills, 'The Metropolitan Protectives' (1851), reprinted in Harry Stone (ed.), *Charles Dickens's Uncollected Writings from Household Words* (Bloomington: Indiana University Press, 1968), 2 vols, vol. 1. For anyone whose first Dickens novel this is, *Little Dorrit* is probably the most comparable, while *David Copperfield* and *Great Expectations* are most relevant comparisons as texts written in the first person. *Dombey and Son*, which also discusses industrialisation, Benthamism and the daughter, is equally relevant.

The following bibliography makes no attempt at completeness, and readers should also consult the texts referred to in the notes to the Introduction and to the various essays. I have divided it into three: books on Dickens, which have substantial discussions of the novel; articles; and lastly, a section which could go on for ever: general studies for Dickens, for Victorian studies and for contemporary critical theory. The list reflects my own preferences throughout.

BOOKS

Jonathan Arac, *Commissioned Spirits: The Shaping of Social Motion in Dickens, Carlyle, Melville and Hawthorn* (New Brunswick: Rutgers University Press, 1979).

John Carey, *Dickens: The Violent Effigy: A Study of Dickens's Imagination* (London: Faber, 1973).

Philip Collins, *Dickens and Crime* (London: Macmillan, 1962).

Steven Connor, *Charles Dickens* (Oxford: Blackwell, 1985).

Kate Flint, *Dickens* (Brighton: Harvester Press, 1986).

Lawrence Frank, *Charles Dickens and the Romantic Self* (Lincoln: University of Nebraska Press, 1984).

John Kucich, *Excess and Restraint in the Novels of Charles Dickens* (Athens, GA: University of Georgia Press 1981).

——, *Repression in Victorian Fiction* (Berkeley, CA: University of California Press, 1987).

F. R. and Q. D. Leavis, *Dickens the Novelist* (London: Chatto & Windus, 1970).

Jerome Meckier, *Hidden Rivalries in Victorian Fiction* (Lexington: University Press of Kentucky, 1987).

J. Hillis Miller, *Charles Dickens: The World of His Novels* (Cambridge, MA, Harvard University Press, 1958).

Pam Morris, *Dickens's Class Consciousness* (London: Macmillan, 1991).

Michael Ragussis, *The Family Plot in Fiction* (New York: 1986).

Bruce Robbins, *The Servant's Hand: English Fiction from Below* (New York: Columbia University Press, 1986).

Anny Sadrin, *Parentage and Inheritance in the Novels of Charles Dickens* (Cambridge: Cambridge University Press, 1994).

Michael Steig, *Dickens and Phiz* (Bloomington: University of Indiana Press, 1978).

Jeremy Tambling, *Dickens, Violence and the Modern State: Dreams of the Scaffold* (London: Macmillan, 1995).

Edmund Wilson, 'Dickens, The Two Scrooges', in his *The Wound and the Bow* (Boston: Houghton Mifflin, 1941).

ARTICLES

Jean Frantz Blackall, 'A Suggestive Book for Charlotte Brontë?' *JEGP*, 76 (1977), 363–83.

Martin A. Danahay, 'Housekeeping and Hegemony in *Bleak House*', *Studies in the Novel*, 23 (1991), 416–31.

Lynette Felber, '"Delightfully Irregular": Esther's Nascent *écriture féminine* in *Bleak House*', *Victorian Newsletter*, 85 (Spring 1994), 13–20.

Michael Peled Ginsburg, 'The Case Against Plot in *Bleak House* and *Our Mutual Friend*', *ELH*, 59 (1992), 175–95.

Suzanne Graver, 'Writing in a "Womanly" Way and the Double Vision of *Bleak House*', *Dickens Quarterly*, 4 (1987), 3–15.

Barbara Gottfried, 'Fathers and Suitors: Narratives of Desire in *Bleak House*', *Dickens Studies Annual*, 19 (1990), 169–203.

Gordon S. Haight, 'Dickens and Lewes on Spontaneous Combustion', *Nineteenth-Century Fiction*, 10 (1955), 53–63.

Thomas Hanzo, 'Paternity and the Subject in *Bleak House*', in Robert Con David (ed.), *The Fictional Father: Lacanian Readings of the Text* (Amherst: University of Massachusetts Press, 1981).

Christopher Herbert, 'The Occult in *Bleak House*', *Novel*, 17 (1983–4), 101–15.

Albert Hutter, '"The High Tower of His Mind": Psychoanalysis and *Bleak House*', *Criticism*, 19 (1977), 296–316.

Valerie Kennedy, '*Bleak House*: More Trouble with Esther?' *Journal of Women's Studies in Literature*, 1 (1979), 330–47.

Leonard F. Manheim, 'The Law as "Father"' *American Imago*, 12 (1955), 17–23.

Helena Mitchie, '"Who is this in Pain?": Scarring, Disfigurement and Female Identity in *Bleak House* and *Our Mutual Friend*', *Novel*, 22 (1989), 199–212.

Robert Newsom, '*Villette* and *Bleak House*: Authorizing Women', *Nineteenth-Century Literature*, 46 (1991), 54–81.

Allan Pritchard, 'The Urban Gothic of *Bleak House*', *Nineteenth-Century Literature*, 43 (1991), 432–52.

Garrett Stewart, 'The New Mortality of *Bleak House*,' *ELH*, 45 (1978), 443–87.

Douglas Thorpe, '"I Never Knew My Lady Swoon before": Lady Dedlock and the Revival of the Victorian Fainting Woman', *Dickens Studies Annual*, 20 (1991), 103–25.

Ann Y. Wilkinson, '*Bleak House*: From Faraday to Judgement Day', *ELH*, 34 (1967), 225–47.

Judith Wilt, 'Confusion and Consciousness in Dickens's Esther', *Nineteenth-Century Fiction*, 32 (1977–8), 285–309.

Alex Zwerdling, 'Esther Summerson Rehabilitated', *PMLA*, 88 (1973), 429–39.

GENERAL STUDIES

Michel Foucault, *Discipline and Punish: The Birth of the Prison* (1975: trans. Alan Sheridan, Harmondsworth: Penguin, 1979).

——, *The History of Sexuality: Vol. 1: An Introduction* (1976, trans. Alan Sheridan, Harmondsworth: Penguin, 1981).

Ernest Mandel, *Delightful Murder: A Social History of the Crime Story* (Minneapolis: University of Minnesota Press, 1984).

Marty Roth, *Foul and Fair Play: Reading Genre in Classic Detective Fiction* (Athens, GA: University of Georgia Press, 1995).

Diane Sadoff, *Monsters of Affection: Dickens, Eliot and Brontë on Fatherhood* (Baltimore, MD: Johns Hopkins University Press, 1982).

Sheila Smith, *The Other Nation: The Poor in English Novels of 1840s and 1850s* (Oxford: Clarendon Press, 1980).

Jeremy Tambling, *Confession: Sexuality, Sin, the Subject* (Manchester: Manchester University Press, 1990).

Anthea Trodd, *Domestic Crime in the Victorian Novel* (London: Macmillan, 1989).

Alexander Welsh, *George Eliot and Blackmail* (Cambridge, MA, Harvard University Press, 1985).

Raymond Williams, *The English Novel from Dickens to Lawrence* (London: Chatto & Windus, 1970).

——, *The Country and the City* (London: Chatto & Windus 1973).

S. Susan Williams, *The Rich Man and the Diseased Poor in Early Victorian Fiction* (London: Macmillan, 1989).

Notes on Contributors

Virginia Blain is Associate Professor of English at Macquarie University in Sydney. Co-author (with Patricia Clements and Isobel Grundy) of *The Feminist Companion to Literature in English: Women Writers from the Middle Ages to the Present* (Yale, 1990), she is currently preparing an anthology of Victorian women poets for Longmans.

Christine van Boheemen-Saaf is Professor of English at the University of Amsterdam, and author of *The Novel as Family Romance* (Cornell, 1987) and *The Languages of Joyce* (Amsterdam, 1993).

Kate Cummings is Associate Professor of English at the University of Washington where she teaches courses in contemporary American culture, critical theory, modern and postmodern literature. She is the author of *Telling Tales: The Hysteric's Seduction in Fiction and Theory, In the Family Name: Readings of 'Home' and 'Exile' in Late-Twentieth Century US Culture* (forthcoming); and numerous articles on such subjects as 'AIDS', representational politics, and subjectivity.

Audrey Jaffe is Associate Professor of English at Ohio State University, Columbus. She is the author of *Vanishing Points: Dickens, Narrative, and the Subject of Omniscience* (University of California, 1991) and essays on Victorian literature.

Dominick LaCapra is Bowmar Professor of Humanistic Studies and Director of the Society for the Humanities at Cornell University. He has published in areas of history, literary criticism, and social theory. His books include *'Madame Bovary' on Trial* (1982), *Rethinking Intellectual History: Texts, Contexts, Language* (1983), *Soundings in Critical Theory* (1989), and *Representing the Holocaust: History, Theory, Trauma* (1994).

Kevin McLaughlin teaches courses on nineteenth-century English and Comparative Literature at Brown University. He is the author of *Writing in Parts: Imitation and Exchange in Nineteenth-Century Literature* (Stanford, 1995) and co-translator with Howard Eiland of Walter

Benjamin's *Arcades Project* (Cambridge, MA, forthcoming). He is currently at work on a study of financial debt in nineteenth-century literature, philosophy, and economic theory provisionally entitled 'Active Debts'.

D. A. Miller teaches English at Columbia University. He is the author of *Narrative and its Discontents* (Princeton, 1981), *The Novel and the Police* (California, 1988), and *Bringing Out Roland Barthes* (California, 1992).

J. Hillis Miller is Distinguished Professor of English and Comparative Literature at the University of California at Irvine. He taught for 19 years at The Johns Hopkins University and 14 years at Yale University before coming to Irvine in 1986. His most recent books are *Versions of Pygmalion* (Harvard, 1990), *Illustration* (Harvard, 1992), and *Topographies* (Stanford, 1995). He is at work on two books, one on the present state of the University, *Black Holes*, the other on the study of narrative continuity entitled *Diegesis*.

Timothy Peltason teaches at Wellesley College. He is the author of *Reading 'In Memoriam'* (Princeton, 1985) and of numerous articles on Mill, Ruskin, Arnold and other Victorian writers. He is currently editing a manuscript called *Cognitive Heroism: Essays on the Victorian Imagination*.

Bruce Robbins maintains a professional affiliation with the English Department of Rutgers University. He is the author of *The Servant's Hand* (New York, 1986), and the editor of *Intellectuals: Aesthetics, Politics, Academics* (Minnesota, 1990).

Index

There are no entries for *Bleak House* or for the characters or events in the novel. References in footnotes are not included here, unless there is substantial additional material about them there.